Night Whispers

'Stirring Passions'

Volume 01-Q1

January-February-March

Edition 01-Revision 08

Victor Robert Farrell

Night Whispers
All current
Contact & Sales Information
Can be found at
www.NightWhispers.com

Night Whispers
'Stirring Passions'
Volume 01–Q1

January-February-March

Copyright © Rev. Victor Robert Farrell

December 2019

All Rights Reserved

No part of this book may be reproduced in any form, by photocopying or by any electronic or mechanical means, including information storage or retrieval systems, without permission in writing from both the copyright owner and the publisher of this book.

ISBN Number 978-1-910686-00-3

First published in this format December 2014 by Whispering Word

All current contact and sales information can be found at

www.Night-Whispers.com

Printed in The United Kingdom

for

WhisperingWord Ltd.

Night Whispers
'Stirring Passions'
Volume 01–Q1

January-February-March

DEDICATION

This book is dedicated, very simply,

to the now four most important people

in the whole wide world to me.

My daughter **Gemma,**

My son **Jonathan,**

My Grandaughter **Ellie May,**

and of course,

My wife

Bridget.

PREFACE

I am Pastor, Rev. Victor Robert Farrell, and these everyday Bible insights called 'Night-Whispers' have long since been a global endeavor to communicate the God of the WHOLE Bible in very raw terms to very real people. This is my passion and the reason why I founded The 66 Books Ministry, who, through our 66 Cities project, over the course of the next 25 years, by the grace of God and according to His will and favor, shall be preaching consecutively from each of the 66 Books of the Holy Bible, the Gospel of the Lord Jesus Christ in 16,500 of the most influential cities of the world on an annual and ongoing basis! In this regard, these Night-Whispers accompany our endeavors by providing Every Day Insights into the whole Bible.

These Night-Whispers are presented in such a way as to be read each day. They are produced on a regular basis, and the 366 daily readings for each year are presented with a unique volume number. That 'Volume' year is then divided into four Quarters. For example:

Year 01= Volume 01-Q1 | January-February-March
Year 01= Volume 01-Q2 | April-May-June
Year 01= Volume 01-Q3 | July-August-September
Year 01= Volume 01-Q4 | October-November-December
Year 02= Volume 02-Q1 | January-February-March
Followed by Volume 3, 4, 5, 6 etc., and the associate four Quarters for the consecutive years. I am sure you get the picture!

The point is, that you can start any volume of Night-Whispers IN ANY YEAR you wish, and AT ANY TIME you choose, because whilst these Everyday Bible Insights are fresh and relevant to each day, they are not interconnected in a way which means you have to read one volume before another. Indeed, Night-Whispers are produced as stand-alone products rather than connected volumes. Therefore, if you wish, you can also consecutively read any Quarter from any Volume you choose! For example: Volume 02-Q3 might easily be followed by Volume 05-Q4, because each book is a standalone product. Got it? Excellent! So, now that I have most thoroughly confused you, may I say that along with the team at The 66 Books Ministry and Whispering Word, I do hope and pray that these particular *Night-Whispers,* will be an enormous blessing to you in *revealing just a little more to you of the God of the WHOLE BIBLE.*

Rev. Victor Robert Farrell, December 2015, England.

INTRODUCTION TO NIGHT-WHISPERS

VOL 01-Q1-'Stirring Passions'

This is our first standalone quarterly volume of Night-Whispers and we hope that these provocative readings will begin to stir those immense spiritual passions laid up by God within you for following the Lord Jesus Christ, the Savior of the world, and for seeking His Father, the God of the whole Bible, with your whole heart. To that end, Night-Whispers will present the God of the Bible in very raw and very real terms, therefore, as you find us pursuing Biblically correct truth, you will find that we are not politically correct in the least. In addition to that, I am sure you might find a few of my observations a wee bit of a challenge, as you also might do with the way I communicate them. That's fine. All we earnestly desire is that you check the Scriptures to see if these things are so.

Some global and historical acknowledgements

Now then, I have been writing these Bible Insights for many years and I have gleaned in a multitude of fine meadows and otherwise. For me to give credit where credit is due then, would not only increase the size of this quarterly volume many, many times, but I would undoubtedly miss many more people out of that massive list of those which I have not tried to give credit to. It is Solomon who said that *"there is nothing new under the sun"* and I believe it! Therefore, please then take it for granted that when someone like myself, who almost sees 'cut and paste' as an unspoken gift of the Holy Spirit, says that he might have gleaned from another person's work, in someplace, somewhere, and at some point in time and has done so without giving appropriate credit where credit is due, that I probably have! If this is the case, it was not my intention to rob you of any rightly due glory, but if I have, then please inform me of the same and the necessary changes and/or credits will be made. Remember, I have borrowed from everywhere; I have taken from everyone. 'Everywhere' and 'everyone;' there you go, that should have you covered!

US, UK or elsewhere, or, "How do you spell that?"

To be British, is to be somewhat like 'the last of the Mohicans.' The United Kingdom I grew up in is breaking apart. Even so, I am of Irish & Scottish great-grandparents, grandparents and parents, and I was also born in England. Therefore, I am British and a Celt at that. Even so, I love North America. Does this make me a Yankophile, or loving the South and its battle flag, more especially a Dixiophile? Alternatively, maybe I could be an Americophile or a Canameriphile? Who knows? Suffice to say, that as our nations are divided by a common language, America being the residence of the majority of our English readers, I have tried to adopt the spelling and grammar of the Americas. Even so, I have no doubt failed, and in the so doing, both mixed and matched the UK and US spelling and grammatical styles as I have compiled these Night-Whispers. I confess that I am a double-minded man, unstable in all my editorial ways. The purists, either side of the pond, I am sure will never forgive me. The rest do not care. Either way I need your help. So, if you spot any 'howlers,' do let me know. Please Email me your corrections on:

getyouracttogetherman@whisperingword.com

Bible Versions

As the The New Separatist's Bible (NSB) is in process of production and being released 'Book by Bible Book,' I have endevoured to use this Bible as it becomes available.

The NSB is is a 'Confluence Bible,' and is rooted mainly in the Pure Cambridge Edition of the 1611 King James Authorized Version and shaped by the 1560 AND 1599 Geneva Bibles and 21st century English. It is, therefore, a confluence of these three great rivers, the Authorized Version, the Geneva Bible and modern English. Therefore, the NSB is NOT a translation, it is a confluence. As it brings together these rivers of translation into the 21st century, it is very happily NOT politically correct and NOT gender neutral.

Preferring the 'Textus Receptus' or the 'Majority Text,' when the NSB has not been available I have tried to use the New King James Version (NKJV) throughout these readings, though where necessary, for mere contemporary clarity of course, I have deviated from this norm, and at that time I have clearly indicated which other Bible Version has been referenced....... Hopefully.

In addition to this, though I have removed verse numbers from the Bible text, I have retained the Capitalization of the beginning of new lines within the text, which would indicate its NKJV poetic form as well as the start of a new verse.

Where possible, all Scripture is taken from the New King James Version®. Copyright © 1982 by Thomas Nelson. Used by permission. All rights reserved.

.

NIGHT-WHISPERS ARE WRITTEN FOR........

There is so much 'devotional' material available nowadays for the Christian that a great part of me says that no more should be written. Yet I do believe that we are moving speedily to the time of the end. What devotionals are written to truly address the needs of Christians living in the approach to this period, or in this period? In my opinion, there are none. Night-Whispers then, are written for those people of this darkening time in particular. Therefore, you will find that Night-Whispers are battle rations that demand your time, attention, study and consideration. If you need a little ear tickler folks, a quick little cuddle before you go to bed at night, a sleeping pill even, indeed, if you have sold out the truth, your calling and your very self for ten shekels and a shirt, then these Bible Insights are NOT for you. They demand your thoughtful consideration and further investigation and ardent application. They need your time! Night-Whispers are written for those seekers who are looking for the God of the whole Bible. They are written for those who hate the color grey but love black and white. They are written for those who want to know the truth, even if it is unpalatable to them. They are written for the awakened; that is, for those people who know that the darkness is alive and like a black incoming tide, is infiltrating every area of present life. They are written for those people who know that a Night is coming when no man can work. They are written for those people who refuse to be spoon-fed. They are written for Bible hungry people. They are written for those who are done with distractions. They are written for those people who have not sold out to cultural compromise and refuse to sell themselves to social niceness and religious self-righteousness. They are written for those who want to cease being unpaid social workers for the unthankful and want to love and arm the saints. They are therefore written for fighters, even that growing band of brothers who are no ragged or rag-tag remnant, but rather, are the released people of 'The Revolution,' that back to the Bible, boots on the ground, present movement of God, who are done with everything that has silenced the one true church and with the removal of its voice, have killed our nations. They are written for the sold out the followers of Christ who have at last found their proclamation voice. They are written for the rooted, fruited and flowering stump. Therefore, to all you great and holy people then, who, even in this darkness might just turn the world right ways up once more, I say then this to you this very night: *"Welcome to Night-Whispers, Volume 01-Q1- 'Stirring Passions.' "Be strong and keep looking up for your salvation draweth nigh."*

JUST A HUCKSTER

Some young preacher will study until he has to get thick glasses to take care of his failing eyesight because he has an idea he wants to become a famous preacher. HE'S JUST A HUCKSTER buying selling and getting gain. They will ordain him and he will be known as Reverend and if he writes a book, they will make him a doctor. And he will be known as Doctor; but he's still a huckster buying and selling and getting gain.

And when the Lord comes back, HE will drive him out of the temple along with the other cattle.

A.W. Tozer

(from 'Tozer on Christian Leadership,' compiled by Ron Eggert)

John 3:30 *He must increase but I must decrease.*

STILL LOOKING

Wise men speak of trees
From the Cedar to the Hyssop
Springing from the wall
From the Aspen to the Alder
Beside the water fall

Wise men speak of animals of creeping things and fish
Of birds and bees and smooth black cats
That lap the dainty dish

Wise men sing of love and capture moments in a jar
Wise men suck the juice of days
Wise men shop at Spar!

Wise men count the fallen ticks
Of old clocks running down
Wise men number muscles
That help create the frown

Wise men follow after
Wise men follow far
Wise men seek the Savior still
Beneath the wandering star

1 Kings 4:33 Also he spoke of trees, from the cedar tree of Lebanon even to the hyssop that springs out of the wall; he spoke also of animals, of birds, of creeping things, and of fish. (NKJV)

The Old 100th!

All people that on earth do dwell,
Sing to the Lord with cheerful voice.
Him serve with fear, His praise forth tell;
Come ye before Him and rejoice.

The Lord, ye know, is God indeed;
Without our aid He did us make;
We are His folk, He doth us feed,
And for His sheep He doth us take.

O enter then His gates with praise;
Approach with joy His courts unto;
Praise, laud, and bless His name always,
For it is seemly so to do.

For why? the Lord our God is good;
His mercy is for ever sure;
His truth at all times firmly stood,
And shall from age to age endure.

To Father, Son and Holy Ghost,
The God whom Heaven and earth adore,
From men and from the angel host
Be praise and glory evermore.

From 'Fourscore and Seven Psalms of David'
(Geneva, Switzerland: 1561); attributed to William Kethe

CONTENTS

DEDICATION vii
PREFACE ix
INTRODUCTION TO NIGHT-WHISPERS xi
VOL 01-Q1-'Stirring Passions' xi
Some global and historical acknowledgements xi
US, UK or elsewhere, or, "How do you spell that?" xiii
Bible Versions xiii
NIGHT-WHISPERS ARE WRITTEN FOR......... xv
JUST A HUCKSTER xvii
STILL LOOKING xix
The Old 100th! xxi

| Vol 01 | Q1 | NW00001 | January 01st | 1
   NIGHT-WHISPER | **LOVE** 1
The O.V.E.N. of burning love! 1
   Psalms 139:23-24 .... *1*

| Vol 01 | Q1 | NW00002 | January 02nd | 4
   NIGHT-WHISPER | **FREEDOM** 4
The breaking of security's shackles 4
   Luke 14:33 .... *4*

| Vol 01 | Q1 | NW00003 | January 03rd | 6
   NIGHT-WHISPER | **SERVE** 6
The Foulis foghorn and the fools that don't listen 6
   Ezekiel 33:4,5 .... *6*

| Vol 01 | Q1 | NW00004 | January 04th | 8
   NIGHT-WHISPER | **LIVE** 8
The silent witness 8
   Ecclesiastes 12:6 .... *8*

| Vol 01 | Q1 | NW00005 | January 05th | 10
    NIGHT-WHISPER | **SACRIFICE** 10
Jesus, my 'Googleganger' 10
    Colossians 2:13 10

| Vol 01 | Q1 | NW00006 | January 06th | 12
    NIGHT-WHISPER | **RESCUE** 12
The legend of Omega man 12
    Revelation 1:8 12

| Vol 01 | Q1 | NW00007 | January 07th | 14
    NIGHT-WHISPER | **SERVE** 14
The Bible, the Facebook 14
    John 14:12-14 14

| Vol 01 | Q1 | NW00008 | January 08th | 17
    NIGHT-WHISPER | **RESCUE** 17
"Arise, let us go from here." 17
    Luke 2:10-12 17

| Vol 01 | Q1 | NW00009 | January 09th | 19
    NIGHT-WHISPER | **CHOOSE** 19
The gift of celery 19
    Matthew 19:11-12 19

| Vol 01 | Q1 | NW00010 | January 10th | 21
    NIGHT-WHISPER | **CHANGE** 21
Signs of softening 21
    Genesis 28:8-9 21

| Vol 01 | Q1 | NW00011 | January 11th | 23
    NIGHT-WHISPER | **COST** 23
Of bursting bags and guilt by association 23
    Matthew 22:32-36 23

| Vol 01 | Q1 | NW00012 | January 12th | 26
    NIGHT-WHISPER | **PREPARE** 26

The beginning of sorrows – The arrival of joy 26
    Matthew 24:6-8 26

| Vol 01 | Q1 | NW00013 | January 13ᵗʰ | 28
    NIGHT-WHISPER | **PREPARE** 28
God the Gazumper 28
    1 Corinthians 6:18-20 28

| Vol 01 | Q1 | NW00014 | January 14ᵗʰ | 30
    NIGHT-WHISPER | **MONEY** 30
Murder meadow 30
    Matthew 27:6-10 30

| Vol 01 | Q1 | NW00015 | January 15ᵗʰ | 33
    NIGHT-WHISPER | **MONEY** 33
The hiring of Larry lightning face 33
    Matthew 28:1-3 33

| Vol 01 | Q1 | NW00016 | January 16ᵗʰ | 36
    NIGHT-WHISPER | **CHOOSE** 36
Splitting dialect and divisive dialogue 36
    Genesis 31:45-48 36

| Vol 01 | Q1 | NW00017 | January 17ᵗʰ | 38
    NIGHT-WHISPER | **RESCUE** 38
Gracious assimilation 38
    Genesis 46:10 38

| Vol 01 | Q1 | NW00018 | January 18ᵗʰ | 40
    NIGHT-WHISPER | **POWER** 40
The dance of death 40
    Romans 12:1-2 40

| Vol 01 | Q1 | NW00019 | January 19ᵗʰ | 43
    NIGHT-WHISPER | **LEAD** 43
Jam and Jerusalem 43

Revelation 21:2-4 43

| Vol 01 | Q1 | NW00020 | January 20th | 46
NIGHT-WHISPER | **WORK** 46
Dare you taste some of Robertson's most generous jam? 46
2 Corinthians 12:15 46

| Vol 01 | Q1 | NW00021 | January 21st | 49
NIGHT-WHISPER | **GRACE** 49
The real cost of some of our Reheboths 49
Genesis 26:19-22 49

| Vol 01 | Q1 | NW00022 | January 22nd | 53
NIGHT-WHISPER | **PERSEVERE** 53
The Irreconcilables 53
Revelation 6:9-12 53

| Vol 01 | Q1 | NW00023 | January 23rd | 57
NIGHT-WHISPER | **CHANGE** 57
Of changing chains to licorice 57
Exodus 14:19-20 57

| Vol 01 | Q1 | NW00024 | January 24th | 60
NIGHT-WHISPER | **BE** 60
"Eimi Ho Eimie" - the resolute declaration of self 60
1 Corinthians 15:9-11 60

| Vol 01 | Q1 | NW00025 | January 25th | 62
NIGHT-WHISPER | **PERSEVERE** 62
The ploughman's poet 62
Proverbs 19:21 62

| Vol 01 | Q1 | NW00026 | January 26th | 65
NIGHT-WHISPER | **CONNECT** 65
On my finger and on my thumb 65
Ecclesiastes 4:9-10 65

| Vol 01 | Q1 | NW00027 | January 27th | 68

NIGHT-WHISPER | **CONFIDENCE** 68
Countdown conundrums 68
Exodus 28:30 68

| Vol 01 | Q1 | NW00028 | January 28th | 71
NIGHT-WHISPER | **CONSIDER** 71
Troubling the tripartite connection 71
Proverbs 23:31-34 71

| Vol 01 | Q1 | NW00029 | January 29th | 73
NIGHT-WHISPER | **CLEAN** 73
Tainted love 73
Zechariah 14:20-21 73

| Vol 01 | Q1 | NW00030 | January 30th | 77
NIGHT-WHISPER | **CHOOSE** 77
Of milksop men & weeping women 77
Job 40:7 77

| Vol 01 | Q1 | NW00031 | January 31st | 80
NIGHT-WHISPER | **SERVE** 80
There were only fish fingers until along came Hans! 80
Isaiah 1:18 80

PAUSE FOR PRAYER | 66CITIES 83

| Vol 01 | Q1 | NW00032 | February 01st | 85
NIGHT-WHISPER | **INTEGRITY** 85
The making of righteous reputations 85
1 Samuel 22:1-2 85

| Vol 01 | Q1 | NW00033 | February 02nd | 88
NIGHT-WHISPER | **PERSEVERE** 88
Building on the body line 88
Hebrews 11:4 88

| Vol 01 | Q1 | NW00034 | February 03rd | 91

NIGHT-WHISPER | **TRUTH** 91
Wringing pigeon's necks 91
    Leviticus 5:1 91

| Vol 01 | Q1 | NW00035 | February 04th | 95
NIGHT-WHISPER | **SERVE** 95
A man with his wholeness wholly attending 95
    John 8:29 95

| Vol 01 | Q1 | NW00036 | February 05th | 98
NIGHT-WHISPER | **WISDOM** 98
Problems from the perplexing king of frolic 98
    Deuteronomy 6:5 98

| Vol 01 | Q1 | NW00037 | February 06th | 102
NIGHT-WHISPER | **HOPE** 102
Of ashes and eye lashes, all curled high on 'Expectation Day' 102
    Psalms 51:1-2 102

| Vol 01 | Q1 | NW00038 | February 07th | 105
NIGHT-WHISPER | **TRUTH** 105
My empire of dirt 105
    Psalms 119:133 105

| Vol 01 | Q1 | NW00039 | February 08th | 108
NIGHT-WHISPER | **STRENGTH** 108
Dealing with the different lava flows of both Levite and Leviathan 108
    Proverbs 15:1 108

| Vol 01 | Q1 | NW00040 | February 09th | 111
NIGHT-WHISPER | **RESCUE** 111
Of plumbers and 'disrememberment' 111
    Deuteronomy 15:15-18 111

| Vol 01 | Q1 | NW00041 | February 10th | 114
NIGHT-WHISPER | **WISDOM** 114
Weeping women 114

Jeremiah 31:15 .... *114*

| Vol 01 | Q1 | NW00042 | February 11ᵗʰ | 117
   Night-Whisper | **WORK** 117
Of good starts and better endings 117
   1 Peter 2:6,7 .... *117*

| Vol 01 | Q1 | NW00043 | February 12ᵗʰ | 120
   Night-Whisper | **DISCOVER** 120
The one necessary root 120
   Matthew 13:20-21 .... *120*

| Vol 01 | Q1 | NW00044 | February 13ᵗʰ | 123
   Night-Whisper | **TRUTH** 123
The sound of sharpening knives 123
   James 5:12 .... *123*

| Vol 01 | Q1 | NW00045 | February 14ᵗʰ | 125
   Night-Whisper | **LEAD** 125
The flags of our father's 125
   Numbers 2:1-2 .... *125*

| Vol 01 | Q1 | NW00046 | February 15ᵗʰ | 127
   Night-Whisper | **FAITHFUL** 127
True friendship is eternal 127
   2 Samuel 19:30 .... *127*

| Vol 01 | Q1 | NW00047 | February 16ᵗʰ | 130
   Night-Whisper | **PROSPER** 130
The color purple and some big news from Baghdad 130
   Mark 8:36 .... *130*

| Vol 01 | Q1 | NW00048 | February 17ᵗʰ | 133
   Night-Whisper | **GIVE** 133
The money in God's pocket 133
   Mark 8:17-19 .... *133*

| Vol 01 | Q1 | NW00049 | February 18th | 135

    NIGHT-WHISPER | **FOCUS** 135

The waking of zombies 135

    2 Corinthians 4:3, 4 .... *135*

| Vol 01 | Q1 | NW00050 | February 19th | 138

    NIGHT-WHISPER | **CONSIDER** 138

The trouble with complacent canaries 138

    Psalms 40:1-3 .... *138*

| Vol 01 | Q1 | NW00051 | February 20th | 140

    NIGHT-WHISPER | **CLEAN** 140

Good for gonads 140

    Exodus 34:6-7 .... *140*

| Vol 01 | Q1 | NW00052 | February 21st | 143

    NIGHT-WHISPER | **CONSIDER** 143

All about Eve 143

    Colossians 1:16-17 .... *143*

| Vol 01 | Q1 | NW00053 | February 22nd | 146

    NIGHT-WHISPER | **DANGER** 146

The disappearance of a duck's quack 146

    2 Kings 3:1-3 .... *146*

| Vol 01 | Q1 | NW00054 | February 23rd | 149

    NIGHT-WHISPER | **CLEAN** 149

Jalousie strudel 149

    Song of Solomon 2:9 .... *149*

| Vol 01 | Q1 | NW00055 | February 24th | 152

    NIGHT-WHISPER | **FAITHFUL** 152

Rings of gold on beds of fulfilment 152

    Numbers 30:1 .... *152*

| Vol 01 | Q1 | NW00056 | February 25th | 155

    NIGHT-WHISPER | **REPENT** 155

The Borsalino back step 155
> *Numbers 16:1-3* *155*

| Vol 01 | Q1 | NW00057 | February 26th | 158
NIGHT-WHISPER | **DESTINY** 158
The making, the breaking, and the branding of mavericks 158
> *Exodus 3:1-2* *158*

| Vol 01 | Q1 | NW00058 | February 27th | 161
NIGHT-WHISPER | **DESTINY** 161
A consideration of destiny or saving and shaping 161
> *Lamentations 1:9* *161*

| Vol 01 | Q1 | NW00059 | February 28th | 163
NIGHT-WHISPER | **ACTION** 163
Trading for the Transjordan-pondering the Ponderosa principle 163
> *Deuteronomy 3:19* *163*

| Vol 01 | Q1 | NW00060 | February 29th | 166
NIGHT-WHISPER | **PREPARE** 166
Coming out from behind the coward's castle 166
> *Acts 17:17-18* *166*

It's time to order your next Quarter of 169

| Vol 01 | Q1 | NW00061 | March 01st | 171
NIGHT-WHISPER | **CONSIDER** 171
Of black cocks and mad March misconceptions 171
> *Ecclesiastes 10:12-13* *171*

| Vol 01 | Q1 | NW00062 | March 02nd | 174
NIGHT-WHISPER | **MONEY** 174
Dealing with the Reverend William Fold 174
> *Deuteronomy 12:19* *174*

| Vol 01 | Q1 | NW00063 | March 03rd | 177
NIGHT-WHISPER | **PERSEVERE** 177

Of magic fairies and velveteen rabbits 177
    1 Thessalonians 2:6-9 .... *177*

| Vol 01 | Q1 | NW00064 | March 04th | **180**
    NIGHT-WHISPER | **HONOR** 180
Rough and ready **180**
    Malachi 1:6a *180*

| Vol 01 | Q1 | NW00065 | March 05th | **183**
    NIGHT-WHISPER | **FIGHT** 183
'The Big E' - her stars and His scars **183**
    John 20:27-28 .... *183*

| Vol 01 | Q1 | NW00066 | March 06th | **186**
    NIGHT-WHISPER | **DESIRE** 186
How's your sex life? **186**
    Isaiah 26:9a *186*

| Vol 01 | Q1 | NW00067 | March 07th | **189**
    NIGHT-WHISPER | **CARE** 189
Oh, for such slippy feet! **189**
    Deuteronomy 33:24-25 .... *189*

| Vol 01 | Q1 | NW00068 | March 08th | **192**
    NIGHT-WHISPER | **HAPPY** 192
The House of Fun **192**
    Deuteronomy 32:15 .... *192*

| Vol 01 | Q1 | NW00069 | March 09th | **195**
    NIGHT-WHISPER | **FOCUS** 195
Singleness of heart **195**
    1 Corinthians 7:1a *195*

| Vol 01 | Q1 | NW00070 | March 10th | **199**
    NIGHT-WHISPER | **BE** 199
God is still a poet and He's wearing a construction hat! **199**
    Ephesians 2:10 .... *199*

| Vol 01 | Q1 | NW00071 | March 11th | 202

    NIGHT-WHISPER | **WISDOM** 202

Cut loose..**202**

    Luke 7:36-37 ....*202*

| Vol 01 | Q1 | NW00072 | March 12th | 204

    NIGHT-WHISPER | **CARE** 204

Resurrection always follows the last supper..........................**204**

    Lamentations 5:1-4 ....*204*

| Vol 01 | Q1 | NW00073 | March 13th | 207

    NIGHT-WHISPER | **WISDOM** 207

The wisdom of not doing the dirty on your own doorstep **207**

    Proverbs 11:29...*207*

| Vol 01 | Q1 | NW00074 | March 14th | 209

    NIGHT-WHISPER | **ASK** 209

Progenitor proceedings, pious ingenuity and permissible percussion ..**209**

    Numbers 27:1 ....*209*

| Vol 01 | Q1 | NW00075 | March 15th | 212

    NIGHT-WHISPER | **GRACE** 212

Refuge! Refuge! Refuge!...**212**

    Deuteronomy 19:10-13...*212*

| Vol 01 | Q1 | NW00076 | March 16th | 216

    NIGHT-WHISPER | **CONSIDER** 216

Grace has its dangers..**216**

    Joshua 24:13 ....*216*

| Vol 01 | Q1 | NW00077 | March 17th | 219

    NIGHT-WHISPER | **HOPE** 219

The last man standing...**219**

    Judges 1:1 ....*219*

| Vol 01 | Q1 | NW00078 | March 18th | 221

NIGHT-WHISPER | **RESCUE** 221
The marketing of God **221**
    John 16:7-11 ....*221*

| Vol 01 | Q1 | NW00079 | March 19th | **224**
NIGHT-WHISPER | **HOPE** 224
If I could turn back time **224**
    2 Kings 20:9-11 ....*224*

| Vol 01 | Q1 | NW00080 | March 20th | **227**
NIGHT-WHISPER | **CONSIDER** 227
The manufacture of the spiritually retarded and crippled clowns **227**
    Jeremiah 3:15 ....*227*

| Vol 01 | Q1 | NW00081 | March 21st | **232**
NIGHT-WHISPER | **PREPARE** 232
Turning aliens into citizens **232**
    Judges 15:11 ....*232*

| Vol 01 | Q1 | NW00082 | March 22nd | **235**
NIGHT-WHISPER | **INTEGRITY** 235
Food for thought by the mining of memory **235**
    Leviticus 25:22 ....*235*

| Vol 01 | Q1 | NW00083 | March 23rd | **238**
NIGHT-WHISPER | **DANGER** 238
Nabel wasn't able to be bound in the bundle of the living **238**
    Isaiah 32:6-8 ....*238*

| Vol 01 | Q1 | NW00084 | March 24th | **241**
NIGHT-WHISPER | **DANGER** 241
The dire desire of a deadly divinity **241**
    1 Samuel 2:22-25 ....*241*

| Vol 01 | Q1 | NW00085 | March 25th | **244**
NIGHT-WHISPER | **WORK** 244
The 7 marks of a dream maker & 3 scales to measure them by **244**

Proverbs 18:9 .... *244*

| Vol 01 | Q1 | NW00086 | March 26th | 246
NIGHT-WHISPER | REST 246
When you bust a gut 246
1 Kings 19:3,4 .... *246*

| Vol 01 | Q1 | NW00087 | March 27th | 248
NIGHT-WHISPER | RESCUE 248
Cow zombies 248
1 Samuel 6:3-9 .... *248*

| Vol 01 | Q1 | NW00088 | March 28th | 251
NIGHT-WHISPER | PERSEVERE 251
Catch the wind 251
Exodus 2:11-15 .... *251*

| Vol 01 | Q1 | NW00089 | March 29th | 254
NIGHT-WHISPER | WISDOM 254
Messing with the Marabouts 254
Exodus 7:11-13 .... *254*

| Vol 01 | Q1 | NW00090 | March 30th | 256
NIGHT-WHISPER | CHANGE 256
Crushing the cockroaches of crowd pleasing 256
1 Samuel 18:7-9 .... *256*

| Vol 01 | Q1 | NW00091 | March 31st | 258
NIGHT-WHISPER | PREPARE 258
Stones of fire on the mount of angels 258
Ezekiel 28:14c *258*

THE MISSION STATEMENT OF THE 66 BOOKS MINISTRY 263

MORE ABOUT 'THE 66 BOOKS MINISTRY' 265

AUTHOR BIO | PURPLE ROBERT 267

| Vol 01 | Q1 | NW00001 | January 01ˢᵗ |

Night-Whisper | **LOVE**

The O.V.E.N. of burning love!

There is presently in our world an all-pervading sexual promiscuousness. It's on our TVs, it's on our mobile phones, it's on the internet, indeed, it's all over the place! Now then, the main maxim of such marketing is this: "If you want to sell it, make it sexy, make it appealing, then, make it eye candy!"

Psalms 139:23-24

"Search me, O God, and know my heart; try me, and know my anxieties; and see if there is any wicked way in me, and lead me in the way everlasting." NKJV

Applying this maxim to an all pervading sexual promiscuity has resulted in a multitude of scantily clad gyrating and twerking women all wiggling their way across our world. This kind of nakedness is plain wantonness, just distant and very unreal, wantonness. This kind of nakedness is sex, but it is not intimacy. Seared consciences have made embarrassed and public nakedness a thing of the past, today though, anything goes. Yet, intimacy is what we truly desire, but the sad thing is that we have come to equate all of this conscience seared sexual promiscuity with intimacy. Of course it isn't. So, our continued and unsatisfied desire for true intimacy, true connectivity, leads us ever onwards to even more sexual promiscuity. Remember, hot sex is not intimacy but hot love is! You see, if at the beginning of this year we earnestly hunger to get real intimate with God, then we need to share with Him the burning **O.V.E.N.** of our love.

First then, let me talk about **'Openness.'** This year, let us commit to more openness with the Lord. We need to tell Him exactly how we feel about situations, about relationships, about ourselves, about Him. Don't hold anything back! Real intimacy, you see, always begins with naked openness. Commit to be completely open and honest with God.

Second, let me talk about **'Vulnerability.'** We must allow God to go wherever He wants to go with us. We must allow Him full and open access to our spirits. We must allow Him to investigate us, to search us and to know us! Remember, God the Holy Spirit might very well want to speak more about our sin than we do ourselves! This year, let God choose the agenda for once.

Third, let me talk about **'Ecstasy.'** Don't forget folks, the purpose of marriage, of faithful intimacy, is both procreation and recreation. God is intent on our joy, even our deepest joy! We too must therefore be intent on His joy, we must be intent on pleasing Him. Therefore make God's joy, your joy friend and you won't go wrong. We must be intent on His pleasure. Imagine that! You see, to truly please ourselves, we must always seek to please Him first. This is the foundation of our glorifying God and that is our primary and secondary purpose, even our chief end, to both glorify God and enjoy Him forever. **Commit this year to pleasing Him.**

Lastly, let me talk about **'Nearness.'** This is the real intent of spiritual intimacy, even the banishment of our cosmic and sin laden loneliness by the presence and the felt nearness of the person you have set your love upon, even God Himself.

Tell you what friend, if this year, you turn yourself into 'a hunk, a hunk of burning love' for your Lord, then your deepest desires will be fully realized. Go on, give it a try. Take responsibility and take some action here! Purposely choose to put God in the **O.V.E.N.** of your own burning love. THIS is your responsibility. **DO IT!**

THIS is your responsibility. **DO IT!**

Listen: *"The Lord has appeared of old to me, saying: 'Yes, I have loved you with an everlasting love; therefore with loving kindness I have drawn you. Again I will build you, and you shall be rebuilt, O virgin of Israel! You shall again be adorned with your tambourines, and shall go forth in the dances of those who rejoice. You shall yet plant vines on the mountains of Samaria; the planters shall plant and eat them as ordinary food. For there shall be a day when the watchmen will cry on Mount Ephraim, "Arise, and let us go up to Zion, to the Lord our God."' (Jeremiah 31:3-6 NKJV)*

Pray: Like the sweet song of a choir, O Lord Almighty come and lift me higher. Let the flame of Your passionate love, this year, come like tongues of fire and lick my soul aflame! Raise my temperature toward You Jesus, and come and light my morning sky with Your burning love for me, that I might be inspired to please You with the offering of myself and my own well decided and applied, all devoted and burning LOVE. Amen, and let it be so.

Night-Whisper | **FREEDOM**

The breaking of security's shackles

The possession of security is a thing of great comfort. I have identified the what we think as human beings are the most important handful, which I believe are also the securities which we all strive to maintain every single day. Here they are:

Luke 14:33
"So likewise, whoever of you does not forsake all that he has cannot be My disciple." NKJV

- *Job security*
- *Housing security*
- *Financial security*
- *Relationship security, and*
- *Health security*

I have observed that the first four of these items of security are the paramount possessions in our Evangelical circles. Health security, however, though desired, carries amongst us conservative Evangelicals, a grudging expectancy of loss and lack of the same. Nevertheless, it would be nice to possess such a health security if we could. Now then, despite the latter so often being out of our reach, the truth is that most of us Evangelicals do spend our lives servicing, maintaining and striving after all of these five items of security and oh my goodness, the high protestant price tag we attach to such man made and seemingly God blessed respectability is gigantic!

It is very true, however, that the pursuance and maintenance of such securities does not really allow time for reflective change and if that is the case, then it rarely allows for real spiritual expansion and growth. For when God comes to us and says: "Leave, forsake, give, sacrifice, and grow," and we say, "Lord, hell no! We will not do so. You've got to be kidding me! What, give up these, Your God blessed securities?" Unfortunately, most church leaders will agree with your conclusions, though they would state it in more respectable terms of course.

I wonder then if in this respect, such shining securities become to us respectable Evangelicals nothing but shackles! Now, if I am correct, we need to be a little concerned about this because Jesus is very much into the shattering of shackles and therefore the shattering of our seeming securities!

A fine Christian businessman spoke with me just this morning. His company like many others in this global village is struggling with cheaper foreign imports. It looks as though his company might not last out the year. Now, concerning this matter, I was impressed with both his heart and his hope for he said to me, "Robert, sometimes you need change forced upon you because security sets in like concrete, and when that happens, then you find it very difficult to move." This man might well have been in the process of closing down his factory but I tell you, he was actually planning for some real spiritual expansion.

I have no doubt that in this coming year change will be forced upon many of us and maybe even upon you reading this right now. Some of your securities, maybe even all of them, will be shattered before your shaking ankles. In this, be assured that for whatever reason, God wants you to be released! Yes, in this, God wants you to grow. So, why not make a covenant with your mouth right now to stop all the whining and to start all the praising instead! Thus, you shall save bleeding the ears of others watching on and also salve your own heart with a certain hope of the goodness of God toward you in Christ Jesus, no matter what seeming securities might be removed. God is for you and don't you ever forget it. Now, go and grow some. Go and expand both your faith and your horizons.

God is for you and don't you ever forget it!

Listen: *"Salt is good; but if the salt has lost its flavor, how shall it be seasoned? It is neither fit for the land nor for the dunghill, but men throw it out. He who has ears to hear, let him hear!" (Luke 14:34-35 NKJV)*

Pray: Now Lord, tonight, give me peace as maybe You take Your hammer to those things which bind me in false securities. May Your mercy and Your joy become the music masters of all my shackle-broken dances, in Jesus name I pray, amen and let it be so!

Night-Whisper | **SERVE**

The Foulis foghorn and the fools that don't listen

Glaswegian, Robert Foulis, was born in Scotland in 1796. Devastated by the death of his first wife whilst giving birth to their daughter, Foulis decided to leave those sad Scottish shores and start a new life in America. Heading for Ohio, it was rough weather which forced his ship ashore in Nova Scotia Canada. It seems that bad weather, the sea, and the providence of God, took him from Old Scotland to New Scotland.

Ezekiel 33:4,5

"Then whoever hears the sound of the trumpet and does not take warning, if the sword comes and takes him away, his blood shall be on his own head. He heard the sound of the trumpet, but did not take warning; his blood shall be upon himself. But he who takes warning will save his life." NKJV

Foulis eventually settled in Saint John and here this talented inventor and business entrepreneur, for quite some time, blessed himself, his family and his community. You see, at that time, Foulis was not the only person wanting to start a new life in the new world. No, ship-loads of European immigrants would enter North America through the Saint John Harbor and would initially be housed (from 1785-1942) at the very first quarantine station of Partridge Island. It was on this desperate island gateway, for well over two thousand people died there, that Foulis the inventor erected a warning signal that would save thousands of other people's lives. His invention: The Foulis steam foghorn.

It is said that Foulis heard his daughter playing piano in the distance on a foggy night, and noticed that the low notes were more audible than the higher notes. Low frequency sound is more audible than high frequency to the human ear, and when fog as thick as molasses can block the strongest of lights, the haunting sound of a low frequency fog horn can still keep a captain safe, can still make speak low of dangers through the fog and guide a sailor safely home.

When we learn to feel into the spiritual realm, when we learn to receive through the feelings of our soul the true sounds and sensations of our spirit, when we receive in this context that felt contact of the spiritual realm, if you will, then we too, on cold and spiritual fog bound days, shall hear the warm low frequency bellow of many an heavenly fog horn, even many a guardian sentinel placed by the great God of all waters there for our guidance, there for our help, there for our health and for our protection. Truly then I can say to some of you mariners this night, some of you tired sailors seeking out a new world in God, blown off your course into foggy seas and rocky coasts, "He who has ears to hear, let him hear!" God IS speaking to your spirit. In the cool of this evening, feel the sound of Him walking in your garden

> *God IS speaking to your spirit. In the cool of this evening, feel the sound of Him walking in your garden!*

Listen: *"And I looked, and I heard an angel flying through the midst of heaven, saying with a loud voice, 'Woe, woe, woe to the inhabitants of the earth, because of the remaining blasts of the trumpet of the three angels who are about to sound!'" (Revelation 8:13 NKJV)*

Pray: Lord, let me not be counted as a fool. Help me hear Your voice, help me feel it. And where You have made me a foghorn, even a sentinel and even a watchman to the house of Israel, make me a loud and fearless open-mouthed proclaimer. Lord, when I am in need of hearing warnings and receiving guidance, give me big and flapping, open ears. In Jesus name I ask these things, amen, and let it be so!

Night-Whisper | **LIVE**

The silent witness

Recently, I have been very sick. So sick that I have been as listless as a dying fish void of the last flap of its flipper. So sick, that I could do nothing but lay still and moan, loudly. So sick, that I wanted no visitors, which is good because no one came anyway. More importantly and most disturbingly for me though is the fact that not even God came to visit me in my sickness.

Ecclesiastes 12:6

"Remember your Creator before the silver cord is loosed, or the golden bowl is broken, or the pitcher shattered at the fountain, or the wheel broken at the well." NKJV

Some of you will say, "Ah Robert, you just could not see Him, your sickness blinded you to His presence." Maybe. Either way, His felt presence was not felt. His healing hand did not touch me. So, in effect, even if God was there, He may as well not have been.

There is a deep mystery in the sometimes seeming silence of God in the sickness of men and women. In this, God requires no defense, neither does He ask for any, for all sickness is a swirling fog of green and foul pestilent mists, that takes us regularly toward the edge of the same cold river that one day, will receive us, when a final and fatal sickness will plunge us, yes each and every one of us, way, way above our necks, into its stiff Rigor-mortis running icy coldness. Sickness and its regular revisits, are a reminder, even a preparation, for such an inevitable cold passing and thus sickness allows us a regular little sniff of what is to eventually to come. This is not a bad thing.

Such silent sicknesses, I mean sickness with the felt absence of God in it all, challenges my faith. Yet, it is in a good way, for I emerge reminded and knowing that God is in light, God is in life, God is in the praises of His people, yes, God is to be found in my day, God is to be sought after and rejoiced in, in the full and present measure of my health and strength. Yes, such silent sickness is in fact a 'silent witness' for us to both live loud and live hot, should life be allowed once again to come into these ever failing bodies of ours.

So, if God in His manifest presence doesn't visit you in your sickness, or in your prison, in your loneliness and in your tortures, and sometimes He does not, then let us make sure we are banging on His door when we are well and entering into close fellowship with Him then. Maybe it is these remembrances that will be hot water bottles to our soul when the cold days shall surely come, those lonely days, when sickness hides God from us. Maybe it is these remembrances that shall also warm us when we cross that last icy river alone, on our last crossing home. Be prepared for these times and for that day, by being hot both for God and with God, right now.

> *"let us make sure we are banging on God's door when we are well and entering into close fellowship with Him then."*

Listen: *"My God, My God, why have You forsaken Me? Why are You so far from helping Me, and from the words of My groaning? O My God, I cry in the daytime, but You do not hear; and in the night season, and am not silent." (Psalms 22:1-2 NKJV)*

Pray: You who fear the Lord, praise Him! All you descendants of Jacob, glorify Him, and fear Him, all you offspring of Israel! For He has not despised nor abhorred the affliction of the afflicted; nor has He hidden His face from Him; but when He cried to Him, He heard. My praise shall be of You in the great assembly; all the ends of the world shall remember and turn to the Lord, and all the families of the nations shall worship before You. For the kingdom is the Lord's, and He rules over the nations. All the prosperous of the earth shall eat and worship; all those who go down to the dust shall bow before Him, even he who cannot keep himself alive. Posterity shall serve Him. It will be recounted of the Lord to the next generation, they will come and declare His righteousness to a people who will be born, that He has done this. (From Psalms 22:23-31 NKJV)

Night-Whisper | SACRIFICE

Jesus, my 'Googleganger'

I remember reading of a group of wordsmiths from the American Dialect Society who chose the word 'subprime' as the word of the year for 2007.

Colossians 2:13

"And you, being dead in your trespasses and the uncircumcision of your flesh, He has made alive together with Him, having forgiven you all trespasses" NKJV

Now, although this word has been around for some time in banking circles, with the collapse of the subprime mortgage markets at that time, it soon became a word affecting all kinds of people in all kinds of places. The bottom line is, that this word now means something that is far, so very far below the best. "This food is subprime!" "My preparation for this test is subprime." "This man's heart is subprime and God, my God, that heart is mine!"

This is more than any other time in history, the time of identity theft. Anyone, and today that means just about everyone, can now have their identity hijacked and utilized for fraudulent means to the benefit of the thief. Speaking as a subprime individual, sometimes I wish that someone would steal my identity and give me a new one! Some reverse identity theft, if you will. That's what I need folks, I tell you the truth. It's this last thought that brings me tonight to Jesus my 'Googleganger.'

Yes, coming a close second to being chosen as word of the year in 2007 was the new word 'Googleganger!' Literally, a 'Googleganger' is someone with the same name whose online records are intermixed with your own when you Google yourself. Now, bear with me please, for it struck me as a saving thought and a delightful muse at that, that whenever a search for the eternal records of the Rev. Victor Robert Farrell might be made on the heavenly internet, mixed in with my details, indeed overlaying all the poverty, all the moral bankruptness and low moral credit ratings of every kind of mine, shall be the goodness of my Savior, Jesus Christ my Lord. All His righteous records shall be written to my account. Do you see that?

Of course dear friends, I am so very pleased to say that tonight this is more than an idle thought, it is an ever present reality! Jesus is my Googleganger, make sure to make Him yours as well.

> *Jesus is my Googleganger, make sure to make Him yours as well.*

Now then, take this this to bed with you tonight and sleep in perfect peace.

Listen: *"Having wiped out the handwriting of requirements that was against us, which was contrary to us. And He has taken it out of the way, having nailed it to the cross. Having disarmed principalities and powers, He made a public spectacle of them, triumphing over them in it. So let no one judge you in food or in drink, or regarding a festival or a new moon or sabbaths, which are a shadow of things to come, but the substance is of Christ. Let no one cheat you of your reward, taking delight in false humility and worship of angels, intruding into those things which he has not seen, vainly puffed up by his fleshly mind, and not holding fast to the Head, from whom all the body, nourished and knit together by joints and ligaments, grows with the increase that is from God." (Colossians 2:14-19 NKJV)*

Pray: Lord, overlay my details, my actions, my thoughts, my very self with all that You are, with all that You have purchased for me O Jesus, my eternal Googleganger. Amen and let it be so!

Night-Whisper | **RESCUE**

The legend of Omega man

Richard Matheson, a former WWII Infantry soldier turned writer, actually penned a number of episodes of the famous *Twilight Zone*, and is a most prolific writer, having many of his novels turned into films. I suppose his most abiding writing is the one that has produced, so far, three films and was written in 1954 and is called: *I am Legend*. The other two films are *The Last Man on Earth* and *Omega Man*.

Omega Man, starring Charlton Heston, is most important to me, as it was the only movie which both my parents ever took me to see! Despite the fact that all three movies, (the third one takes the title of the book itself) stray from the original novel in many respects, they maintain one consistent theme and that is: the redemption of mankind by the shed blood of one man, a Messiah-Savior figure.

Revelation 1:8

"'I am the Alpha and the Omega, the Beginning and the End,' says the Lord, 'who is and who was and who is to come, the Almighty.'" NKJV

Blood which is sacred. Blood which is prohibited as food. Blood which contains the life. Shed Blood, which is to be avenged. Sprinkled blood, the splattering sign of the sure covenant. Protective blood, even lintel dripping and death protecting blood. Crying blood, condemning blood, seeking justice, all these kinds of blood are all bottled up in the Bible. Yes friends, the covers of the Bible should never be calf-skin and smooth black, but rather, sticky red, for its pages are sodden with red blood, they are even irrigated with rivulets of this red blood, all running down each of the dotted 'i's and dripping off all the curly ended 'y's, pooling in the guts of 'g's even, and yet, unlike the blood in a Stephen King novel, this Bible blood not only horrifies us but also smiles at us in all its pages, for the witness of Scripture is clear, in that blood is equated with but one thing, and that is: "Life given up in death for the purpose of the redemption of others!"

Into an infected world Christ came, pure and lovely, seeking the lost, intent on birthing life amongst the dead. Against unrelenting evil He came and at last shed His blood for our redemption. In short, remember this tonight, Christ gave His life in death for the whole world, for His church and for You in particular. Yes He did all that for you. He shed His blood for me. In this, He Jesus is 'legend,' He is the last Adam, He is the Omega man, who made it all right in the end! If you see blood running down the doors of your dreams tonight, it is not a nightmare friends, it is a vision of His redemptive love for you.

In this, Jesus is 'legend,' He is the last Adam, He is the Omega man, who made it all right in the end!

Listen: *"For the life of the flesh is in the blood, and I have given it to you upon the altar to make atonement for your souls; for it is the blood that makes atonement for the soul. Therefore I said to the children of Israel, 'No one among you shall eat blood, nor shall any stranger who dwells among you eat blood.'" (Leviticus 17:11-12 NKJV)*

Pray: Because of the blood of your covenant, set the prisoners free from the waterless pit. May all the prisoners of hope return to the stronghold of Your love and hear You declare even today that You will restore double to us all. For You have bent Judah, Your bow, fitted the bow with Ephraim, and raised up Your sons O Zion and set them against the enemies of Your blood. Be seen over us O God, let loose Your arrows, let them go forth like lightning. Amen and let it be so! NKJV (from Zech 9:11 onwards)

| Vol 01 | Q1 | NW00007 | January 07th |

Night-Whisper | **SERVE**

The Bible, the Facebook

In the early 19th century a congregational minister in Topeka, Kansas was having not a few problems in keeping the younger people of his congregation interested in his messages during the evening service. To gain and keep their attention he developed a narrative style of communication by reading aloud his made up stories of a fictional minister, 'Dr. Henry Maxwell.'

John 14:12-14

"Most assuredly, I say to you, he who believes in Me, the works that I do he will do also; and greater works than these he will do, because I go to My Father. And whatever you ask in My name, Word that I will do, that the Father may be glorified in the Son. If you ask anything in My name, I will do it."
NKJV

The fictional Maxwell, was the respected pastor of the equally fictional First Church of Raymond, who now, at each weekly evening service, unpacked in narrative style before the now well gripped younger crew, the idea that "Christian discipleship demanded more than mere mental assent." Maxwell's weekly movements of transferring grace to goodness, of putting Christ back on two legs with two hands, an open heart, mouth and wallet, was done so by prefacing every attitude and action of his own full, but fictional life, with one very simple yet quite profound question, "What Would Jesus Do in this situation if He were me?" The Rev. Charles Sheldon's narrative style became so popular that his sermon series was turned into a book called, *In His Steps* and the rest, as they say, is history.

The mass marketing of this little phrase "What Would Jesus Do?" and everything branded **WWJD** can drive you to distraction! "What would Jesus do with His kidneys? What would Jesus drive? What would Jesus bomb first? What would..." well you get my drift. Nevertheless, make no mistake about it, this little phrase is the second biggest question that we who are trying to be the "imitation of God" can ever ask of ourselves. "What Would Jesus Do?"

Tonight, however, I want to challenge us all with a far greater question. For before we can answer the question of "**What Would Jesus Do?**" we must know exactly just who Jesus is. Now there it is, there is the greater question. Do you know who Jesus is? No, not "have you accepted Him as your personal Savior and Lord?" No, that's too easy, that's just become another tick in a box that's often only a distraction and God help us, in our day, is more often than not, the point where our affirmation to this question becomes nothing but a big fat lie! No, the more important question for you tonight is this, "Do you know Jesus? Do you know who He is, what He likes and dislikes, what makes Him tick, who His friends are, where He likes to go, who He likes to hang out with? Do you know what annoys Him, indeed, do you know what gets His gander up! Do you know how to please Him? Do you know the Jesus of the Bible?"

The sad indictment for Christians at the beginning of the 21st century is that they do not know the Jesus of the Bible. Tell me then tonight, how can we begin to answer the question of **What Would Jesus Do**, if we do not know who on earth or in heaven, He truly is?

The sad indictment for Christians at the beginning of the 21st century is that they do not know the Jesus of the Bible.

We need three things to get to know Jesus:

First we must let His word dwell in us richly. We need to get into the Bible and get the Bible into us. Some of you may shortly be cast into prison, and I doubt very much if a Bible will be given to you. Listen now, memorize the Word of God. This takes time, effort, dedication, regurgitation. My commitment this year is to get to know Him more? How about you?

Second, we need to obey what we read. Doing the Word, makes our hearing of the word most effective on the memory of our hearts. Are you obeying the Word of God now? If you are obeying it in comparative ease, then you shall obey it in hardship, and I tell you, hardships are coming.

Lastly, in both of these things, you must prayerful and humbly ask for the help of God the Holy Spirit in enabling you to study the Word, understand the Word, illuminate the Word, apply the Word and remember the Word. Remember that the Word of God is a book of Spirit words and there is no better interpreter of the same than God the Holy Spirit Himself.

Take time to let the Word of Christ dwell in you RICHLY. Morning and evening, day and night, let His words be upon your lips.

Listen: *"Many will say to Me in that day, 'Lord, Lord, have we not prophesied in Your name, cast out demons in Your name, and done many wonders in Your name?' And then I will declare to them, 'I never knew you; depart from Me, you who practice lawlessness!'" (Matthew 7:22-23 NKJV)*

Pray: Lord, You have put Your face in Your book. All Your groups, all Your friends, all Your likes and all Your dislikes are there for me to see. Come and poke me in the morning, O Lord my God, come and write an invitation on my wall to come and walk with You today, that I might know You more. Amen, and let it be so.

| Vol 01 | Q1 | NW00008 | January 08ᵗʰ |

Night-Whisper | **RESCUE**

"Arise, let us go from here."

The most prescribed drugs in the Western world are anti-depressants. The most widely taken drugs in the Christian world are anti-depressants. The basic conclusion from this is that there appears to be no apparent connection or correlation between the words and works of Jesus and the practice of His followers. When the "so called" sons of His love are sustained by pills there has to be a problem here, doesn't there?

Luke 2:10-12

"Then the angel said to them, 'Do not be afraid, for behold, I bring you good tidings of great joy which will be to all people. For there is born to you this day in the city of David a Savior, who is Christ the Lord.'" NKJV

Now tonight before I go any farther, let me say that I am not condemning in any way whatsoever, anyone who is using anti-depressants. I am very simply pointing out the massive mismatch that exists between the proclamations of the Gospel and the necessary anti-depressant practices of many of its its recipients. Why is this?

I believe Henry Noweun was correct when he says that: "Our culture has become most sophisticated in the avoidance of pain, not only our physical pain but our emotional and mental pain as well." Now friends, in no way can this meditation of a few minutes at the end of this day fully provide an answer to the problem of our depression. Nevertheless, may I make a suggestion to us all this evening, that somewhere we need to find a space and a place where our pain can arise, be remembered, be seen, be dealt with and then be healed? I wonder if the Christian problem with this, oh so common and cosmic depression, is indeed the avoidance of our pain? If this is the case, then not only must our pain not be dismissed but also in a very positive way, it must be allowed to both live and express itself to death! Indeed, I wonder if God's light, even loves pain to death?

This kind of emotional healing, like the casting out of epileptic demons, takes both the time and the attention of even the active, believing and fighting disciple. That being the case, maybe we can use our pills as an emotional bridging loan, if you will, whilst the raw materials of our spiritual healing and health are gathered within ourselves, so, that in this coming year, we might build a home in which we might dwell at peace with both God and ourselves.

Maybe tonight, maybe tomorrow, is the time when some of us should earnestly begin this healing work within us, maybe with friends, certainly with God, and hopefully with true spiritual shepherds, this deep healing of our depressions can begin so that we might be delivered from all our manufactured bottles of branded hope and solace once and for all?

> *Maybe we should only use our pills as an emotional bridging loan?*

For all of us, at some point, the time arrives when we should turn and face our pain, our sadness, our anger, our whatever, and then express it all to death and where it is necessary, even confess it all to death.

Listen: *"Peace I leave with you, my peace I give to you; not as the world gives do I give to you. Let not your heart be troubled, neither let it be afraid. You have heard Me say to you, 'I am going away and coming back to you.' If you loved Me, you would rejoice because I said, 'I am going to the Father,' for My Father is greater than I. 'And now I have told you before it comes, that when it does come to pass, you may believe. I will no longer talk much with you, for the ruler of this world is coming, and he has nothing in Me. But that the world may know that I love the Father, and as the Father gave Me commandment, so I do. Arise, let us go from here.'"* (John 14:27-31 NKJV)

Pray: Lord, I come to You, let my heart be changed, renewed, flowing from the grace, that I found in You. Lord, I've come to know, the weaknesses I see in me, will be stripped away, by the power of Your love. Hold me close, let Your love surround me, bring me near, draw me to Your side and as I wait, I'll rise up like the eagle and I will soar with You, Your Spirit leads me on in the power of Your Love. Lord, unveil my eyes let me see You face to face, the knowledge of Your love, as You live in me. Lord renew my mind, as Your will unfolds in my life in living every day, in the power of Your Love. (Lyrics by Lincoln Brewster)

Night-Whisper | **CHOOSE**

The gift of celery

As a man, I have come to appreciate the gift of celery. It has been some years since this marvelous plant was discovered to be rich in the male steroid, Androsterone, and now the latest research seems to indicate that this male hormone enhances pheromones, which in turn physically attracts women, especially those whose genetic makeup does not overlay our own, and apparently, this same hormone also subjugates other men! So, pass me the celery! When such a vegetable enhances my male sexuality, then this is a great green gift that I can personally and most readily accept.

Matthew 19:11-12

"But He said to them, 'All cannot accept this saying, but only those to whom it has been given: For there are eunuchs who were born thus from their mother's womb, and there are eunuchs who were made eunuchs by men, and there are eunuchs who have made themselves eunuchs for the kingdom of heaven's sake. He who is able to accept it, let him accept it.'" NKJV

Jesus today, however, speaks of another gift. A gift of celibacy. Now let me cut to the chase, if you will excuse my pun, for Jesus is talking about a man with no testicles. He is talking about a man, who is devoted to his calling above all the natural inclinations and relations of life. In this, Jesus says there are three kinds of testicular-absent males: those born that way, those made that way and those you who choose to live that way!

Now this is serious stuff, for it was Origen of Alexander who famously castrated himself (ouch!), having literally interpreted and applied this passage so as to allow him the ability to teach female disciples without their being any hint of scandal! In his later life, he regretted this personal action and most thoroughly railed against the continued and weird practice in parts of the church and against anyone following in his footsteps! So, let us all agree with the Origen of more mature years, that this passage is not to be taken literally. (Some of you men can let go of them now!)

Jesus says two rather amazing things in our text for tonight. He first says that "Yes, it's a difficult one, but some people can choose to forego their righteous sexual and social relationship expressions for the sake of the Kingdom." Celibacy then, implies Jesus, is quite clearly a choice! This means there is a cost to this choice. This is hard for the individual and not many can accept it because the choice is not made in the absence of desire or the absence of need, but rather, in the full-blown presence of both! Celibacy then is a choice, not a response to the inability to find a mate, not a desperate decision made in response to any outplay of homosexual or asexual tendencies, no, celibacy is a hard and righteous choice of sexual sacrifice, for the sake of more a focused service choice in the Kingdom of God.

> *Celibacy then, implies Jesus, is quite clearly a choice! However, with every choice, there is also a cost.*

The second thing that Jesus says is that if you choose to accept this way of living and are able to be celibate, then you have received a hard gift. Did you get that, the gift did not make the choice easy, but the choice made the hard gift acceptable! Think about that.

I believe there is a principle here for us all to embrace in that in our lives we have to make many hard choices for the sake of the Kingdom. Here it is: When we make these hard and righteous choices, (not just celibacy) and are able to accept them for what they are, then in some majestic and marvelous way, these hard choices will transform themselves into solid gifts to us and into tremendous blessings to others.

As for me, give me celery each and every time!

Listen: *"Do not deprive one another except with consent for a time, that you may give yourselves to fasting and prayer; and come together again so that Satan does not tempt you because of your lack of self-control. But I say this as a concession, not as a commandment. For I wish that all men were even as I myself. But each one has his own gift from God, one in this manner and another in that." (1 Corinthians 7:5-7 NKJV)*

Pray: Lord, there are hard choices to be made for the sake of the kingdom. Please Lord, give me the courage and the grace to make these hard choices, then O Lord, would You please make them Your special gift to me, and of tremendous blessing to others, in Jesus name I pray, amen.

| Vol 01 | Q1 | NW00010 | January 10th |

Night-Whisper | **CHANGE**

Signs of softening

I like Esau. Indeed, I like him much better than Jacob. The problem is that God loves Jacob more, much, much more. Frankly I don't get it but then I am not supposed to get it! God is God and I am not. Let the facts then stand:

Genesis 28:8-9

"Also Esau saw that the daughters of Canaan did not please his father Isaac. So Esau went to Ishmael and took Mahalath the daughter of Ishmael, Abraham's son, the sister of Nebajoth, to be his wife in addition to the wives he had." NKJV

"And not only this, but when Rebecca also had conceived by one man, even by our father Isaac (for the children not yet being born, nor having done any good or evil, that the purpose of God according to election might stand, not of works but of Him who calls), it was said to her, 'The older shall serve the younger.' As it is written, 'Jacob I have loved, but Esau I have hated.'" Romans 9:10-13 NKJV

The plain reading of the Old Testament text regarding the outworking of this Divine favor does in fact reveal the outworking of this election to have been carried out callously, maliciously and surreptitiously by the human beings involved. So much so, that Esau is on many points simply left to scratch his head as he repeats to himself, "just what the heck was going on here!"

Certainly our text for today comes from the outworking of one of those Esau head scratching musings. I wonder if Esau was saying to himself, "How on earth did I get here? Why does my dad despise me in his actions and why does my mom hate me in her heart?" His conclusion to his musings was that his two Canaanite wives had done more harm than good to their family relationships, more harm than he had anticipated or even cared about at the time of his wedding and bedding them. Or maybe he knew exactly what he was doing when he married them and just what damage and hurt they would inflict upon his parents. Yes, maybe Esau was now simply reaping both the rejection and the discord which he had so intentionally and freely sown among his parents?

In any event, Esau's next action, be it clumsy in the extreme, (and it was), nevertheless, shows a welcomed softening and change of heart. Esau, you see, marries again and this time for the sake of love! Unfortunately, not for the sake of the love of the woman he married, but for the sake of the love of the parents whose affirmation and affection he so now obviously craved after. Now this was a very wrong action, yet might I suggest, very indicative of a softening of heart and of a deep desire to change.

In the mess that is humanity and in the depths that are God's good and gracious sovereignty, let us look for the softening and changing of hearts of people who have been found in the most stupid and stressful of situations. I tell you, all softening and change is to be rejoiced in and built upon. Look for it, yes, look for the rise of such regretful repentance, for I tell you, I believe the Lord Himself most certainly looks for it.

Celibacy then, implies Jesus, is quite clearly a choice! However, with every choice, there is also a cost.

Pity the person, I say pity the person that has no regrets to shepherd them home.

Listen: *"Jesus said to them, 'Assuredly, I say to you that tax collectors and harlots enter the kingdom of God before you. For John came to you in the way of righteousness, and you did not believe him; but tax collectors and harlots believed him; and when you saw it, you did not afterward relent and believe him.'" (Matthew 21:31b-32 NKJV)*

Pray: Lord, grant to me and to many others the gift of regret. Then please lead us through our regret into the valley of relent and the safe and sure shores of repentance, in Jesus name we pray, amen.

Night-Whisper | **COST**

Of bursting bags and guilt by association

In our text for tonight there is most definitely I think, a Pharisaic spirit that Jesus is judging here. He is not happy! Most frighteningly though is the fact that Jesus joins the Pharisees of His day to a spiritual genealogy of both judgment and persecution. The association is so complete in His eyes that He calls them the murderers of prophets from another age and of the prophet Zechariah in particular.

Matthew 22:32-36

"Fill up, then, the measure of your fathers' guilt. Serpents, brood of vipers! How can you escape the condemnation of hell? Therefore, indeed, I send you prophets, wise men, and scribes: some of them you will kill and crucify, and some of them you will scourge in your synagogues and persecute from city to city, that on you may come all the righteous blood shed on the earth, from the blood of righteous Abel to the blood of Zechariah, son of Berechiah, whom you murdered between the temple and the altar. Assuredly, I say to you, all these things will come upon this generation." NKJV

Physically of course, these particular Pharisees were not even born then, but spiritually, I suppose, their present expression of malice toward Jesus showed their 'spiritual DNA,' as it were, to be so rooted and connected with what happened 'way back then,' that Jesus condemns them now for those murderous actions as well! It is as though Jesus says "you Pharisees are the spiritual progeny of the prophet murderers of the past." That being the case, judgment, the severest and most terrible of kinds would come upon this present and living brood of vipers, because they were so intrinsically connected with that wriggling serpent who had swished his tail in murderous assault throughout the generations against God's messengers. There is most definitely I think, a Pharisaic spirit that Jesus is judging here. He is not happy!

Jamieson, Fausset and Brown, commenting on that particular generation says "As it was only in the last generation of them that 'the iniquity of the Amorites was full' (Genesis 15:16), and then the abominations of ages were at once completely and awfully avenged, so the iniquity of Israel was allowed to accumulate from age to age until in that generation it came to the full, and the whole collected vengeance of Heaven broke at once over its devoted head." In the first French Revolution the same awful principle of the bursting bag of the fullness of sin was also exemplified against an uncaring and disconnected monarchy and ruling class, and I fear that Christendom has not seen the last of bursting bags just yet.

> *Look now! Judgment is begun in the house of God and the church is under His rod of railing anger! How dare the Prophets NOT point this out. How dare the Pastors NOT tell the church the truth?*

There is a Laodicean laziness among the professing church at the end of this age, even a blind quietness born of full bellies, born of an attitude of 'sin and let sin,' born of the seeming inactivity and ignoring of Almighty God. For those that listen, however, time is heard running in its fullness to the top of the containers of God's judgment. The sound of filling these containers of judgement is coming to an end and I fear that the whole boiling water pot is about to fall off the stove and onto the pink and bared flesh of all our on-looking spiritual children, those pale and poor young youths who have been sold a yapping puppy of a faith.

Those of us still in the Kitchen have but very little time to call these goggle eyed singing goons back to the God of the Bible, lest they and their milksop teachers both, have the full and red hot bags of skubalastic judgment burst over their guilty by association little heads Look now! Judgment is begun in the house of God and the church is under His rod of railing anger! How dare the Prophets NOT point this out. How dare the Pastors NOT tell the church the truth?

When, the discipline is over, the remnant will find themselves in a very different church and world. I tell you, it is then and only then that the refining will begin.

Listen: *"Then the Spirit of God came upon Zechariah the son of Jehoiada the priest, who stood above the people, and said to them, 'Thus says God: "Why do you transgress the commandments of the Lord, so that you cannot prosper? Because you have forsaken the Lord, He also has forsaken you."' So they conspired against him, and at the command* *of the king they stoned him with stones in the court of the house of the Lord. Thus Joash the king did not remember the kindness which Jehoiada his father had done to him, but killed his son; and as he died, he said, 'The Lord look on it, and repay!'" (2 Chronicles 24:20-22 NKJV)*

Pray: Restore us, O God of our salvation, and cause Your anger toward us to cease. Will You be angry with us forever? Will You prolong Your anger to all generations? Will You not revive us again, that Your people may rejoice in You? Show us Your mercy, Lord, and grant us Your salvation. (Psalms 85:4-7 NKJV)

Night-Whisper | **PREPARE**

The beginning of sorrows – The arrival of joy

Erected at a time when it was possible to be born in this small island of Britain and then choose the whole wide world to die in, at the bottom of Regency Square in Hove stands an old Royal Sussex regimental war memorial. A bronze bugler surrounded by four artillery shells gazes over the English Channel and blows a long forgotten sound regarding the loss of local men in the first South African Boer War.

Matthew 24:6-8

"And you will hear of wars and rumours of wars. See that you are not troubled, for all these things must come to pass, but the end is not yet. For nation will rise against nation, and kingdom against kingdom. And there will be famines, pestilences, and earthquakes in various places. All these are the beginning of sorrows." NKJV

The majority of people walking past this now unknown memorial to unknown conflict in unknown countries on continents long since changed; this green and weathered testament to the fact that wars, kingdoms and empires, all come and all go; are now mostly from other countries and like what remains of the local population, they are completely ignorant of the losses and the battles that this bugle blowing bronze tries to recall, tries to remember, tries to commemorate. All who would remember them, are gone!

Thus the moving collage of this changing world, runs its colors into one another, as one kingdom overlays another with acquisitions and aspirations and like dirty frothed water spiraling down an emptying plughole, slowly but surely, yes, like black vultures, the changing nations now circle themselves over that nation that refuses to be rubbed out of history: the nation of Israel.

In our text for tonight, Jesus clearly tells us that toward the time of the end, like a woman in labor, the Kingdoms of this world will begin to heave and pant, as the 'apex' nation of the conclusion of time is at last called into the revelation, even Israel with its capital as Jerusalem.

It is my delight to tell you tonight that amidst all the coming sweat and trouble, amidst all the artillery shells of war, through the giving birth to that 'apex' baby in 1948, it was God's clear and good purpose for the miraculous nation of Israel to pop itself out from between the open legs of Lady history, and bring with that birth, that further blessing, of not only greater trouble, but also an ever greater redemption though Jesus Christ her Lord. Truly, like never before, we need to look up and listen up, for amongts the ignorance of the milling masses, the bugle is now sounding loud and very clear, and with it, our redemption draweth nigh.

> *It was God's clear and good purpose for the miraculous nation of Israel to pop itself out from between the open legs of Lady history!*

Therefore, I tell you tonight, in the tumult of the nation's now upon us, (and it is, and the tumult will get worse), keep both eyes on Jesus and keep your spare eye on Israel and Jerusalem in particular!

Listen: *"For the earnest expectation of the creation eagerly waits for the revealing of the sons of God. For the creation was subjected to futility, not willingly, but because of Him who subjected it in hope; because the creation itself also will be delivered from the bondage of corruption into the glorious liberty of the children of God. For we know that the whole creation groans and labours with birth pangs together until now. Not only that, but we also who have the first fruits of the Spirit, even we ourselves groan within ourselves, eagerly waiting for the adoption, the redemption of our body. For we were saved in this hope, but hope that is seen is not hope; for why does one still hope for what he sees? But if we hope for what we do not see, we eagerly wait for it with perseverance." (Romans 8:19-25 NKJV)*

Pray: Help us O Lord in this time of increasing wars to proclaim the Gospel of peace with God through the shed blood of Jesus Christ our Lord, amen and let it be so!

Night-Whisper | **PREPARE**

God the Gazumper

The term, 'Presumed consent,' in the arena of organ donation is: "the right to harvest organs from the dead unless explicit instructions have been given to the contrary." I believe this is a most personal violation of human rights, for allowing the State to decide how our dead bodies should be dealt with is just another gross raping of our individual choice, even another indecent and disrespect of our personal decision. All the cries for the saving of people dying for lack of organs, are overshadowed by the real reason for this violation of human rights and that is: "the saving of money."

It is in economic terms, far less expensive to bung a cadaver kidney into a patient rather than maintain their dialysis over long periods of time. The same economic truths apply to all other patients in need of a transplant and frankly, though I am personally only in favor of informed consent, it is never the less obvious that the harvesting of organs from conscripted corpses will reduce the health service medical bills by hundreds of millions of monies. Make no mistake, health is business, big business! For now, money can buy life extension, health enhancement, good looks and sexuality like never before. The raw materials of fresh dead people are all around us and the technology available to utilize their quickly wasting parts, increases every single day. Our bodies, it would appear, are increasingly becoming a composite of artificial enhancements and other people's parts. I wonder, if both in the respect and application of governmental 'presumed consent,' that our bodies are increasingly not our own. Look now. The Non-Christian state simply regards you as a piece of meat. Never forget that.

1 Corinthians 6:18-20

"Flee sexual immorality. Every sin that a man does is outside the body, but he who commits sexual immorality sins against his own body. Or do you not know that your body is the temple of the Holy Spirit who is in you, whom you have from God, and you are not your own? For you were bought at a price; therefore glorify God in your body and in your spirit, which are God's."
NKJV

In Christian terms, of course, this dispossession has always been the case. Our bodies our not our own but rather are the indwelling of God the Most High and consequently are sacred places, places for His use. God is not the tenant here, no, God does not pay any rent, but rather God owns our whole kit and caboodle, body soul and spirit and it is we who are in effect tenants of His even within the walls of our own bodies. God has 'gazumped' the devil in that He has raised the price of our purchase and bought us out from under his dirty and scaly little feet and made us the most precious of His purchased possessions, all shiny and new in His most glorious sight! Now then, the devil is not very happy about this and consequently is out for or diminishment at worse and our demolition or destruction at best. We must not help him this! No, as tenants in our own body then, we need to make sure we maintain this dwelling place of God, for God, because in both actuality and in effect, the temple of our body, even every member and every organ, every muscle tear and long black nasal hair, are not ours at all! They are God's.

We need to re-read the terms of our own lease once more, yes, we need to lay down our so called 'ownership rights' once and for all time, for we are truly not our own.

Now and in the future, we shall surely have to fight all the ethical battles of organ donation and body manipulation, even trans-humanism, but more than anything tonight dear friends, we need to re-read the terms of our own lease once more, yes, we need to lay down our so called 'ownership rights' once and for all time, for we are truly not our own. Let me ask you then: "are you taking care of His stuff?"

Listen: *"You were bought at a price; do not become slaves of men." (1 Corinthians 7:23-24 NKJV)*

Pray: You have called me O Lord, bought and bagged me, right where I am. Truly then, I am not my own. Help me to care of this body, Your most precious possession, as a temple of health where possible and a temple of holiness at all times, in Jesus name I ask it, amen and let it be so.

| Vol 01 | Q1 | NW00014 | January 14th |

Night-Whisper | **MONEY**

Murder meadow

The following words in our text for tonight are of course not recorded in the prophecy of Jeremiah at all!

Matthew 27:6-10
"But the chief priests took the silver pieces and said, 'It is not lawful to put them into the treasury, because they are the price of blood.' And they consulted together and bought with them the potter's field, to bury strangers in. Therefore that field has been called the Field of Blood to this day. Then was fulfilled what was spoken by Jeremiah the prophet, saying, 'And they took the thirty pieces of silver, the value of Him who was priced, whom they of the children of Israel priced, and gave them for the potter's field, as the Lord directed me.'"

'And they took the thirty pieces of silver, the value of Him who was priced, whom they of the children of Israel priced, and gave them for the potter's field, as the Lord directed me.'

Nevertheless, under the guidance of the Holy Spirit, Matthew does say they were 'spoken' by Jeremiah. Even if indeed the scroll of Jeremiah was the opening parchment to that collection which contained Zachariah, Matthew is in fact interjecting a parenthesis from that prophet Zachariah as a fuller and substantiating explanation as to the fact that both the incident and the occurrence recorded here by him, was in fact a fulfilment of prophecy.

This parenthetical interjection from the prophecy of Zachariah regarding the thirty pieces of silver, was in fact the price Israel put on Zachariah's original prophetic ministry, even the pitiful price of a common slave! In other words, Israel of old were saying that Zachariah's prophetic shepherding ministry was valueless and saying it in the same way that the leaders of Israel were also now regarding the powerful prophetic ministry of the Great Shepherd of the sheep, Jesus Himself. The leaders of Israel, thought the ministry of Christ as worthless. Many still do.

In many mega churches today there is a massive problem of secret over-payment, and I mean outrageous overpayment of so many, so called Pastors. However, at the opposite end of the scale, so many of Christ's under-shepherds, even today, also seem to have their ministry regarded as worthless by those who should know better. This is indeed reflected in the wages that their congregations are willing to pay for them. Though it is less so than it was, there are still many congregations praying that God will keep their shepherds humble as they try and keep them poor.

Worse than that both this nauseating overpayment and this disgusting underpayment I suppose, is the dreadful Laodicean laziness of shepherds who make their own ministries worthless to their sheep. by providing them with nothing but stale bread, poor protection and no real spiritual direction at all. This worthless kind of pastoral ministry, this laziness that leaves people hungry, might be clothed in boasting busyness and seeming success, might be either very entertaining or very boring, yet I tell you, it is still worthless. If you are not getting fed my friends, then you are not getting led and you are not getting truly cared for. Get out while you can!

> *If you are not getting fed my friends, then you are not getting led and you are not getting truly cared for. Get out while you can!*

I suppose in both respects, such a valueless shepherding ministry can amazingly produce only fine charnel houses and sculptured ossuaries, but in the end, they rarely produce life and such churches and religious organizations have simply become fields full of dead men's bones. The churches left in the United Kingdom at the beginning of the twenty first century are ample testimony of this and I wonder if a contributing factor to this was poor Biblical preaching and even poorer Biblical shepherding?

My fellow sheep, may I encourage you tonight to encourage your shepherds in both words and in deeds as they minister the bread of life toward you. My fellow ministers, may I encourage you tonight to labor such amongst the sheep of your pasture that your ministry would be greatly valued by them. For you see, the absence of good ministry which the absence of good shepherds bring with them, means the sheep of God shall essentially be sold into the emaciated slavery of either entertainment or boredom. Whatever you do Pastor and church member, do not turn the green pastures of God, running beside the silver springs of still waters, into meadows of murder where wolves run wild. In the second decade of the 21ˢᵗ century, most churches are murder meadows, all filled with wolves. **We need a culling and we need it now.**

Listen: *Let the elders who rule well be counted worthy of double honour, especially those who labour in the word and doctrine. For the Scripture says, "You shall not muzzle an ox while it treads out the grain," and, "The labourer is worthy of his wages." (1 Timothy 5:17-19 NKJV)*

Pray: Father, help me to rightly value those ministries and ministers of eternal preciousness, in Jesus name I pray, amen.

| Vol 01 | Q1 | NW00015 | January 15th |

Night-Whisper | **MONEY**

The hiring of Larry lightning face

A long, long time ago, Jesus posted some job adverts up on an angelic notice board. It was one angel in particular, old 'Larry lightning face,' a friend of Jesus who liked surprises and loved talking about the new stuff he had found out about God and His creation, who actually was intrigued enough to apply for the position of 'Temporary tomb tour guide.'

Matthew 28:1-3

"Now after the Sabbath, as the first day of the week began to dawn, Mary Magdalene and the other Mary came to see the tomb. And behold, there was a great earthquake, for an angel of the Lord descended from heaven, and came and rolled back the stone from the door, and sat on it." NKJV

This job was a very short term appointment for sure, and there was not much money in it, but it caught Larry's eye, because like I said, he loved showing the other angels the stuff he had found out about God and His creation, and anyways, both he and Jesus were, like I said, very good mates indeed.

"So anyway, it's not a tough job." Says Jesus.

"What do you want me to do then Lord? How many folks will I be showing around and more importantly will You be there, 'cause I want You to see what I do, for though I say so myself, I'm pretty good at this you know. I love it! Do you remember when I found that secret solar system You tucked away behind that red dwarf, well..."

"Ahem, yes," says Jesus, "Another place now overrun with the angelic mob relaxing on holy days and what's with that whole Germanic lot claiming the beach for sunrise praise? Anyways, let's not get sidetracked here Larry, I know you like this kind of stuff, which is why I know you'll do a good job and I can leave you to get on with it?"

"You'll not be there then?" says Larry with some disappointment.

"No, no, I'll not be there because you see, I'll already be up and around but I'd like you to come and roll away the stone anyways and then show a few folk around the tomb for a bit. A select few mind you, good friends of mine?"

"OK. Is that all then?"

"Well you know, I want you to do this with some gusto Larry, some noise if you want, put on a show even! You do like noise don't you Larry?"

"Love noise Lord, love it! Rumbling earthquakes, cracks of lightening, all that kind of stuff, love it!"

"Well with a face like yours Larry, I know you can do this job with some pizzazz, some shazzam! Put the wind up the guards a bit of course, not too much, but enough so they'll get the message.

"OK, OK, sounds good, then what Lord?"

"Well, then you can relax, sit down a bit even. The guards will have fainted or run off, so just chill a little. I know you'll be excited after your sound and light show and what with me defeating death and all that, but just calm yourself down a little, hang around and be that very temporary tomb guide I need you to be. You know, show the punters around a bit, let 'em have a little "look see" and then remind them, because they will have forgotten, to go and tell the those dozy and dazed disciples of mine, that I am making my way to Galilee to meet them at the appointed place. Simple really Larry. Really simple"

"Yes, yes, OK I get it, but what will You be doing then Lord?"

"I've just told you, I'll be in my way to Galilee Larry! You know what it's like when you've just gotten back from somewhere and done really well! It'll be nice to just turn up and surprise a few folk, maybe even jump out on them, on the road somewhere, maybe over a meal! Hilarious! Anyways, we'll see. So, Larry! That's the job mate, 'temporary tomb tour guide.' Do you want it?"

"Do I get a ticket machine?"

"No, of course you don't get a ticket machine Larry, what's wrong with you?"

"How about a uniform? A green one maybe with a cap?"

"Well, now you're just being silly! Do you want the job or not?"

"I'd love it Lord!" Says Larry, " I'd just love it."

Jesus gets up, shakes Larry's hand and turns him around to escort him out of the meeting room. The angel, still excited and still talking says, "Thanks for the job Jesus. I know it's only for a bit but I promise You, I'll make You proud! Do you want me to tidy the place up a bit? You know, neatly fold the old grave clothes up, dust around a little, sweep maybe?"

"Yeah, if you want? That'll be nice"

"Of course Lord, presentation! That's what's it all about, presentation. Like I said on Andromeda..."

The Lord, looking over the shoulder of the excited and chattering angel at the long line of angelic host queuing up in the distance, waves to a smiling face and with great relief shouts: "Next! Excuse me now will you Larry, I've got to see this next chap, he wants to spook some shepherds at the beginning of the show, so, until the empty tomb then Larry, until the empty tomb, G'bye! "

Listen: *"His countenance was like lightning, and his clothing as white as snow. And the guards shook for fear of him, and became like dead men. But the angel answered and said to the women, 'Do not be afraid, for I know that you seek Jesus who was crucified. He is not here; for He is risen, as He said. Come, see the place where the Lord lay. And go quickly and tell His disciples that He is risen from the dead, and indeed He is going before you into Galilee; there you will see Him. Behold, I have told you.'" (Matthew 28:3-7 NKJV)*

Pray: Oh to be so confident of You O Lord, to be able to perform my God appointed task and then sit down upon it and wait in watching wonder at what You will do next. Oh for such relaxed confidence in all my coming days O Lord. In Jesus name Father, I ask you to grant me such an expectant confidence. Amen, and let it be so.

Night-Whisper | **CHOOSE**

Splitting dialect and divisive dialogue

Jacob, of course, will graduate from God's College of True Faith and Worship, (T.F.W.). He's earned the school colors of black and blue and though his education is far from over, he is about to graduate, Baccalaureate in hand, to a master's level training course. That particular story, however, is for another night.

Genesis 31:45-48
"So Jacob took a stone and set it up as a pillar. Then Jacob said to his brethren, 'Gather stones.' And they took stones and made a heap, and they ate there on the heap. Laban called it Jegar Sahadutha, but Jacob called it Galeed."
NKJV

Jacob's present professor at arms has for some years been his old uncle Laban. For twenty years, Laban has messed with Jacob's head, used him, abused him, stole from him, and generally has tried to rob Jacob of everything that was rightfully his. My, oh my, how the chickens have now finally come home to roost in Jacob's life, but like I say, that's a story for another day.

The bottom line and background of our text for tonight is that Jacob has "done a runner!" Without informing Laban, he has left town and done so with all of his family, all of his goods and a few stolen bits thrown in for good measure. Laban has loaded up his six guns and high tailed it after him with but one purpose on his mind, that being the utter and final destruction of Jacob and the forceful taking back of everything Laban thought rightfully belonged to him, which was, by the way, in Laban's eyes, quite literally, everything Jacob owned and loved. Now, make no mistake about it, except that God had intervened in a most threatening dream the night before Laban's face-to-face encounter with Jacob, this would have been the outcome. Jacob would have been left destitute, and maybe even dead.

The fact that God stepped in meant Jacob and Laban, probably for the first time in twenty years or more, had to 'talk turkey' with one another. The main problem with these two rascals relatives, was that they didn't communicate and they didn't communicate because they didn't even speak the same language! The naming of this rock pile, this cairn of witness, this watchtower of mutually assured destruction, is testimony to that fact. They both call the cairn the same name, however, Laban gives it an Aramaic name, 'Jegar Sahadutha,' and Jacob a Hebrew one, 'Galeed.'

If you are with someone with whom you have no depth of communication tonight and consequently and in all probability, a growing hostility, then may I suggest that without sinning, it is time to separate. It is time to leave and in the leaving set up a rock pile where God is witness to your blessing of the other and your leaving the other alone!

Who is out to kill you? Who do you need to separate from tonight?

I believe in heaven that no such 'Mizpah' like rock piles exist between those who are His. On God's good earth however, setting up a few stones of separating testimony is often the wisest and safest thing we can do. Who is out to kill you? Who do you need to separate from tonight?

Listen: *"And Laban said, 'This heap is a witness between you and me this day.' Therefore its name was called Galeed, also Mizpah, because he said, 'May the Lord watch between you and me when we are absent one from another. If you afflict my daughters, or if you take other wives besides my daughters, although no man is with us - see, God is witness between you and me!' Then Laban said to Jacob, 'Here is this heap and here is this pillar, which I have placed between you and me. This heap is a witness, and this pillar is a witness, that I will not pass beyond this heap to you, and you will not pass beyond this heap and this pillar to me, for harm. The God of Abraham, the God of Nahor, and the God of their father judge between us.' And Jacob swore by the Fear of his father Isaac. Then Jacob offered a sacrifice on the mountain, and called his brethren to eat bread. And they ate bread and stayed all night on the mountain. And early in the morning Laban arose, and kissed his sons and daughters and blessed them. Then Laban departed and returned to his place." (Genesis 31:48-55 NKJV)*

Pray: Lord, if there is any leaving to do, let me do it with both righteousness and love. Help me in the spirit to set up clear boundaries of blessing and protection, in Jesus name I pray, amen, and let it be so!

Night-Whisper | **RESCUE**

Gracious assimilation

Born in France in 1040, it was Rabbi Shlomo Yitzhaqi, better known as 'Rashi' the famed author of the first comprehensive commentaries on the Talmud, Torah and Tanakh, who first suggested that the 'Shaul' of our text for tonight, was in fact Dinah's son by lusty young Shechem!

Genesis 46:10

"The sons of Simeon were Jemuel, Jamin, Ohad, Jachin, Zohar, and Shaul, the son of a Canaanite woman."
NKJV

Rashi relates that following the rape of their sister Dinah, Simeon and Levi later killed all the men in the city, including Shechem and his father. At that time, records Rachi, Dinah refused to leave the bloody palace of Shechem unless Simeon removed her pregnant shame, by agreeing to marry her! Of course Rashi goes on to say that Dinah only lived in Simeon's house and did not have sexual relations with him. In any event, Rashi relates that because of this redemptive and shame covering marriage, Dinah's son Shaul, is counted among Simeon's children and consequently, Shaul also received a portion of land in Israel in the time of Joshua. Rashi suggests that Dinah, apparently because of her stupidity, because of her rape by Shechem and because of her being buried in the land of Canaan, is regarded as that 'Canaanite woman' of our text for tonight!

Well what can we say regarding this text and this Rash'ite recounting of a very strange story?

In this strange time in which we live, we are surrounded by women who have children by multiple fathers. The rise of divorce and remarriage, or marriage by any other name, has led to a multitude of composite families, of both composite colors and composite cultures. These are mere observations rather than condemnations of those truths. These are just a fistful of frightening facts at the beginning of the twenty first century. It seems that both the world and the church are a mass and a mess of relationships all gone wrong!

I wonder then if our text for tonight, mentions Shaul as a special son of Simeon, because he is a figurehead of redemptive assimilation? Shaul's free acceptance and full adoption into Israel of old, is then a picture of the way in which we need to try and adopt all the unasked for sons of Canaan into the fantastic family of God.

Speaking as a son of a Canaanite woman myself, I know that God puts His love on all sorts of folks and brings them into the blessings of His family and into the very heart the Promised Land. Let's make sure in the coming days that we can all, with righteousness and grace, widen our own tent pegs both to righteous accommodation and redemptive assimilation.

> *Shaul's free acceptance and full adoption into Israel of old, is then a picture of the way in which we need to try and adopt all the unasked for sons of Canaan into the fantastic family of God.*

Listen: *"And they sang a new song, saying: 'You are worthy to take the scroll, and to open its seals; for You were slain, and have redeemed us to God by Your blood out of every tribe and tongue and people and nation, and have made us kings and priests to our God; and we shall reign on the earth.'" (Revelation 5:9,10 NKJV0*

Pray: Worthy is the lamb who was slain, to receive power and riches and wisdom, and strength and honor and glory and blessing! Yes, blessing and honor and glory and power be to Him who sits on the throne, and to the lamb, forever and ever! Amen, and let it always be so!

Night-Whisper | **POWER**

The dance of death

The local soccer team in the city in which I presently reside at the time of writing, bears a name similar to many soccer teams in the United Kingdom. It is called Brighton & Hove Albion.

Romans 12:1-2

"I beseech you therefore, brethren, by the mercies of God, that you present your bodies a living sacrifice, holy, acceptable to God, which is your reasonable service. And do not be conformed to this world, but be transformed by the renewing of your mind, that you may prove what is that good and acceptable and perfect will of God." NKJV

Albion of course, has become the ancient name for these islands of mine, even for this "other Eden, this demi-paradise, this little world, this nurse, this teeming womb of royal kings, feared by their breed and famous by their birth, this precious stone set in a silver sea." (Well on rare sunny days anyways!) Yes, Albion I think, refers in particular to the spirit of the ancient people of these islands, more than its place, pointing back to that strong and certain, happy breed of men.

It was Leanardo DaVinci, who in around 1492 drew what is now the growing medical icon of 'Vitruvian Man.' Da Vinci, drawing heavily on a treatise on the geometrical proportions of man written by the Roman architect Vitrivius, drew this nude male figure in two superimposed positions. Both with their arms and legs apart and each one simultaneously surrounded by both a circle and a square. Believing the workings of the body to picture the workings of the universe, Da Vinci acknowledges both the symmetry of this the spirituality of it, by placing the center of the man's hips in the center of the square (material) and the man's naval in the center of the circle (spiritual).

It was this Da Vinci drawing that some 400 years later, William Blake took, and in both picture and in prose, released Da Vinci's Vitruvian man from both the confines of the circle and the square, of the material and the spiritual. Depicting a dancing and naked man then, Blake penned the following inscription above the released and now happy Da

Vinci Vitruvian which said, *"Albion rose from where he labour'd at the mill with slaves: Giving himself for the nations he danc'd the dance of eternal death."*

Blake, commenting on the social revolutions at the time and in particular the American revolution, associated himself most fully with that freed and democratic spirit and pictured his own people, the people he associated with, as offering themselves as living sacrifices for the sake of the nations and of America in particular.

This post-Christian land of lost Albion, this Britannia, this England, has in the past, offered up hundreds of thousands of living sacrifices for other nations. My fellow countryman, this muddied, yet green and verdant land of ours, has not only been the birth and womb of parliamentary democracy to the whole world but in its past, has birthed such members of the Holy Nation and Royal Priesthood, that hundreds and thousands of them, danced with gladness the dance of death, giving themselves as a living sacrifices to the Great Commission of their Captain, so that the nations might know Jesus Christ as their Savior and Lord.

> *Brothers and sisters, it is time to fearlessly proclaim the Gospel once again in these islands. What a blessing that might be to the rest of the world once more. Selah.*

The glad days of Albion are now long gone and a gross spirit of indifference, fear and sordid selfishness has stained the chalky cliffs of white, upon which we daily build our lives. I tell you, unless a new and dancing generation arises in these islands and raises it up above its broken parapets, the waters of the world shall rise and flood in upon us and drowned us in their sea and then like Atlantis of old, Albion and it's glorious dancing spirit shall be lost forever more beneath the angry waves. Brothers and sisters, it is time to fearlessly proclaim the Gospel once again in these islands. What a blessing that might be to the rest of the world once more. Selah.

Listen: *"Yet I have set My King on my Holy hill of Zion. I will declare the decree: The Lord has said to Me, 'You are My Son, today I have begotten You. Ask of Me, and I will give You the nations for Your inheritance, and the ends of the earth for Your possession.'" (Psalms 2:6-8 NKJV0*

Pray: Along with the other "blessed of the Lord," we put our trust in You O God, yes, we rejoice with fear and trembling and we kiss the Son, lest He be angry with us all the time and we perish beneath these angry, pounding waves. Lord, let your anger diminish. Lord, let it become little toward us. Lord, have mercy upon these islands and its people. Lord, revive Your remnant and set our feet to dancing. Give birth O Lord, give birth to a new and dancing generation and then, within these stained and fallen chalky walls of ours, give us a happy land once more. Yes Lord, as an inheritance, as an eternal reward for us and as an eternal emblem of Your love, give us all the nations that now lodge in Albion, long since gone. In Jesus name we ask it, amen and let it be so!

Night-Whisper | **LEAD**

Jam and Jerusalem

As a former village pastor, I remember going to my first local Women's Institute (W.I.) Christmas party and being entertained by several older women in their sixties, all dressed in emerald green leotards, spangly clad and high-kicking, singing old war songs whilst wearing black top hats and tapping silver canes on the dirty, old and creaky wooden floor of the village hall. My cheek muscles suffered severe 'giggle-ation' that afternoon and I was facially, forever ruined by that laughter, for my cheeks have never returned to their former firmness since that fun-filled and fateful afternoon! Once you've seen a perm rinsed old lady, sporting shiny dentures and pulled into in a spangly leotard like a string tied pork roast, wearing top hat and fish net tights, you will never be the same again!

Revelation 21:2-4

"Then I, John, saw the holy city, New Jerusalem, coming down out of heaven from God, prepared as a bride adorned for her husband. And I heard a loud voice from heaven saying, 'Behold, the tabernacle of God is with men, and He will dwell with them, and they shall be His people. God Himself will be with them and be their God. And God will wipe away every tear from their eyes; there shall be no more death, nor sorrow, nor crying. There shall be no more pain, for the former things have passed away.'" NKJV

It was during WWII whilst running government sponsored Preservation Centers and making and canning using excess food produce, that the W.I. acquired their mythical focus on jam making! Interestingly, it was some thirty years previous to this during the Great war to end all wars, when in the United Kingdom, the disappearance of men from the land, especially from rural areas, began to take a toll on the economy of Britain. It was John Nugent Harris, secretary of the then Agricultural Organizations Societies, who met with Mrs. Madge Rose Watt, formerly of British Columbia, to begin in these Islands, the famed Women's Institute. As I write today, the W.I. have over 225,000 members nationwide and for ninety years or more have been a force and influence in local communities as well as at a national level. Yes indeed, though many local WI meetings begin with the singing of Blake's 'Jerusalem,' this organization is far from being just about 'jam and Jerusalem.' The list of issues the W.I. have tackled is enormous. To name but two examples: it was in 1986 that the W.I. became the first organization to lobby the Government into tackling the Aids crisis, and then who can forget the year 2000 and the giant 'hand-bagging' of Prime Minister Tony Blair, when the W.I. delegates administered the longest, most public and most broadcast, slowest handclapping of disapproval ever given! On both counts, the nation took notice of the W.I.

As a Christian, I do seek 'jam tomorrow.' I am looking for a better time to come, in the better world to come, where I also seek my New Jerusalem, my eternal home, my city, whose builder and maker is God. In many respects then, the Christian life is indeed about embracing that old jocular of jam and Jerusalem.

To the watching world of course, though they are not watching us so much nowadays that's for sure, but to the world, we the church must never allow ourselves to be consigned to the irrelevant and the laughable 'tea at three brigade.' No, we can take a leaf from the W.I. manual here and organize ourselves into both cells of local goodness and a growing body of national influence. We Christians need to get organized like never before. Yes, let's support the organizations we've already got but quite frankly, they're just not enough to do the job! We need to organize yet more and more. Good grief, I mean there is a war on folks after all!

We Christians need to get organized like never before.

The difference between us and the W.I. however, is that in the end, all our organizations, all our local goodness projects must point to heaven's hope and all our national pressure must be about the jammy goodness of God toward us in Christ Jesus! Yes, dear friends, without the superb silliness of scantily clad old ladies in emerald green leotards and the tea at three brigade cheering them on, in the end, we Christians must indeed be all about jam and Jerusalem, and let me tell you tonight that being so, is a long, long way from being old, out of date and irrelevant!

Think about this. How can we get more better organized? I tell you, get cracking today, for tomorrow is coming and a darkness when no man can work. It is time to truly prepare for a transformational change. This means putting boots on the ground, it means getting back to a New Testament five-fold ministerial and itinerant connected and growing church.

Listen: *"If anyone among you thinks he is religious, and does not bridle his tongue but deceives his own heart, this one's religion is useless. Pure and undefiled religion before God and the Father is this: to visit orphans and widows in their trouble, and to keep oneself unspotted from the world." (James 1:26-27 NKJV)*

Pray: Lord, thank you for jam and for Jerusalem. Now with this hope of Your goodness and vision of our completeness, help us to offer hope and goodness to others, in Jesus name we pray, amen, and let it be so.

Night-Whisper | **WORK**

Dare you taste some of Robertson's most generous jam?

I was walking down a street in the city of Brighton & Hove not too long ago, when I came across another historical plaque fixed to an old house. It read "Robertson of Brighton – Philosopher and Preacher." Certainly this great Anglican preacher of the later Regency period, knew exactly what pugnacious preaching was, for he loved the Word, he loved the public publishing of the Truth and proclaimed it well, and at great personal cost.

2 Corinthians 12:15

"And I will very gladly spend and be spent for your souls; though the more abundantly I love you, the less I am loved."
NKJV

In his pugnaciousness Robertson was not given to the gross denunciation of others who were not in full agreement with his beliefs. Neither was he given to the dissemination of his own pet doctrines either but was rather, in great love and practicality, given over to the proclamation of the truth, the whole truth and nothing but the truth. In this, Robertson was a man of eloquence, of fire and of compassionate understanding. Preaching on 'The Tongue' on April 28th 1850, he remarks in this magnificent sermon that, "The Church of Rome hurls her thunders against Protestants of every denomination: the Calvinist scarcely recognizes the Arminian as a Christian: he who considers himself as the true Anglican, excludes from the Church of Christ all but the adherents of his own orthodoxy; every minister and congregation has its small circle, beyond which all are heretics." Yes, Robertson was concerned about the composite flower of both 'Truth and Grace' breaking forth from the seeds of practicality and goodness. His style of pugnacious preaching was the Gospel style of proclaiming revealed truth, rather than that of pushing the party denunciation of others. Robertson's zeal for this kind of preaching and all its arduous demands and consequences, in the end, cost him his life.

Born to an Evangelical army officer, Robertson entered the ministry with a soldier's zeal and much self-discipline. While at Oxford for example, he memorized the New Testament in both Greek and Hebrew, and had already broken his health in service and study prior to his arrival in Brighton. In the final six years of his life and ministry there, he filled his church each time he preached, appealing to both the rich and especially the working class, yes especially the poor, and was also monumental in helping found the Brighton Working Men's Institute. Here, his practical political views led him to be ostracized from many of his colleagues and his earnest zeal and ardent duties led him to be worn out with his work. At last, sick, in pain, lonely and depressed, thinking his short life's work wasted and futile, he died, aged just 37. Nevertheless, around 1,500 people, mainly from those well helped poor, formed a column nearly half a mile long to walk behind his coffin as it went to the cemetery and nearly all the shops en-route, closed as a mark of respect.

As I write these thoughts tonight, Holy Trinity, the church this great preacher ministered from in Ship Street Brighton, has long since closed its doors as a sacred place and is now a curious contemporary art gallery. A couple of plaques and a double decker bus bearing Robertson's once respected and revered name now driving around these Godless streets, are the only real remains of all the great preaching and good works this man did in the now gay capital of this far fallen Kingdom of ours.

We need to encourage and challenge our preachers to preach the truth in all its fullness. Then, we need to stand with them shoulder to shoulder in all its arduous demands and subsequent consequences. Tell me tonight, are you ready to do just that? Are you ready to pay that price? Are you ready to taste of real Robertson's jam?

> *Are you ready to pay that price? Are you ready to taste of real Robertson's jam?*

I wonder if a few more preachers of similar substance and courage, might step off that bus one day, clothed with the spirit of Robinson, settle down, serve six demanding years and save the day at last. Some of you ministers need to be putting a few more hours in. Some of you will have to. Labor on brothers, labor on! Expend yourself for Jesus.

Listen:

Go, labour on: spend, and be spent,
Thy joy to do the Father's will:
It is the way the Master went;
Should not the servant tread it still?
Go, labour on! 'Tis not for naught

Thine earthly loss is heav'nly gain;
Men heed thee, love thee, praise thee not;
The Master praises: what are men?
Go, labour on! Enough, while here,
If He shall praise thee, if He deign
The willing heart to mark and cheer:
No toil for Him shall be in vain.

Go, labour on! Your hands are weak,
Your knees are faint, your soul cast down;
Yet falter not; the prize you seek
Is near—a kingdom and a crown.

Go, labour on while it is day:
The world's dark night is hast'ning on;
Speed, speed thy work, cast sloth away;
It is not thus that souls are won.

Men die in darkness at thy side,
Without a hope to cheer the tomb;
Take up the torch and wave it wide—
The torch that lights time's thickest gloom.

Toil on, faint not, keep watch and pray,
Be wise the erring soul to win;
Go forth into the world's highway,
Compel the wand'rer to come in.

Toil on, and in thy toil rejoice!
For toil comes rest, for exile home;
Soon shalt thou hear the Bridegroom's voice,
The midnight peal, "Behold, I come!"

Horatius Bonar

Pray: So strengthen me tonight and even so, come Lord Jesus, amen and let it be so.

Night-Whisper | **GRACE**

The real cost of some of our Reheboths

Less than thirty miles away from the city of Brighton, is one of my favorite old market towns, Horsham. There survives here, an old historical Strict and Particular Baptist church called 'Reheboth,' whose composite meaning would be 'a broad, made space.' This Reheboth in Horsham was 'Strict' in terms of membership and membership access to the communion table, and 'Particular' in terms of the Calvinistic, some might even say hyper-Calvinistic thought, which stated that Christ died for the elect and only the elect.

Genesis 26:19-22

"Also Isaac's servants dug in the valley, and found a well of running water there. But the herdsmen of Gerar quarreled with Isaac's herdsmen, saying, 'The water is ours.' So he called the name of the well Esek, because they quarrelled with him. Then they dug another well, and they quarrelled over that one also. So he called its name Sitnah. And he moved from there and dug another well, and they did not quarrel over it. So he called its name Rehoboth, because he said, 'For now the Lord has made room for us, and we shall be fruitful in the land.'" NKJV

In our text for tonight, Isaac had tried to dwell with some peace, space and safety in the land of his sojourn, only to have his first two attempts end in dreadful failure, pictured by the naming of wells once dug, called 'Esek' and 'Sitnah,' or better still, 'contention' and 'hatred.'

The naming of the Baptist Chapel in Horsham bears the marks of similar disappointment in its own personal history in that it was, like many Baptist churches, borne out of a church split, where just six people at that time, set out on their own from the talking, teaching and practice which they considered to be contrary to their understanding of the Gospel. They were not alone, for in the 1800s this 'Strict and Particular' viewpoint and action was gathering some steam.

Even so, these disgruntled six souls met in an old farmhouse and grew enough in numbers to acquire the monies to rent a vacant chapel building. Here they grew still and soon purchased the property in which they met. Over the next fourteen years, with the help of one man in particular, the wee flock grew further in finances, enough to call and pay for their very first full time Pastor.

I am an ordained Countess of Huntingdon minister, proud of both my Selina heritage and her most famous of Chaplains and preachers, the Rev. George Whitfield. Indeed, it was from a Connexion Chapel in Tottenham, and one of Whitfield's churches, that a young man who "didn't even know" there was a God, eventually came to faith in Jesus under the then resident preacher, the Rev. John Hyatt. This new convert was Edward Mote.

After apprenticing and functioning as a cabinet-maker Edward Mote felt himself 'called to preach' and I do believe was himself ordained as a Countess of Huntingdon Minister. However, it is this same man, who we now find being that one man in particular in Horsham, who secured the building for a group of Christians most definitely not in line with the beliefs of the Connexion. It was this one man in particular who was also called as Reheboth's first full time pastor, and was also offered the trust deed of the property. Mote declined however, saying: "I do not want the chapel, I only want the pulpit; and when I cease to preach Christ, then turn me out of that."

> *"I do not want the chapel, I only want the pulpit; and when I cease to preach Christ, then turn me out of that."*

The history of heaven's church militant is one most unfortunately marked by consistent contention and hatred, even as we all seek spaces and places to be and to grow. Born today in 1797, I think Edward Mote, the Reheboth Baptist Chapel and their joint history, is a colorful snapshot of the church, which for centuries has been rent asunder by various ungracious divisions. Often, while seeking the true peace of righteousness, the Christian experience of one another in all our fragmentation has been far from gracious. Though its title is often opposite to our personal experience of one another, Mote, in one of many hymns of his, has left us all with an enduring focus of hope. Mote called this hymn, "The Gracious Experience of a Christian." I hope it is your gracious experience as well, despite those 'other' Christians!

Listen:

My hope is built on nothing less
Than Jesus' blood and righteousness.
I dare not trust the sweetest frame,
But wholly trust in Jesus' Name.

(Refrain)'On Christ the solid Rock I stand,
All other ground is sinking sand;
All other ground is sinking sand.'

When darkness seems to hide His face,
I rest on His unchanging grace.
In every high and stormy gale,
My anchor holds within the veil.
(Refrain)

His oath, His covenant, His blood,
Support me in the whelming flood.
When all around my soul gives way,
He then is all my Hope and Stay.
(Refrain)

When He shall come with trumpet sound,
Oh may I then in Him be found.
Dressed in His righteousness alone,
Faultless to stand before the throne.
(Refrain)

Pray: Lord, help us, the receivers of Your great grace, be so secured in Your righteousness, that we might be gracious to one another and stand so firm in You, that the sinking of ten thousand times ten thousands of our own and homemade Reheboths, our own broad and often ungracious spaces upon this broken planet, will make such little difference to our experiential standing in You, that we would always be found rejoicing in

You, yes in You, the great rock of our salvation. In Your great name we pray, amen and let be so.

Night-Whisper | **PERSEVERE**

The Irreconcilables

One of the many places our text for tonight can be found is on an original memorial plaque erected in 1706 to commemorate the death of 'Covenanter Irreconcilables' held in a section of Grey Friars Churchyard in Edinburgh. It is true that their chief persecutor, Sir George Mackenzie of Rosehaugh, or 'Bloody Mackenzie' as his epitaph exclaims, is interred in a fine mausoleum not too far away from those he most horribly persecuted. However, in these long fought over bloody islands of Britain, it is not strange to find it so.

Revelation 6:9-12

"When He opened the fifth seal, I saw under the altar the souls of those who had been slain for the word of God and for the testimony which they held. And they cried with a loud voice, saying, 'How long, O Lord, holy and true, until You judge and avenge our blood on those who dwell on the earth?' Then a white robe was given to each of them; and it was said to them that they should rest a little while longer, until both the number of their fellow servants and their brethren, who would be killed as they were, was completed."
NKJV

Not many years ago, for the first time in over a century, charges of 'disturbing a sepulcher' were brought against some miscreant youths who broke into this same 'Bloody Mackenzie's' tomb, stole his skull and at the very least, used it as a glove puppet! The law of 'disturbing a sepulcher' had its original intent in trying and deter the actions of the 'resurrectionists,' those body snatchers, those "Burke and Hares" of the day, from removing freshly planted corpses and then selling them to medical science. No wonder then, that this particular portion of Grey Friars, noted for human violation and so much un-sacred disturbance, is reported to be fraught with paranormal activity, even today.

Mackenzie was no fool. A learned man, a man of writing and letters, a legal whizz of his day if you will, became the willing glove puppet of the law of prerogative, that is, the law of the 'Divine Right of Kings,' which allowed Royalty to do what they will, with whom they will, when they will, and all within the boundaries historically set for them by their nobles and the church of Rome. Scotland, in the complicated reformation malaise of that day, almost as one man, had entered into what I would call the national covenant of the 'Divine Right of the Church' as expressed especially in Presbyterian government, to declare the outworking of the Word of God as directed by its appointed preachers. A bloody clash of national proportions therefore was inevitable in Scotland.

Essentially, this Scottish and National Covenant was a rejection of all independent protestant and non-conforming preaching and especially that form of Episcopal government, so neatly arrived at by Elizabeth, which not only brought some peace to England, but allowed monarchical government to be expressed through the Bishops of the Church of England. Scotland would have no intrusion of any hint of Papish power as they saw expressed in Episcopalian government and the order of service in the Book of common prayer. No! In Scotland, it was Presbyterianism or death!

> *Essentially, this Scottish and National Covenant was a rejection of all independent protestant and non-conforming preaching*

After the English Civil War and the restoration of the monarchy it was James Stuart who tried to fully unite the Kingdoms of Scotland and England, first by pleading and politics and when that failed, by violent coercion. Fines imposed on dissenting Covenanter meetings and the giving of their livings back to once disenfranchised Covenanter preachers, was a great political pincer movement which left none but the 'Irreconcilable' hardliners to stand by the great Scottish National Covenant. These same 'Irreconcilables' were eventually rounded up and imprisoned. Some dying there, some deported from there, and some being martyred there.

Mackenzie, swayed and ruled, moved and made, by the old law of prerogative, had the opportunity not only to line his deep pockets, but also to be used as the glove puppet of Satan against the people of God. For if we remove the political ranting and the nationalistic rabble-rousing, which some would call rebellion, then so forcibly made by the Covenant preachers against the government of the day, then we are left with the awful slaughter of the people of God during what has become to be so terribly known as 'The killing time.'

Politics is always a complicated affair, and has always been streaked with red when played out amongst the people of these often cold, grey islands. Even so, whenever we see the deaths head skull, so gleefully displayed toward and applied against the people of God, then we can be assured that the mover of this open mouth of death, is none but Satan himself.

Christian, a battle is going on around you and amidst all the clamor and dreadful shrieks of the centuries, through the blinding gun smoke of the front line, know this one thing, that the Devil is out to kill you! Indeed, he is out to slaughter all the people of God. You are the cause of such spiritual confusion, yes, you are the point of it all, and your death is the purpose of it. On every continent and in every time, it has always been so and always will be. Christians are at war with the devil. The devil is at war with Christians.

Christian, a battle is going on around you and amidst all the clamor and dreadful shrieks of the centuries, through the blinding gun smoke of the front line, know this one thing, that the Devil is out to kill you! Indeed, he is out to slaughter all the people of God.

If you were the only Christian alive on planet earth, then the whole of the cosmos, indeed, the whole multidimensional space-time continuum, the whole of heaven, earth and hell, would revolve around you, your prayers, your power in Jesus and your actions in, for and through Him. So then, go and get a good night's sleep for tomorrow, it is time to start living out of your enormous importance to this world and the world to come. You are God's representative in this great place of darkness. When the sun comes up, make sure you shine along with it.

Listen: *"Now all things are of God, who has reconciled us to Himself through Jesus Christ, and has given us the ministry of reconciliation, that is, that God was in Christ reconciling the world to Himself, not imputing their trespasses to them, and has committed to us the word of reconciliation. Now then, we are ambassadors for Christ, as though God were pleading through us: we implore you on Christ's behalf, be reconciled to God. For He made Him who knew no sin to be sin for us, that we might become the righteousness of God in Him." (2 Corinthians 5:18-21 NKJV0*

Pray: We the 'Irreconcilable' to this world, do for the rest of our days, covenant ourselves to the great ministry of the reconciliation of the world to God the Father, through Jesus Christ our Lord, amen and let it be so.

| Vol 01 | Q1 | NW00023 | January 23rd |

Night-Whisper | **CHANGE**

Of changing chains to licorice

God, like some great war General, had given very specific instructions to these fleeing slaves about precisely where they would pitch their camp. However, the positioning of that place looked like nothing short of stupidity. Moses, known at court, known for being a trained and practiced military leader amongst the Egyptians, would have looked like a foolish old man to this Pharaoh, for the leader of Israel had obviously been confused by the landscape and had inadvertently led the fleeing and frantic, fledgling of a nation into a giant and inescapable killing zone. On the morrow, Egypt would cut them to pieces.

Exodus 14:19-20

"And the Angel of God, who went before the camp of Israel, moved and went behind them; and the pillar of cloud went from before them and stood behind them. So it came between the camp of the Egyptians and the camp of Israel. Thus it was a cloud and darkness to the one, and it gave light by night to the other, so that the one did not come near the other all that night."
NKJV

Egypt did not realize that Moses was not the real leader! No, God was Israel's true leader and God Himself had instructed precisely where Israel should position themselves. It was God who had in fact laid the trap for Egypt and the killing zone. Israel's positioning was a carrot to bring on donkey Egypt, and in such a complete way, that in the end, they would be utterly destroyed from before the face of Israel, forever! You see, those that Israel saw and worried about that very day, would on the morrow, be seen no more. Forever!

Now, this fiery pillar, this viewing war chariot of the most High God, moved from the front of the Israelite ranks to their rear. What happened that night, the very picture of that position of God, is instructive to us concerning the setting and sealing of hearts, by God. You see, the position of this cloud set the Egyptians heart forever hard and kept the

Israelite hearts quivering in softness. Even though the hard hearts of Egypt were resolute, determined, courageous cruel and confident, and the soft hearts of Israel were in panic, disarray and quivering in cowardly custard yellow, it was they who were in His light! It was Egypt who were in the dark.

You see, once Pharaoh had made the choice to thoroughly come against God, the Lord changed His position. Do you see that? This change is done during the night, even at the beginning of the night. The change takes place when all appears lost to those who earnestly look for their salvation. This change of position separates forever the enemies of God from the friends of God. This positioning maintains a cold dark night over the hearts of the hardened, yet provides a strange light, even an eerie warmth and comfort to 'quiverers and shiverers' who never the less are about to cross into the Promised Land. Our text tonight points very clearly to a God arranged separation between darkness and light and once that die is cast, God Himself appears to maintain that darkness on the one and the soft light on the other. Forever!

Our text tonight points very clearly to a God arranged separation between darkness and light and once that die is cast, God Himself appears to maintain that darkness on the one and the soft light on the other. Forever!

It is important to see that the end of the courageously resolute, determinedly cruel and confident bullies of hard-hearted darkness, was total devastation and utter destruction. They were like many fallen angels kept in the darkness of their hearts in chains of hardness, until the appointed time of judgment and destruction. We all know many on the earth tonight, who are kept in exactly the same way. May God have mercy upon them and shine His light once more toward them.

We must pray for a new enlightenment to shine in the hearts of the hardened. We must ask for a rising softening and a marvelous melting that will change into a running river of sweet and milky chocolate within them. We must ask God for sweetness to begin to flow in them, for until that time, until the heart is softened and changed, until the chains of hardness are softened to licorice black, every word and every work toward them, is to no avail at all. So then, our prayers must be focused and centered around the fortress of their heart, and pleading on their behalf for the light of God to shine once more upon it. If not, then they, like Pharaoh's army, shall be lost beneath the waves of judgment. Forever.

Listen: *"'Then I will give them one heart, and I will put a new spirit within them, and take the stony heart out of their flesh, and give them a heart of flesh, that they may walk in My statutes and keep My judgments and do them; and they shall be My people, and I will be their God. But as for those whose hearts follow the desire for their detestable things and their abominations, I will recompense their deeds on their own heads,' says the Lord God." (Ezekiel 11:19-21 NKJV0*

Pray: Relent Lord. As you did with us, so do with them whose hard and unchanged hearts sadden and make heavy our way. Relent Lord and be gracious to them, as You were to us. Yes, smile upon them and soften their chains to melted licorice black, yes, set Your blazing Son in their dark dungeon O Lord and bring them from their dreadful night into Your glorious day, in His great redemptive name we pray, amen and let it be so.

"Eimi Ho Eimie" - the resolute declaration of self

We know from his writings that the apostle Paul, one born out of due time, a late birth delivery if you will, was almost always having to defend his destiny and his calling, that is, his apostleship. Our text for tonight is the summary of one of those several defenses which he gave in his writings and the capstone of that defense summary, was that most marvelous statement of his:

1 Corinthians 15:9-11
"For I am the least of the apostles, who am not worthy to be called an apostle, because I persecuted the church of God. But by the grace of God I am what I am, and His grace toward me was not in vain; but I laboured more abundantly than they all, yet not I, but the grace of God which was with me. Therefore, whether it was I or they, so we preach and so you believed." NKJV

"By the grace of God," says Paul, "Eimi Ho Eimie – I am what I am."

I have on the whole heard this statement used in but one way by Christians and that has always been in terms of 'resignation!' "Oh yes," they whimper, "by the grace of God, I'm just a humble servant of the Lord, just a door keeper in the house of my God. Let me wash your feet. Do you want sugar in your coffee? Can I park your car?" Rather than a resigned deference, the apostle Paul however, uses this term in sharp and pointed crashing wave-breaking resolution, stating in effect? "By the grace of God I am an apostle, so get out my way pumpkin, I'm a comin' thru!"

There is, as always, a world of difference in the fruit of these two couplets, you know, 'deference and determination' and 'resignation' and 'resolution.' If I might examine the roots of those latter two in our hearts, I would say that resignation is rooted essentially in abandoned and dog-beaten depression, whilst resolution is rooted in revealed and pursued, focused determination. By the grace of God, Paul here is most resolutely declaring who he is by the grace of God! Indeed, "Like it or not," he says, "and many of you don't, I am an apostle of Jesus Christ the Lord!"

Paul knew his calling. Paul knew both his commission and his destiny. Believing it to be his particular path to walk upon and despite a multitude of overwhelming obstacles, he pursued the same with his whole being, his whole heart and his whole body soul and spirit. "Those other apostles, those you consider the more authentic ones, the real ones, well listen mateys all," says the great apostle Paul, "I labored more abundantly, more abundantly than them all!"

So, let me ask you tonight? "By the grace of God, who the heck are you?" If you don't know dear friend, then you had better find out and once you do, every day, you too need to hone the point of your calling, your commission and your destiny, focus it and sharpen it with the sharp and pointed resolution of the apostle Paul.

"By the grace of God, who the heck are you?"

Resignation is born of cowardice. Resolution is born of courage. Therefore, be courageous. Who are you?

Listen: *"Now it came to pass, when the time had come for Him to be received up, that He steadfastly set His face to go to Jerusalem, and sent messengers before His face. And as they went, they entered a village of the Samaritans, to prepare for Him. But they did not receive Him, because His face was set for the journey to Jerusalem." (Luke 9:51-54 NKJV)*

Pray: Lord of the Church, Jesus Christ my Savior, please come and show me Your calling and commission for my life. Glimpse to me my destiny and then pour in to me the strongest spirit of resolution, in Your great name I pray. Amen, and let it be so.

Night-Whisper | **PERSEVERE**

The ploughman's poet

Rabbie Burns, the bard of Ayrshire, poet, lyricist, and Scotland's most famous son, is tonight celebrated worldwide especially amongst the Scottish Diaspora, because tonight of course, is 'Burns Night!'

Proverbs 19:21

"There are many plans in a man's heart, nevertheless the Lord's counsel - that will stand." NKJV

Without going into the ritual and content of a 'Burns Night' supper, which is co-centered around a haggis and a speech made to the immortal memory of Rabbie Burns, let me cut to the end of the night, where the proceeding are closed with a favorite collection of some of the songs and poems of this most famous of ploughman's poets.

You see, my favorite Burns poem is 'Tae a Moose' or better still maybe, 'To a Mouse.' This great poem is peppered with sadness, regret, remorse, tenderness and soulish association. The poem centers very simply, around the destruction of a mouse nest, but in the so doing, it most profoundly portrays the basic theme of the piece which is: that mere mortals of all sizes and souls, of all desires and drives, even though they make best their plans for the future, often it is the unexpected, unplanned for and often times disastrous, which shall come upon them.

The last two stanzas read as follows:

> *But Mousie, thou art no thy lane,*
> *In proving foresight may be vain;*
> *The best-laid schemes o' mice an' men*
> *Gang aft agley,*
> *An' lea'e us nought but grief an' pain,*
> *For promis'd joy!*
>
> *Still thou art blest, compar'd wi' me;*
> *The present only toucheth thee:*
> *But och! I backward cast my e'e,*

On prospects dreaer!
An' forward, tho' I canna see,
I guess an' fear!

(and now the understandable version ☺)

But, mousie, thou art not alane,
In proving foresight may be in vain,
The best laid schemes of mice and men,
Go oft astray,
And leave us nought but grief and pain,
To rend our day.

Still thou art blessed, compared with me!
The present only touches thee,
But, oh, I backward cast my eye
On prospects drear,
And forward, though I cannot see,
I guess and fear.

One example of this poem's consistent influence is the fact that Nobel Prize winning author, John Steinbeck, changed the original title of his first play-novelette to one of the lines of this poem and called it, '*Of Mice and Men.*' Set in the American depression of the 1930's this Steinbeck work, currently on the American Library Association's list at no 4 in 'The Most Challenged Books of the 21st century,' portrays in the most magnificent, moving, and yet depressive terms, that no man-made plan is fool-proof and that no one, absolutely no one, can be completely prepared for the future. Yes indeed, knowing that 'the best laid plans of mice and men often go awry,' can indeed fill us with a great and debilitating fear concerning the future.

I am sure of one thing this Burn's Night, and that is that fear concerning the future will rob us of the enjoyment of the present. So, it is ever and always an active decision of ours not to let that happen. Indeed, we cannot have true contentment without a choice of enjoyment that leads to our eventual satisfaction. So, according to our Lord Jesus, let us feast on the day which we have been given, plan and prepare for the future, as much as is

We cannot have true contentment without a choice of enjoyment that leads to our eventual satisfaction.

right and profitable, and then leave it all with God. Whatever that future might be, we must leave it all with God.

My present stage on this personal journey of mine leaves tonight's text filling me with a strange mixture of both confusion and peace. Nevertheless, this statement of God stands solid and secure: the future is His! Therefore, no matter what fears (founded or otherwise) like strange specters stand sentinel like against our pressing ahead, let us be happy for the day, thankful for what we have, and courageous in pressing forward into another day, knowing that God waits for us there.

Listen: *Now godliness with contentment is great gain. For we brought nothing into this world, and it is certain we can carry nothing out. And having food and clothing, with these we shall be content.*

(1 Timothy 6:6-8)

Pray: Rabbie Burns ("The Selkirk Grace")

Some hae meat and cannot eat.
Some cannot eat that want it:
But we hae meat and we can eat,
Sae let the Lord be thankit.

| Vol 01 | Q1 | NW00026 | January 26th |

Night-Whisper | **CONNECT**

On my finger and on my thumb

One of my good friends, founder and director of a multifaceted missions organization, has a long running project whose arms reach out to the street people of his own home city. He spoke to me just recently regarding his concern over the increasing problem and rising percentage of former long term military veterans finding themselves homeless and living on the streets.

Ecclesiastes 4:9-10

"Two are better than one, because they have a good reward for their labour. For if they fall, one will lift up his companion. But woe to him who is alone when he falls, for he has no one to help him up."
NKJV

There are lots of reasons for homeless veterans but I am sure that one of them, is an inability to cope with life after being removed from an organization with purpose, direction, value and most of all, from such a close comrade fellowship, that only people who have been in the armed forces can fully appreciate. As a former submarine sailor, I testify that you never forget the feeling of being part of a very close knit unit. You rarely find such fellowship outside of the armed forces and so consequently, you do feel the loss of such closeness and unity most profoundly and always pine for its return. In my experience, it is never found in 'Civvy Street.' Without some semblance of this manly closeness being found elsewhere, often a black hole of depression and all its consequent ills, forms at the center of an old veterans being, which will eventually suck the life out of him and kill his capacity to hope and cope. Such was the fate of enlisted soldier Voytek of the Polish 2nd Army Corps, 22nd Transport Division, Artillery Supply Troops.

Voytek, having stood shoulder to shoulder with his comrades at the crucial battle of Monte Casino in Northern Italy, loading trucks with artillery shells while under heavy fire himself, was along with his unit, retired to Scotland after WWII. When the exiled Polish army was demobilised in 1947, Voytek, being Iranian by birth, found it difficult to find a home for himself. As his fellow soldiers disappeared one by one, the loss which Voytek felt was both profound and all-consuming, for he pined away over the lost camaraderie, remembering the marching together, the sleeping under canvas together, the driving together, the fused purpose of being, the happy singing, the smokes around the late night fire, the beer, yes the beer and the accompanying drinking songs and of course, the wrestling. Yes, he was good at the wrestling. So good in fact that he would sometimes take on four of his fellow soldiers at a time! He was rarely beaten then but my, how the mighty had fallen now, for the loneliness that fell upon Voytek after the loss of this fellowship, beat him badly and eventually left him behind bars in Edinburgh, a sulky and sullen old man of a bear, unwilling to venture out in the open for anyone, not even for the children who loved him and called regularly upon him.

Voytek had been with the Polish army since they had found him as a youngster being carried in a sack along the roads and in the mountains of Hamadan, Northern Iran. His mother had been killed by hunters and he had been left to fend for himself, though frankly, had not been doing so good a job if it.

Voytek had been with the Polish army since they had found him as a youngster being carried in a sack along the roads and in the mountains of Hamadan, Northern Iran. His mother had been killed by hunters and he had been left to fend for himself, though frankly, had not been doing so good a job if it. The story goes, that the Polish soldiers from the unit had purchased him out of a brown muslin sack, in exchange for a bar of chocolate, a tin of corned beef and a pocket penknife. Once in their company, Voytek was cuddled, loved, adopted and made such a full part of everything the unit did, that he was eventually enlisted! These soldiers treated Voytek like everyone else in the unit and more than anything, they left him feeling part of something, yes, he felt like part of a family! You see Voytek, the old WWII veteran, was a 6ft tall, 500lb, Iranian brown bear who died alone and depressed in Edinburgh Zoo in 1963.

I was out at the pub with this same Mission Director friend of mine after discussing the homeless situation of veterans. A man sat at the table next to us eating alone. Once he had lubricated his social ineptness with a few beers, he began overtly seeking fellowship with others, waving madly at anyone who passed his table, smiling like a loon, laughing loudly and drawing attention to himself, trying to force a conversation, any conversation, to get an invitation into discussions and depth he could never truly be part of. I have seen this man many times, the nice but freaky bag man, employed as the collector of abandoned shopping trolleys at the local super market. The loneliness of mental illness is as deep and black as it is long and sad. It was obvious that this man did not even have a memory of close comrade fellowship. He was a veteran of loneliness. Maybe that was a bitter blessing? Maybe not?

Are you lonely tonight? I am so sorry if you are. It is a most terrible position to be in and is in fact, a cosmic condition which we all share and often experience if we allow ourselves to approach the center of our being. You are not alone in this experience my friend. You are not alone.

However, if you long for a closeness and a fellowship of body soul and spirit, that only a band of like-minded brothers or sisters can provide you with, then Christian, the community of saints is the only place this can possibly be cultivated to the depth we so longingly crave. Such communities are often not pretty, and they are very hard work as well but friends, and you are my friends, the true comrade fellowship of the real church is all we've got, so help us God!

Let us begin this deep cultivation of the spirit ourselves, by becoming a true friend to a few, maybe not so good men in the community of saints

On the morrow then, let us begin this deep cultivation of the spirit ourselves, by becoming a true friend to a few, maybe not so good men in the community of saints, the church of Jesus Christ the Lord. For me thinks that far too many are dying of loneliness behind prison bars, and too many can only count their true friends on one finger and a thumb.

Listen: *"A man who has friends must himself be friendly, but there is a friend who sticks closer than a brother." (Proverbs 18:24 NKJV)*

Pray: Lord, thank You for the circle of friends and level of friendship I enjoy. Help me to be a better friend, cultivating the heart and soul of others for their betterment and our mutual closeness. However Lord, please be that friend of mine, deeper than family, firmer than similar souls, stickier than superglue, both on my finger and on my thumb. In Your great name I ask it, amen.

| Vol 01 | Q1 | NW00027 | January 27th |

Night-Whisper | **CONFIDENCE**

Countdown conundrums

Exodus 28:30

"And you shall put in the breastplate of judgment the Urim and the Thummim and they shall be over Aaron's heart when he goes in before the Lord. So Aaron shall bear the judgment of the children of Israel over his heart before the Lord continually."

The British game show called *Countdown* first aired in 1982 and is one of the longest running game shows in the world. One of its most popular items is the conundrum section, which is a buzzer round where contestants try and become the quickest to solve a nine-letter anagram. I rarely manage to solve the puzzle. How about you?

Almost all of the time for me and I suspect for you as well, discerning the best choices in life, the God choices in life, is rather like deciphering an anagram, except it's not as much fun! Despite my having the Holy Spirit and the whole revealed counsel of God, to my own peace and satisfaction, I rarely manage to solve the puzzles which life often presents to me. How about you?

Maybe a better understood rending of our text for tonight would be to refer to the high priestly breastplate as the "breastplate of decision" rather than the "breastplate of Judgment." Either way, this gloriously beautiful and Divinely designed outfit for the High Priest of Israel to wear before the manifest presence of God and His people, was finally kitted out with what can only be described as: a 'decision making device.' You see, whatever the Urim and Thummin were in reality, in practicality they were a most definitive way of providing a "yes" or "no" answer to questions which were placed before God. Wouldn't you like to get your hand on those little beauties eh? Oh how much easier life would become for us! Or would it?

When we adopt this 'yes or no' kind of thinking we imagine our passage in life to be simply the outcome of a series of 'yes and no' decisions and therefore of 'right and wrong' directional choices. Maybe though life is more than the outcome of 'yes and no' decisions? I wonder if where there is no moral imperative, where there is no command disobedience at stake, that maybe, that life is a matter of choices and frankly, any choice will do?

We do not live in the age of Urim and Thummim, however, we do have a great High Priest of the good things to come, modelled after the eternal order of Melchizedeck, who is undefiled, separate from sinners, holy, harmless, and has, since the eternal sacrifice of Himself, become higher than the heavens and is seated right now at the right hand of the throne of the Majesty on High and imagine this, He ever lives to make intercession for us. We don't need this Old Testament decision making device nor any other.

Because Jesus ever lives to make intercession for us, we don't need this Old Testament decision making device nor any other.

There is a vastness in the goodness of God that encompasses all the full and free decisions which we His people choose. Have we in this way then become the free agents of His will? Do we reign with Him only when we make decisions in His name and for His glory? Have we become, along with Him, part of God the Father's creation process, part of His Son's Kingdom rule? I think so. Maybe there is, as one preacher put it: "The Holy Spirit endowed musical instrument of choice and with it, the ability to improvise in the key of the Gospel." I think all of this is true.

This kind of trouble free decision making then, calls us to stop playing hesitant games and invites us into a Royal maturity which most is us have never yet entered into because of the crippling confusion of the ignorance of who we are in Him and of fear of 'getting it wrong' and messing up God's plan. Hilarious! Who told you that you were that powerful? On the other hand, as we choose and decide, as we say yes and no in the power of the Holy Spirit, we do reign with Him and my oh my, what great power there is in that!

Life is scary. May I say that often, life also feels like a conundrum. Nevertheless, decisions have to be made and I reckon we can have a greater confidence, freedom and even a greater expectant joy in our decisions knowing that Christ ever lives to make intercession for us. Therefore, stop being so fearful man and make your choice in the knowledge that God is good and God is great. Maybe life is not as big as a conundrum as we feel. Just let your "Yes" mean "Yes" and your "No" mean "No," there is power enough in that.

Listen:

> *Worship the Lord in the beauty of holiness,*
> *Bow down before Him, His glory proclaim;*
> *Gold of obedience and incense of lowliness,*
> *Bring and adore Him—the Lord is His Name.*
>
> *Low at His feet lay Thy burden of carefulness,*
> *High on His heart He will bear it for thee;*
> *Comfort thy sorrows and answer thy prayerfulness,*
> *Guiding thy steps as may best for thee be.*
>
> *Fear not to enter His courts in the slenderness*
> *Of the poor wealth thou wouldst reckon as thine;*
> *Truth in its beauty, and love in its tenderness,*
> *These are the offerings to lay on His shrine.*

Pray: These choices we bring then, in trembling and fearfulness, You will accept for the name that is dear. Mornings of joy give for evenings of tearfulness, trust for our trembling, and hope for our fear. Amen and let it be so.

(John S. B. Monsell)

| Vol 01 | Q1 | NW00028 | January 28th |

Night-Whisper | **CONSIDER**

Troubling the tripartite connection

The Paris residence of Charles Maurice de Talleyrand-Périgord, 1st Sovereign Prince of Bénévent, is now owned by the embassy of the United States of America.

Proverbs 23:31-34

"Do not look on the wine when it is red, when it sparkles in the cup, when it swirls around smoothly; at the last it bites like a serpent, and stings like a viper. Your eyes will see strange things, and your heart will utter perverse things. Yes, you will be like one who lies down in the midst of the sea, or like one who lies at the top of the mast" NKJV

Talleyrand is this same, political prince of diplomats, this French rogue who was also a wine bibber, glutton and one of the first people to employ his very own celebrity chef: The famous, chef Carême, also known as the "chef of kings and the king of chefs." I mention Tallyrand tonight, because this great fat French conversationalist has had one of his most famous comments displayed very far and wide in this big old world of ours. It is, of course, his own personal recipe for serving coffee: *"Black as the devil, hot as hell, pure as an angel, sweet as love!"*

It was a few weeks ago now, when my mornings seemed to begin with tiredness, then move swiftly into fraught activity and end in twitching anxiety. After some heart palpitations, I realized that my new regime of espresso with my wife in the morning and then not too much later, a tall latte, to justify my sitting in a coffee shop and writing for a couple hours, was in fact hitting my system with enough caffeine to make an old nag chomp at the bit in a bid to run in the Grand National! My anxiety was not an emotional or a spiritual issue, it was a physical manifestation of a drug taken into my system. The answer to my anxiety was quite simply to have a nice sweet tea to start the day followed by two large glasses of water.

My point tonight, is to remind you that as a tripartite being of body, soul and spirit, and any effect on the body can have repercussions on the soul and the spirit. So, if you are feeling a little distant from Jesus, a little less out of love with Him, then maybe, just maybe, you need to sleep more, drink more water and attend better to your diet and fitness. If you do these three things anyways, I suspect your spiritual life will increase with vigor and your emotional life with fervor as well. Therefore, take care of your whole self! Your spiritual life depends on it. *May all your imbibing then be as "Good as God, as sweet as heaven, as pure as an angel, and as tasty as love!"*

Take care of your whole self! Your spiritual life depends on it.

Listen: *"And in a window sat a certain young man named Eutychus, who was sinking into a deep sleep. He was overcome by sleep; and as Paul continued speaking, he fell down from the third story and was taken up dead." (Acts 20:9-10 NKJV0*

Pray: Father, for my overall health and my spiritual health especially, help me discern what to remove from my body and what to put into my body. Make me wise in this, in Jesus name I pray, amen and let it be so.

Night-Whisper | **CLEAN**

Tainted love

One of the High Priestly objects of splendor, apart from his beautiful breastplate and garments of glory, was the white turbaned head-dress.

Zechariah 14:20-21

"In that day 'holiness to the Lord' shall be engraved on the bells of the horses. The pots in the Lord's house shall be like the bowls before the altar. Yes, every pot in Jerusalem and Judah shall be holiness to the Lord of hosts. Everyone who sacrifices shall come and take them and cook in them. In that day there shall no longer be a Canaanite in the house of the Lord of hosts."

This head-dress was a miter of eight yards of fine twisted linen coiled into a cap, over which was laid a golden plate, fastened by blue ribbon. This golden plate hung down across the forehead of the High Priest, between his hair fringe and his eyebrows and had engraved upon it: **'Holiness to the Lord.'**

I must admit, that my experience of 'holiness' in the church has had more to do with a 'touch not, taste not, handle not,' po-faced, hypocritical irrelevant and repugnant "we don't do that here" kind of philosophy, than real 'Bible Holiness.' So much so, that something in me just kicks and rebels against all these forms of self-righteousness, religious or otherwise! And may I say right now, that one surprising characteristics of the of post-Christian, anti-Christian politically correct world is one of self-righteous mock-holiness, that is grossly judgmental in all its dealings and unnervingly unmerciful in the extreme. Try disagreeing with climate change statistics, or admit that yes actually, you are homophobic (in a very Biblical sense), or that gender rolls do exist, and just watch the carnivorous self-righteous wolves descend upon you to tear you all to pieces. The holy things of this present world system are an abomination to God, and the self-righteous attitudes, practices and people which hold these abominations dear to them, are both vindictive and vicious.

I would say that for me, this kind of mock holiness in the church, provokes me into a mischievous naughtiness, which I am more than eager to succumb to, rather than cause me to honor and glorify Christ. I cannot go with either the po-faced church holiness or the politically correct one which seems now to have mixed themselves so well together in the gatherings of God. It makes me sick. Surely, there must a Biblical holiness which is deeper than those two imposters, there must be a holiness which is more encompassing and wholesome, indeed, I would say there must be a holiness that is, like that golden plate, so at the fore front of who we are that it is all embracing in its projection, and pure and lovely in its application. Well, I am pleased to tell you that there shall be and that there is.

Our text for tonight prophetically tells us of a time to come when everything, from making a living to making a home, shall be considered to be and shall be encompassed by a living holiness. Christian! Our Savior died to make us holy! We are called to be holy because our Lord is holy and that to be Biblically holy is simply to be fully yielded to the Son in the name of the Father by the power of God the Holy Spirit. It is to have our separated-ness to Him, ever and always at the forefront of our being. Indeed, it is to have God's personal name, reputation and glory, like the Old High Priest's, like our Great High Priest's even, hanging in imprinted letters of Gold between our fringe and our eyebrows. Everything in our lives, from mission praise to marriage bed and all things in between, should be offered to God for His namesake and for His glory.

Everything in our lives, from mission praise to marriage bed and all things in between, should be offered to God for His namesake and for His glory.

I hear many of you say today: "Oh Robert, if only you knew how tainted even my most Holy of thoughts and actions can be!" Well, my reply to you is this: "Oh do stop whining! Please, stop both this wormology and defeatism. Why not just move over, you Muppet, and give some other little girl some wasting time in the whimper seat! Of course I know what your heart is like! It is like mine! We all know the taintedness of our holy things. We are all built of the same stuff!"

I hope my ungenerous and seeming uncaring response tilted a few of you that tilted a few of you. Please excuse me for giving you a very big verbal 'slap up the side of the head' tonight, but I need your full attention. I am tired of seeing unholy and defective Christians! You see, you have to know right now dear friend that our Great High Priest IS the Great sin exterminator Himself, and the ability of His person, yes, the testimony of His robes and the power of His office, means that He can even exterminate the ever pox-like pollution of sin in our mortal bodies and daily lives, which clings, even today, like the smell of foul sulphured eggs, to our most Holy of sacrifices.

Look you now: Whenever we do good this side of heaven, evil, at some level it seems, is both present and pungent! It is! So please, be assured then, that our Great High Priest covers even these sins of our own Holy things. Thank God for that! Thank God for that I say, and therefore in the so doing, I encourage you to stop whining, give up your wormology, and keep on yielding yourself to God for He has all of our shortfalls, all the swerve balls and all long balls of our life well covered by His blood. He has to, for even our Holy things are tainted this side of heaven.

Stop making excuses to yourselves for not living a holy life! Stop settling for less than 'holiness to the Lord' in EVERYTHING your are and EVERYTHING you do.

Therefore, stop making excuses to yourselves for not living a holy life. Stop settling for less than 'holiness to the Lord' in EVERYTHING your are and EVERYTHING you do. Let the wholesome holiness of God, irradiate every portal of your being, excluding all the filth that would come in and killing all filth residing therein already. Tonight I say to you then: "You can be truly holy, and enjoy the power and peace of the same."

Therefore my dear friends, keep striving and keep yielding, yes, keep being holy.

Listen: *"You shall also make a plate of pure gold and engrave on it, like the engraving of a signet: Holiness to the Lord. And you shall put it on a blue cord, that it may be on the turban; it shall be on the front of the turban. So it shall be on Aaron's forehead, that Aaron may bear the iniquity of the holy things which the children of Israel hallow in all their holy gifts; and it shall always be on his forehead, that they may be accepted before the Lord." (Exodus 28:36-38 NKJV)*

Pray: Lord, thank You so much that You have all my tainted love also covered by Your blood. Oh hallelujah and amen, thank you for that. Therefore, I yield to You right now an ask you to help me work out my own salvation with fear and trembling, that every thought and every action, and every circumstance of my choosing would be 'holiness to the Lord.' Amen, and let it be so.

| Vol 01 | Q1 | NW00030 | January 30th |

Night-Whisper | **CHOOSE**

Of milksop men & weeping women

I've been doing it again, you know, going to church and looking at all the ladies. I mostly count all the ladies heads in the church when the sermon is predominantly boring, so that's just about every Sunday! At the beginning of the 21st century, from church to church in the West, the percentage figures rarely change for my count, with the local gathering consisting of around 60-70% women, all mostly 50 years of age and up. Women leading, women decorating, women baking, women making at all happen. Thank God for women eh?

Job 40:7

"Now prepare yourself like a man; I will question you, and you shall answer Me," NKJV

The church has become very feminine in its makeup and the men that do attend, though they aren't necessarily effeminate themselves, have maybe as David Murrow, author of: *Why Men Hate Going To Church* has put it, "Become used to it!" Used to it indeed!

It was in the year of our Lord, 2008, for the first time ever, more women than men were ordained in the Anglican church. Indeed, as I make these observations, I am looking for a ministerial position myself, I have already withdrawn my name from three large non-conformist churches (Ha!) having discovered that they have (completely and contrary to the Scriptures) quietly set aside women as elders and preachers in their church. This rampant speeding up of the feminization of the local church is an important fact to be known because already, men in their millions are just not going to church because of it, and over 90% of boys brought up in the church today, will leave it as soon as they can and never return again! We are destined to die out, and in our dotage our gatherings shall be mostly a bunch of old ladies of both the male and female variety.

Spurgeon may have remarked that, "There has got abroad a notion, somehow, that if you become a Christian you must sink your manliness and turn milksop," and unfortunately folks, that perception is obviously correct because many men don't go to church at all and the reason for that is often this, "they have already been!" Look now, the church has gotten so unbiblical that when manliness arises in leadership, it is despised. The spirt of Jezebel resides in both Salome and in Herodius and make no bones about it boys, they are still looking for uncontested power and when they cannot get it, they will have your heads.

The writer David Murrow makes a proposal that men are already pursuing a religion outside of church and it is called masculinity. Now then, and especially in this most thoroughly feminized society of ours, I most certainly believe that to be the case. Those men that want to hang on to their manhood will always avoid places of feminine control. It's just a fact. That being the case, we really do have to pump some holy testosterone back into the church.

However, there is an even more pressing pastoral problem which we have to attend. It is a problem which I have seen on quite a few occasions now and it troubles me greatly, because good men are either getting sick within the church or leaving the church bitter, hurt and disappointed. You see, the longer men remain in a feminized politically correct church the more spiritually aware they become that they have sacrificed their manhood. They have lost themselves. They have become a very nice man but a very nice milksop man, and in their deepest heart of hearts, they despise themselves. When this despising of self finally comes out, it's often in a sideways manner and usually expresses itself at some level in anger and even hatred, both towards Christ and his church. I have had many, man to man, 'exit' conversations over the years and know this reason to be strong and driving unspoken fact.

The longer men remain in a feminized politically correct church the more spiritually aware they become that they have sacrificed their manhood.

In answer to this then, I would say three things tonight:

First, if people in the church don't like you expressing your manhood, then that's their decision. Let them live with it. Be who you are and ask Christ to help you live the life of the man He died for. In the end, you must as a man, be able to live with yourself in true respect. Be a man.

Secondly, the church and especially my sisters in the church must begin to welcome and embrace true Biblical manhood back into the local church. Unless this manhood is mourned for, longed for even, then you may never see it again, and the church will become very simply, a ladies club, even a gay ladies club. Listen, I have had too many good looking, professional and highly desirable weeping sisters crying at our kitchen table over the fact that they cannot find a man to marry in the kingdom of God. Sister, you had better change, or the church will die.

Thirdly, the church and especially the male leaders left in the church must begin to count the cost of both reclaiming their own manhood and making the church a more masculine place to be and that's not just at a greasy Saturday morning men's breakfast, down the local pub. Think about it.

Finally, if these churches cannot be changed, cannot be revived, and by the way, any real revival MUST apply this complementarian view of the Scriptures, then there is no hope for these unbiblical churches, I say again, there is no hope, and they will die and if you stay my friend, then you as a man will also die with them. God has abandoned them. Get out of that Godless place and start again.

For those of you who cannot and will not see, the gender battle is over. Manhood lost. Men lost. The survivors have regrouped and completely separated themselves, in statement, doctrine and practice, from those who have capitulated. The 'separation' is here. There is now a choice to make..

The gender battle is over. Manhood lost. Men lost. The survivors have regrouped and completely separated themselves, in statement, doctrine and practice, from those who have capitulated..

Meanwhile, like I say, that quiet weeping you hear in the church comes from the dwindling remains of godly, strong and beautiful ladies, who whilst remaining faithful to Jesus, just cannot find a strong man to marry and will not settle for a wimp. It's all so very sad.

Listen: *"As for My people, children are their oppressors, and women rule over them." (Isaiah 3:12a NKJV)*

Pray: Lord, help the male leaders of the church to stand fast in the faith, and quit them like men and be strong! In the mighty and manly name of Jesus we pray, amen and let it be so.

Night-Whisper | **SERVE**

There were only fish fingers until along came Hans!

In the ages to come, in eternity, one of the things my wife wishes to do is to fly among the stars. Ever since I sat in front of the first few episodes of Star Trek, I have wanted to do the same really, but in the intergalactic comfort of a star ship of course! My wife, however, wants to fly 'skyclad,' you know, buck naked when on her travels, sweeping and zooming in and out of amber asteroid belts, big red dwarfs, and sparkling suns of every sort. My only objection to all of is: "Baby, it's cold outside!" I tell you tonight, God did not create me for cold climates. "Brrrr. I Hate that cold!"

Isaiah 1:18

" 'Come now, and let us reason together,' says the Lord, 'Though your sins are like scarlet, they shall be as white as snow.' " NKJV

Space is cold. Indeed, even at the edges of our own solar system, the largely unexplored Trans-Neptunian area, which has yielded our tenth planet, or second Dwarf Planet, (depending on how those who designate have thus far designated), is very cold indeed! Here the newly discovered entity sits naked, floating silently in the icy cold depths of black, black space. I wouldn't want to fly there that's for sure. "Brrrr. I Hate that cold!"

Sedan, this second Dwarf Planet at our own solar system's outer edges, is in fact named after the Inuit or the Eskimo, (depending on how those who designate have thus far designated), goddess of the sea. Apparently, in the Inuit mythology of creation, the creator God was so displeased with his daughter, (who by the way, was turning into a big, ugly, fat pig of a woman after eating everything in sight, including portions of the creator God himself,) that he slung her out of his Kayak! When she tried to get back in, he chopped off her fingers one by one, which in turn turned into seals and whales and other creatures of the deep. Now that's what I call fish fingers! Anyway, that cold icy second Dwarf planet, Sedan, is named after her and knowing that particular fact, I definitely would not want to fly there. "Brrrr. I Hate that cold!"

The Inuit goddess of the sea may be located in the watery underworld of the deep, but the Inuit peoples are spread pretty widely across the land, even all the way down to Greenland, which I personally think is a most unfortunate name for a country which is predominantly sub polar in climate and covered in ice! Frankly, unless it was to preach the Gospel, I wouldn't want to go to Greenland either. "Brrrr. I Hate that cold!"

Hans Egede was born today in Norway in 1686. He became a Norwegian Lutheran Minister and because of his sacrificial efforts among the Inuit peoples, he later became known as the 'Apostle to Greenland.' Indeed, he also founded the city of 'Good Hope,' or 'Godthab,' or now as it is known, 'Nuuk,' which actually became the capital city of Greenland.

The problems Egede encountered whilst trying to do his missionary work were enormous, not least the challenges of his own character! Apparently a 'head down, cold nosed man' he had steeled himself for both his calling and the icy weather. This was no two week short term holiday and sightseeing mission he was on, no sir, Egede could lose his life in Greenland and the lives of the forty Christian settlers that went with him, and he knew it! They may have had the command of both The Heavenly King and their own earthly king to go on this Divine venture, but this particular mission could cost him everything. No wonder he was so serious! Someone has commented that "Hans tended to be harsh and overbearing and though he dearly loved the people, like many other Christians, he did not know how to express this in human terms!" An apostolic icy Christian, in an icy heathen world. "Brrrr. I Hate that cold!"

An apostolic icy Christian, in an icy heathen world!

The great thaw of Egede's hearts came, I am afraid, on the back of an Old World disease called smallpox. In most of the New World, the population would be almost totally wiped out by contact with any European carrying viral diseases from the Old World, whether they were Missionaries, explorers, whalers, traders, or whatever. Accidental genocide is one thing, however, as far as I am aware, it was only the British who had deliberately used smallpox as a biological weapon against native American Indians, but that's another grey story, for another cold grey day. "Brrrr. I Hate that cold!"

In this case, Egede, did not bring the disease to the Inuit of Greenland, but he did stay with the now small-pox ridden and diseased people and refused to leave them, caring for them as they fell, leading them as best he could into the arms of Jesus. Egede's wife Gertrude, so expended herself in doing this, that she died of exhaustion shortly thereafter.

Egede's son Paul, raised among the Inuit, took over the work from his father, mastered the language, completed the translation of the New Testament, and later saw many folks come to know the Lord. His father was ecstatic to see him reap, where he had formerly and so sacrificially sown.

> *Would you fly to icy places at the command of your King so that He might make people as white as snow?*

Today's Night-Whisper is about sacrifice, focus and persistence. Tonight is about flying among the cold, cold stars at the outer edges of our own solar system, yes, the cold and very costly, outer edges of known civilization. Would you fly to icy places at the command of your King so that He might make people as white as snow? Tell me would you? It's worth thinking about. As for me, my love for Jesus overcomes my hatred of cold. I will go anywhere for Him. How about you?

"Brrrr. I still hate that cold!"

Listen: *"So Samuel said: 'Has the Lord as great delight in burnt offerings and sacrifices, as in obeying the voice of the Lord? Behold, to obey is better than sacrifice, and to heed than the fat of rams.'" (1 Samuel 15:22 NKJV)*

Pray: Lord, whether it be hot or cold, hard or soft, North or South, East or West, please Lord, help me to obey You fully concerning Your Great Commission to us Your people and You command to me in particular. Amen and let it be so.

PAUSE FOR PRAYER | 66CITIES

Well, I do pray that the first month of this year's Night-Whispers written with you in mind, have prospered you spiritually and pushed you on a little farther down the road in knowing, obeying and immediately following the commands of the God of the whole Bible. This is my desire.

I am Victor Robert Farrell and I am the author of Night-Whispers. I also have the privilege of being the President of The 66 Books Ministry and I want to tell you a little bit about our major project which is: 66Cities. I believe one of the problems with the rapid moral decline of the West coupled with the influx of other religions, has been the compromise of the local church. It is as though we leaders have watered down the wine of the Gospel with the methods and culture of the world and have done so to such an extent that all we are left with is an anemic and slightly rose colored, fluoride-filled cup of poor tepid mouth wash. It is good for nothing except to be poured down the drain. This compromise I speak of, was to stop speaking about the God of the whole Bible and to such an extent that Christians were left in a strange kind of idolatry, worshiping the God of a cultural constructed Christianity, and so much so, that when these same Christians came into contact with the real God of the Bible, He troubled them and offended them. Indeed, they were embarrassed by Him and wanted Him excluded from their parties. The world of course, found more substance in the other gods, especially that kind of unbiblical Trinitarian spirituality which allowed science and hedonism to mate with the X factor of their own particular choosing.

We at The 66 Books Ministry intend to preach the Gospel of Jesus Christ and the God of the whole Bible, from each of the 66 Books of the Bible in the 66 most influential cities of the nations of the world. That's 16,500 cities in an annual and ongoing basis. To make this happen we are prayerfully raising up teams of proclaimers and 'prayer rangers' to go into these cities. We see this is a true prophetic witness to the glory of God. Indeed. This is the main reason why we are doing this: that God the Father and God the Son may be seen and Glorified in the power of God The Holy Spirit. We hope and pray, that many will see the Father, trust in the Son and be saved by the power of the Holy Spirit as well. Brethren, **we covet your prayers as we do this.** Check out WWW.66Books.TV

Night-Whisper | **INTEGRITY**

The making of righteous reputations

I suspect that I have already quoted my most favorite of preachers, Dr. J Vernon McGee, repeating that it was he who said:, "God created the garden and man the cities, but the devil made the small town!"

1 Samuel 22:1-2

"David therefore departed from there and escaped to the cave of Adullam. So when his brothers and all his father's house heard it, they went down there to him. And everyone who was in distress, everyone who was in debt, and everyone who was discontented gathered to him. So he became captain over them. And there were about four hundred men with him."
NKJV

Dr. McGee spoke this way out of his experience as a small town pastor of many years, and he knew this fact to be true: that once you had a bad reputation in a small town, the people in it, rarely allowed you or your family, your kin, the remotest possibility of changing and rising above it.

The truth of this same observation has stuck with me for years and manifested itself most disturbingly in far too many churches of small town mentalities, where the people of God are not allowed the experience of profound, and journeying change. So often then, these now stunted folk of not so good reputation, simply have to move on, at best acquiring a reputation for being spiritual Gypsies and at worst, for never entering a church again. It's a crying shame.

Yes, unfortunately far too many of our old churches are often filled with old misery guts. In Britain I have experienced them as "The Tea at Three Brigade," and in the USA as the "The Prissy and Precise, Religious Matadors of Mice!" Both these sorry, regulated small town regiments, full of fear and led by cardboard cutout men, or women trying to be men, adore niceness and respectability more than any manifestation of raw righteousness, running red in real people who are being lifted out their deepest and darkest pits by the ripped red sash, of Jehova Tsidkenu Himself. Yup, they don't much like that, for when God lifts a person from a pit, there is an awful lot of grunting, and a disturbing amount of groaning, and many, many times, a falling back into the sludge from whence they came. Yet, God Himself, covered with sweat, dripping great drops of blood, still peers over the pit's edge, cajoling those broken legged thieves below to lay hold of Him and His redemption, again, and again, and again. Sanctification, you see, is in reality a very messy affair, and the flower of real righteousness is a many thorn embedded rose. In such a flowered garden City of God, the old small town mentally, will not work at all. No, it really just won't do.

Though many local churches often act like such small towns of restriction, they shouldn't, for they are more, much more than that. Local churches should live out what they truly and twice fold are, in being first, a foreign outpost of the Kingdom of God in a very dangerous land and secondly, of being a superb suburb of the city of God itself! In other words, in the local church, the gold of God's goodness should pave the streets we walk upon. We should be looking for change in people, hoping and praying for it, believing God for it and rejoicing in it when we see it. New names, new possibilities, new beginnings, new horizons, new gifting, new hopes, new dreams, new destinies, all fresh and bursting out of a new and constantly renewed people, should be what we long and hope for. That sounds like an exciting place to be! Yes sir indeedy, that sounds like just the place for me! Ah, but what a smell of manure often goes with such a place of growing. Remember that.

> *Local churches should live out what they truly and twice fold are, in being first, a foreign outpost of the Kingdom of God in a very dangerous land and secondly, of being a superb suburb of the city of God itself!*

We spiritual members of the body of Christ are the makers of our local churches. We are the true people of God who can begin today walking on the streets of golden goodness. What a holy effort of faith it shall be to see people for whom they could be, and then speak to them in the future tense, concerning the righteous reputations of heaven, which are theirs in reality and will be theirs in experience by the mighty changing power of Jesus Christ the Lord. These kind of prophetic faith words need to be spoken over those now being sanctified. We need to call forth resurrection and newness in every disciple.

Christian, tomorrow and forever and ever amen, may I encourage you to have both the faith and the vision to deal sometimes in peoples past but much more in people's futures! Let's stop all the movin' on and encourage much more movin' in! We are the blood bought people of God and the local church belongs to us. Let's take it back.

Listen: *"Do you not know that the unrighteous will not inherit the kingdom of God? Do not be deceived. Neither fornicators, nor idolaters, nor adulterers, nor homosexuals, nor sodomites, nor thieves, nor covetous, nor drunkards, nor revilers, nor extortioners will inherit the kingdom of God. And such were some of you. But you were washed, but you were sanctified, but you were justified in the name of the Lord Jesus and by the Spirit of our God." (1 Corinthians 6:9-11 NKJV)*

Pray: Lord, help me to see both myself and others clothed in Your righteousness, both loving in it and living in it, amen and let it be so!

Night-Whisper | **PERSEVERE**

Building on the body line

I used to live maybe a 10-minute walk from the Sussex County Cricket ground. A long time ago I was also a wicket keeper, however, I only played this position because I found cricket to be one of the most boring games on the planet, and please forgive me CT Studd, but I still do!

Hebrews 11:4

"By faith Abel offered to God a more excellent sacrifice than Cain, through which he obtained witness that he was righteous, God testifying of his gifts; and through it he being dead still speaks." NKJV

At least behind the stumps, I found the adrenalin rush from a 6oz cricket ball being bowled at great speed towards me, kept me somewhat awake and interested through all the other boring cricket proceedings and protocols.

Yup, keeping yourself from getting hurt from a fast moving object certainly kept your attention. That is, unless you were a batsman like Australian born Don Bradman, from the small town Bowral in New South Wales, who in the 1932-33 Ashes series, was subject to the infamous 'bodyline tactics' of the then English national cricket team, who, frightened of defeat at the hands of the Aussies, decided to bowl the cricket ball directly at Bradman rather than the wicket. Don Bradman, was such a threat to the visiting English you see, that they had to get him out of the way. If it meant serious injury to him, then so be it. Remember, that these were days before helmets, and we know today that even international cricketers wearing helmets still die when a fast bowler hits their skull with a 6oz cannon ball travelling at 100 miles per hour.

Two years after the birth of Bradman, today in 1910, the small town of Bowral, New South Wales also produced another famous son in the form of Dr. Paul White, a missionary to Africa who became such a threat to the enemy of our souls, that he had to get him out of the way as quickly as possible as well.

Paul White had a tough up bringing after his father died of meningitis. Though Paul was only just 4 years of age when this happened His father, a soldier in the Boer War, had already planted seeds of the mysterious and dark continent of Africa and the power of story-telling, through his tall tales of jumping Zulu warriors. Paul struggled badly with Asthma as a youngster and a broken arm, badly set as a child, also left him with weakness in his right arm which he would battle with all of his life. Still, aged 16 he became a Christian and despite being fatherless and encumbered with all these setbacks, his perseverance, exceptional sacrifice and hard work, led him into training as a Doctor, marriage and eventually setting sail with his new wife to Africa, the seeds of those dead-dad stories having now come to full flower

White's first wife Mary, who later died of Alzheimer's disease, suffered chronic manic depressive psychosis for most of her life and was only kept sane in Africa by the use of dangerous, and some believe, very cruel, insulin shock therapy treatment. Eventually, Mary's psychosis forced Dr. Paul White to leave the mission field and return to Australia. His dreams of ministering in Africa were shattered.

The bodyline tactics of the enemy had left this man, his family and his ministry in ruins. All was lost. All had been a waste.

Whilst trying to communicate the Gospel in Africa, Paul found his communicative ability to fall far short of what was necessary. Until that is, he investigated the culture, its folklore and it's love of storytelling prowess and then inculcated these into his manner of communication. He found he better proclaimed the stories of Christ when he did so in this much more accessible parable form, which in Tanganyika (Tanzania), was far better received and understood by his hearers. However, now as he returned to Sydney with his very sick wife, it would appear that all his efforts had come to nothing. The bodyline tactics of the enemy had left this man, his family and his ministry in ruins. All was lost. All had been a waste.

It was during that long sail home after just three and half years on the mission field, that Paul occupied himself with turning his medical notes into a book entitled, *Doctor of Tanganyika*. Despite paper shortages during WWII the book was soon published and on the back of being a new and popular, published author, he was offered a radio station to tell his stories and from which was birthed the famous, 'Jungle Doctor' stories.

Dr. Paul White took patient care of his poor wife before her death in 1970, and Mary, by then, had long ceased to recognize her husband Paul or their children. Paul himself, whilst suffering from cancer, did in fact eventually die of a heart attack over dinner in 1992. He had a Tough life. Yet, like many of our lives, his was a troubled tapestry set in a slightly shining, silver frame, for his 'Jungle Doctor' books, have been translated into over a hundred languages, transferred to audio and for many years have been in comic book form. His three and half most difficult years in Africa did in fact lead to millions hearing the Gospel throughout the whole world and now, though he is dead, Paul still speaks of his Saviour through these self same; *Jungle Doctor* stories, which were birthed under the constant duress of the bodyline tactics of the enemy. Maybe, just maybe, your work in the Lord is not in vain. Those cannon ball bowls of the enemy, are trying to hurt you and take you from your wicket. No matter! For the devil cannot win and you cannot lose. What do you think?

Listen: *"Others were tortured, not accepting deliverance, that they might obtain a better resurrection. Still others had trial of mockings and scourgings, yes, and of chains and imprisonment. They were stoned, they were sawn in two, were tempted, were slain with the sword. They wandered about in sheepskins and goatskins, being destitute, afflicted, tormented - of whom the world was not worthy." (Hebrews 11:35b-38a NKJV)*

Pray: Lord, in taking the good examples of better people gone before, please help me, through the trials and twists of life to persevere in my calling, in Your great name I pray, amen!

| Vol 01 | Q1 | NW00034 | February 03rd |

Night-Whisper | **TRUTH**

Wringing pigeon's necks

The local bus service in the city of Brighton and Hove has come a long way from the poorer service it used to be. Now you can stand at a bus stop and with the technological 'miracle' of global positioning satellites, you can gaze at a digital read out which will tell you precisely where any of over 200 buses from their existing fleet are, and more especially, when your bus in particular will arrive at the place you are waiting for it. Amazing!

Leviticus 5:1

"If a person sins in hearing the utterance of an oath, and is a witness, whether he has seen or known of the matter - if he does not tell it, he bears guilt." NKJV

Note this though, that the government manipulated rising cost of petrol-gas, is not only causing increased 'drive offs' without paying' on thousands of garage forecourts, but fuel price rises themselves are also affecting the local bus queue in terms passing rising fares onto customers!

My wife told me just the other day how she saw a tough looking young woman, standing at the front of the bus queue, jump on the newly arrived bus, pay her 'ticket to ride all day fare,' then, whilst the other passengers were paying their fare, she ran to the back, opened the bus window and dropped her newly acquired ticket into the hands of her waiting friend, who, quite calmly, got onto the bus, flashed her newly acquired 'ride all day ticket' and then and went and sat with her friend. Everyone but the bus driver saw the whole incident. No one said a word.

I have pondered the question as to why no one said anything regarding this act of thievery and have come to the following eight conclusions:

1. People don't care, because dealing with this issue of theft carried out before their eyes, may delay their own journey.

2. People don't care, for this minor theft is in the great scheme of things a very little offence and not worth the hassle of confrontation. After all, those Banksters get away with stealing billions and then still get a bonus! That's quite some ticket to ride isn't it! What's the theft of a cheap bus ticket in light of that?

3. People are in collusion, for many of us have done the same thing, maybe in a different area, maybe at a different time of our life, but it is the same sin and in confronting this 'illegality,' we have to confront and condemn ourselves as well. Who wants to do that?

4. People are in collusion, for seeing how easily it was done, means it's a great idea and one they might use themselves at some other time.

Is confronting a small level of moral failure worth a broken nose?

5. People are in collusion, for the service is over-priced anyway, the profits for the providers are too great, and it's good to see some payback. It's always good to see the 'little people' getting little payback sometimes.

6. People do not take responsibility for their community, if the bus driver didn't see it, then frankly, "it's not my bag baby!"

7. People do not want to be seen as being a "grass," or as a "snitch" or as a "talebearer." This is a very powerful cultural peer pressure. No one wants to tell tales.

8. People are frightened, for confrontation often leads to violence being inflicted upon the accuser. This small level of moral failure is not worth a broken nose.

So there you have it. Apathy, collusion, ignorance, lack of responsibility, peer pressure and fear. And do you know what? These are also the six common causes of my own negligent sins.

The opening verse of Leviticus chapter five deals with these sins of fearful apathy and ignorance. 'The Message' translates our verse for tonight as follows:

"If you sin by not stepping up and offering yourself as a witness to something you've heard or seen in cases of wrongdoing, you'll be held responsible." Lev 5:1

Now obviously this has to do primarily with the sin of broken adjuration in the forms of either avoidance or lying. In other words, the context of these verses stands completely in a court of law, such that, if you are on oath and are asked a direct question, then where you refuse to answer, or, in the answering you then deliberately, for whatever reason, give the wrong answer, then you have sinned.

Jesus was keeping silent before His accusers until asked a direct question by someone in authority. Look:

But Jesus kept silent. And the high priest answered and said to Him, "I put You under oath (or I adjure you) by the living God: Tell us if You are the Christ, the Son of God!" Jesus said to him, "It is as you said. Nevertheless, I say to you, hereafter you will see the Son of Man sitting at the right hand of the power, and coming on the clouds of heaven." Matthew 26:63-64 NKJV

Jesus is the only person I know of, who has never sinned in terms of broken 'adjurement.' We, however, break it all the time, and in a way, we break it even when we are waiting for a bus!

Jesus is the only person I know of, who has never sinned in terms of broken 'adjurement.' We, however, break it all the time, and in a way, we break it even when we are waiting for a bus!

Fortunately, Leviticus chapter 5 goes on to provide regulations for a bloody sin offering for these unpremeditated sins, for these unintentional sins, for these sins of forgetfulness, for these sins of negligence and for these sins of fear. The sin offering prescribed covers all social and financial levels of society, for at every level, this sin is most prevalent. My God, those little foxes, you know, can burn down our houses once their tales are lit by lies!

Why is attending to these comparatively little sins so important then? Well, understand that not seeing these seeming slight sins is dangerous stuff, for not dealing with them in the first instance, in the shallow waters, if you will, leads us to deeper levels of collusion and association, and from the sticky 'gloop' of these minor misdemeanors, there then rises the more haunting and condemning sins of cowardice and betrayal. Think about that. Banksters, are after all, are the ultimate betrayers of nations. They are the treasonous traitors of the treasury and some would say, even self-serving cowards. Yet are they in the dock? Are they in prison? No. Therefore woe to the nations who allow money to buy morality. Our nations have most certainly done so. Look you though, I bet some of those Banksters started out by getting a free ride one day.

Yes, it's all dangerous stuff and we all need to have the forgiveness that comes through the blood of Christ, coupled with the wisdom which comes through a maturity of walk and a courage which comes from a close companionship with Jesus Himself. Forgiveness, an active righteousness, wisdom, courage, maturity and the companionship of Christ. Now then, there are six holy answers to the six common causes of all our negligent sins! Well that and a bloody pigeon! That and dealing with all the little misdemeanors at the bus queue.

Listen: *"Let the rivers clap their hands; let the hills be joyful together before the Lord, for He is coming to judge the earth. With righteousness He shall judge the world, and the peoples with equity." (Psalms 98:8-9 NKJV)*

Pray: Almighty and most merciful Father, we have erred, and strayed from Thy ways like lost sheep. We have followed too much the devices and desires of our own hearts. We have offended against Thy holy laws. We have left undone those things which we ought to have done; and we have done those things which we ought not to have done; and there is no health in us. But Thou, O Lord, have mercy upon us, miserable offenders. Spare Thou them, O God, which confess their faults. Restore Thou them that are penitent; according to Thy promises declared unto mankind in Christ Jesus our Lord. And grant, O most merciful Father, for his sake, that we may hereafter live a godly, righteous, and sober life, to the glory of Thy holy name. Amen.

(Evening Prayer, from The Book of Common Prayer)

Night-Whisper | **SERVE**

A man with his wholeness wholly attending

I am re-reading again, one of my favorite books of all time, which is, *The Man Who Mistook His Wife for a Hat, and other clinical tales*, by Oliver Sacks. Apart from being a genius of a man and a most engaging writer, I have consistently found his clinical neurological analyses to also contain profound spiritual and pastoral content.

John 8:29
"And He who sent Me is with Me. The Father has not left Me alone, for I always do those things that please Him." NKJV

In part four of his book entitled: *The World of The Simple*, in section 22, he recounts the story of 'Martin A,' a 61 year old 'idiot savant,' or, known more appropriately today as an 'autistic savant,' who was admitted late in life to Sack's hospital, with Parkinson's disease.

Whilst in infancy, Martin also had near fatal meningitis causing retardation, impulsiveness, seizures and some spasticity on one side. Nevertheless, because Martin's father was a famous singer at New York's Metropolitan opera, Martin consequently had amazing musical gifts, musical sensibilities and an eidetic, photographic, vivid and total recall, musical memory!

However, when Martin entered Sacks' hospital he regressed into the form of a dirty, belligerent and snotty child. Consequently, no one liked him and his nurses knew that Martin was in fact killing himself, as something seemed to be gnawing away inside of him, even eating him to death! Eventually, Martin blurted out the reason for his sad and forthcoming demise saying: "I've got to sing, I can't live without it, and it's not just the music, I can't pray without it. Music to Bach, was the apparatus of worship. I've never spent a Sunday without going to church, without singing in the choir. I first went there with my father when I was old enough to walk, and I continued going after his death. I've got to go! It'll kill me if I don't."

Sacks ensured that Martin was at church, singing in the choir every Sunday thereafter. He writes that Martin "Became a different man...recovered himself, recollected himself, became real again. The pseudo person, the stigmatized, the snotty, spitting boy disappeared; as did the irritating, emotionless, impersonal eidetic. The real person reappeared, a dignified, decent man, respected and valued now by other residents. But the marvel, the real marvel, was to see Martin when he was actually singing, or in communion with music, listening with an intentness that verged on rapture, he was 'a man in his wholeness wholly attending.' Martin was, in a word, transformed. All that was defective or pathological fell away, and one saw only absorption and animation, wholeness and health."

> *'a man in his wholeness wholly attending.'*

Oh to have the ability my friends, oh to have the capacity, the opportunity, to be 'people in our wholeness, wholly attending.' There is a glimpse of heaven in that phrase don't you think? There is a sniff of what is to come, even the enjoyment and focus of being without any destructive distractions. The pain we see in those we love; evil expressed in the world, in our world; the unmet need; the unfulfilled desire; the daily mocking of often years of particular prayers still remaining unanswered; yes, it is these kind of destructive distractions that rob most Christians of their focused wholeness. Is a savant sickness the only way for us to become so enraptured? No. However, I do think that we need a 'fool for Christ,' kind of servant sickness, rather than savant sickness, to help us in our focus.

Let us discover the Father's desire for us, in gifting, in providential opportunity, in sacrifice and in satisfaction. Let us then pursue it with all of our might and in the so doing, pursue Him our Lord as His most willing servants. He then must become our focus, our pleasure, and our delight. I am convinced that it is only when we have such a 'servant's sickness,' that we too shall become a people in their wholeness, wholly attending.

It's worth contemplating. It's worth trying. Don't you think?

Listen: *"No one engaged in warfare entangles himself with the affairs of this life, that he may please him who enlisted him as a soldier. And also if anyone competes in athletics, he is not crowned unless he competes according to the rules. The hardworking farmer must be first to partake of the crops. Consider what I say, and may the Lord give you understanding in all things." (2 Timothy 2:4-7 NKJV)*

Pray: Father, remove far from me all my unnecessary busy work and help me to be truly focused, even a man in his wholeness, wholly attending. In Jesus name I ask it, amen and let it be so!

Night-Whisper | **WISDOM**

Problems from the perplexing king of frolic

Not many people know this but I am in fact a male model. It's quite a few years ago now but a great artist friend of mine once asked me to pose as St Francis of Assisi for a wall mural she had been commissioned to paint. "I wanted someone who could look spiritual, insane and emaciated all at the same time," she said. At that time, I was most definitely the man for the job. Though I am far from emaciated nowadays!

Deuteronomy 6:5

"You shall love the Lord your God with all your heart, with all your soul, and with all your strength." NKJV

I am reminded of this today as I have just come from a day's retreat where the life of this saint was unfolded before us. Throughout the last eight centuries the intriguing nature of Francis has never ceased to attract further examination and at the end of the age, he is still proving increasingly popular in terms of ecumenism, ecology, animal rights, and a varied array of other skewwhiff pseudo-spirituality. But really, is there anything more we might learn from Saint Francis of Assisi?

Born in Italy in 1182 and named by his French mother as Giovanni, his father, returning late from a foreign trading trip nevertheless renamed him 'Frances,' after his love of all things French!

A much over indulged child, Francis, this 'king of frolic' joined the troubadours, partied down and then partied on, fully financed by his wealthy parents, and in the so doing, growing increasingly strong willed as he went. Excessive, proud and boastful, he was later taken into captivity for nearly a year when an attempt at soldiering led to disaster. His mother had no doubt pumped him up about his future religious greatness, which I feel, led to many of his private aspirations and dreams. These, coupled with the deep mother stirred thoughts about his future, those deeper thoughts that only a forced incarceration can conjure up, no doubt began to unfurl the future sails of this very unhinged ascetic mystic.

Francis, the little poor man, was eventually permanently estranged from his earthly father over the selling of stolen goods. His father's goods that is! Through his whole life, Francis remained irreconcilable to his rich father. This was chiefly because of Francis's most public rejection of his father's all too late discipline. The forsaken father's constant provision and material goodness begged for an acknowledge honor from his oh so spoiled son, but unfortunately, it never came.

Emotional and excessive eccentrics have always gathered a crowd and St Francis was no different. His visions of speaking crucifixes, dreams of sacrificial seraphs sending bolts of lightning blessings upon him, his increasingly and eccentric public displays and overt clashes with rising capitalism, especially manifested amongst the clergy, led him to become a fascinating and living artefact in the church, even an irritating little speaking stone in its tight fitting shoes. He was a distraction maybe, but in the right political hands, he might become someone's very profitable tool. Yes, once Francis became the first recorded case of church accepted, 'true stigmata,' I think his eventual fate was sealed. For despite his marriage to 'Lady Poverty' it did not stop, especially in later days, many penitential gifts of property being made to the newly founded orders, especially that of the female version of the Franciscans, the 'Poor Clare.'

He was a distraction maybe, but in the right political hands, he might become someone's very profitable tool.

The Roman church seemed to somewhat smile on the giving away of goods by Francs, even church goods, yes, even goods gained by Crusades and Indulgences, but it did not smile in the giving away of property! For property is power and any property held by any order was in fact property held by the Pope. Innocence III made the man 'Ugolino' his 'protective Bishop' in these property matters, and it was this same 'mystic minder' who later became Pope Gregory IX, who also made Francis a Saint. After this was done, the money and the property just came rolling in friends, it just came rolling in! Funny, people thought they were giving property to the ministers to the poor but in effect they were giving it to the pope! Unless you think this was not a big deal, know that in later days, anyone disagreeing with the real estate property rights of the Pope were deemed to be heretics, and handed over to the inquisition before being burned at the stake. Franciscan or otherwise.

St Francis himself, suffering from infections and blinding trachoma, ostiomalacia (rickets) through bad diet, probably died of a chronic parasitic disease called schistosomiasis. His stigmata made him famous and profitable for the church, but his self-induced poverty killed him. To get to my question then: is there anything we can learn from Saint Francis of Assisi? Yes, I think there are many things and tonight let us consider but five of them.

> *God can use lunatics - especially if they are undaunted in their actions and dedicated to their task..*

• First, that God can use lunatics - especially if they are undaunted in their actions and dedicated to their task.

• Secondly, that political powers use lunatics, especially when there is profit in the so doing. Especially if its property profits.

• Thirdly, that people follow lunatics, even to great excess, especially if there is seeming spiritual profit in the so doing and spiritual peer prowess in the practice. You know, the given admiration of others. People like to be adored. To be looked up to in some measure at least.

• Fourthly, that good hygiene and good nutrition, though important to healthy living, and balanced ministry, will not keep you alive forever. Be sure then that you are living with all your might for the things you believe in with all your heart. Eat well! For you just might minister longer and minister better.

• Lastly, the powerful and consistent, seen and sacrificial dedication of such servants of God, though not good rules to base our lives upon, are never the less, glaring ultraviolet beams of shining and deep scanning revelation, revealing the pox marks on our own halfhearted and over indulgent souls.

What can we learn from the life of St Francis? Be balanced. Don't be used and abused. Live well. Love better.

Listen: *"Then Jesus, looking at him, loved him, and said to him, 'One thing you lack: Go your way, sell whatever you have and give to the poor, and you will have treasure in heaven; and come, take up the cross, and follow Me.' But he was sad at this word, and went away sorrowful, for he had great possessions." (Mark 10:21-22 NKJV)*

Pray: Lord, make me an instrument of Thy peace; where there is hatred, let me sow love; where there is injury, pardon; where there is doubt, faith; where there is despair, hope; where there is darkness, light; and where there is sadness, joy. O Divine Master, grant that I may not so much seek to be consoled as to console; to be understood, as to understand; to be loved, as to love; for it is in giving that we receive, it is in pardoning that we are pardoned, and it is in dying that we are born to Eternal Life. Amen, and let it be so.

Night-Whisper | **HOPE**

Of ashes and eye lashes, all curled high on 'Expectation Day'

In the Western Christian calendar, Ash Wednesday is the first day of Lent and occurs, excluding Sundays, forty days before Easter. Because it is dependent on the lunar date of Easter, it falls on a different date each year and can occur as early as February 4th or as late as March 10th. The day of my writing this Night Whisper (though not of your reading) is indeed Ash Wednesday and though the day is celebrated by a number of Christian denominations, it is especially utilized by Roman Catholics.

Psalms 51:1-2

"Have mercy upon me, O God, according to Your loving kindness; according to the multitude of Your tender mercies, blot out my transgressions. Wash me thoroughly from my iniquity, and cleanse me from my sin." NKJV

Having been brought up as a Roman Catholic, one of my most earliest religious recollections is that of being taken from school to church (again), and above the violently swung olfactory charge of burning incense, hearing the voice of a Bishop, marking all the lined up child supplicants, with a black grey cross on their forehead, his old and worn out voice, full of tired old words echoing like an ethereal and disembodied warning, sliding down the cold brick walls and perching like black crows upon all the twelve stations of the cross, I hear it even today, repeated incessantly in my mind and underlined by every area of bodily arthritis: "Remember man that thou art dust and unto dust thou shalt return; remember man that thou art dust and unto dust thou shalt return; remember man that thou art dust and unto dust thou shalt return…"

Ash Wednesday is in effect a day of repentance, marking the beginning of the 40 days of preparation for Holy Week. I have always found it a piously pompous, marked and miserable day and don't ask me how, but almost always in my childhood, the dark internal tone and tenor of the day was always in direct contrast with the outside weather, where the sun seemed to be always shining.

Puberty, play, life, light and love were all calling outside. Inside Ash Wednesday was full of skeletons and dust, even though they were then only the stuff of harmless hammer horror movies, or of old graveyards in the grey dusk light, or those dark indeterminable shadows which inhabited the hushed sentences of sad adults, when whispering regrets and wiping quiet tears from their sad and mascara marked faces, always turned away from the children. It was the adults who had death and regret. It was we children who had hope and a future.

"Remember man that thou art dust and unto dust thou shalt return;"

What was this Bishop trying to do to me with these words? "Remember man that thou art dust and unto dust thou shalt return; remember man that thou art dust and unto dust thou shalt return; remember man that thou art dust and unto dust thou shalt return…"

Whenever God the Holy Spirit at first removes the cataracts of self-justification from our eyes and all our many sins come into focus before our unprepared and peering peepers, the hurricane of horror, the gale of grief and the storms of sorrow which come upon us, are initially so powerful, that they bowl us over into the dirt of our past lives and all we can do, all we must do, is abhor ourselves for a while, covering our miserable heads in dust and ashes. This is not a religious practice I am referring to, no, it is a consequence of true and spiritual, ophthalmic surgery. We see ourselves in sin, we abhor ourselves, we repent and when we do this, God touches the forehead of our minds in this self-loathing, and He does it where no ceremony can, for when God brushes our foreheads with His loving thumb, the words: "Remember man that thou art dust and unto dust thou shalt return," have no place in this particular, forehead touch divine.

You see, when repentance is allowed to have its place and allowed to have its work, not only is our sight more keener but the trepanned tears of our broken heart, pour out through our now opened mind, somehow miraculously releasing the love of God into our limbs, His active life pouring into our astonished little legs, and so much so, that the command to stand upon our feet, is heard, is obeyed and is speedily actioned. Sure, the bridegroom is away and fasting shall occur, but now, they are not fasts of preparation to be marked by words of death and signs of hopeless ashes, but fasting's of longing, all marked by the shining and oily hope of anointed heads, washed faces, and bright eyes, which brim full of the forgiveness of the Son of God Himself and oooh yes, they are signs marked by eyelashes, yes of eyelashes, clean and curled up high to heaven, like palm fronds raised in happy expectation. The voice we now hear says: "Remember man, that art loved and to Him that loves thee, thou shalt return, with joy unspeakable and full of glory."

I think that Ash Wednesday should be clothed in Orange and instead of ashes rubbed into the forehead with worrying words, each child should be given a green topped shining carrot, which, as we all know, is the very best of vegetables for the preservation of eyesight. After all, you never see a rabbit wearing glasses. I wonder then if Ash Wednesday should also be given a new name maybe! How about, "Expectation Wednesday!" There is a time to remember our coming earthly demise, but this time, this 'Carrot Wednesday,' this new 'Expectation Day' should be prepared by delight and met with joy, washed faces and joy anointed heads, in the amazing fact that Christ has died for all of our sins.

> *Ash Wednesday should also be given a new name maybe! How about, "Expectation Wednesday!"*

Listen: *"Moreover, when you fast, do not be like the hypocrites, with a sad countenance. For they disfigure their faces that they may appear to men to be fasting. Assuredly, I say to you, they have their reward. But you, when you fast, anoint your head and wash your face, so that you do not appear to men to be fasting, but to your Father who is in the secret place; and your Father who sees in secret will reward you openly." (Matthew 6:16-18 NKJV)*

Pray: Father, thank You for the forgiveness I have received through Jesus Christ the Lord, Your Son and my Savior. Holy Spirit, lifter of my head, bore my ears with the sign of my much satisfied servant hood, yes, come, trepan my skull and open my mind to who I am in You, come breathe again the kiss of life, up my flared and open nostrils and raise me again and again in my daily experience, to life and light and love and hope, in Jesus name I pray, amen?

| Vol 01 | Q1 | NW00038 | February 07th |

Night-Whisper | **TRUTH**

My empire of dirt

It was Trent Reznor from Cleveland Ohio who founded the American industrial rock band called Nine Inch Nails. Almost immediately before his death, it was, however, 'The Man in Black' himself, Mr. Johnny Cash, who covered one of Reznor's songs entitled 'Hurt.'

Psalms 119:133

"Direct my steps by Your word, and let no iniquity have dominion over me."
NKJV

Nominated for 7 MTV awards and a Grammy for the best short form video, the 71–year-old Johnny Cash, made this song his very own. Profound in the extreme, Cash turned this song not only into one of the best anti-drug songs ever recorded but from his old twisted mouth, with an aged and broken voice, he made it a stunning personal testimony of regret and repentance regarding the selfishness of his past life, which was embodied in utterly sinful hedonism and the seeking of sparkling pots, which in turn, Cash found in the end to be only full of dust and rust and rot. I think it is one of the most magnificent music videos ever made. Jonny Cash died just days after making this video.

I have great experience with selfishness and too much experience of drugs. It is amazing how similar the destructive consequences are when you indulge in either of these. Largest of all, is the unseen but enormously evident stunting of emotional development. You see, I have observed that those who indulge in drug taking, remain at a most juvenile and selfish stage of emotional development for a long time. Those not indulging in these same sinful practices, develop as individuals, they move on, they move away, they grow up. Drug users, however, like lost men over the stern of a fast moving ship speeding through the cold spray filled night, are in seconds lost over the darkest of horizons, drowning in a vast, slow eating sea of emptiness and utter loneliness. No matter if more juveniles may join them, no matter if they manage to temporarily get hold of those sparkling pots of gold, they eventually lose themselves, for everyone they know, goes away in the end, and worst of all, they lose their sweetest friend. They lose their very selves.

Cash's closing utterance to Reznor's lyrics, expressed in sobbing tears to the rising heart pounding music is this:

> *If I could start again*
> *A million miles away*
> *I would keep myself*
> *I would find a way*

What have you become my sweetest friend? What holes are torn into your own soul? Your empire of dirt has only let you down and hurt you, robbed you of true feeling, leaving you with unfixable and broken thoughts, whilst seating you as King on your own selfish throne and lying to your face. The drugs and the drug of utter selfishness in particular, have turned you into nothing short of a rotting retard, rolling in regret. This is the truth of your terrible situation.

Dear drug user, and all other people consumed in selfishness, Christ died to save you, Christ died to make you His very own, Christ died to restore your humanity and His most secret and greatest gift to you, is the return of your lost self into your very own desperate and open arms, but this time healed, whole and complete in Him, with Him, for Him, by Him. Yes, I am convinced that Christ wants to give you back to yourself. Turn to Him for help and deliverance tonight.

> *Yes, I am convinced that Christ wants to give you back to yourself. Turn to Him for help and deliverance tonight.*

Sin is a drug. Sin persisted in is addictive. Addiction to any form of selfish sin robs you of your true self. Sinner, repent of your secret and persistent sins tonight. Sinner, you self-deluded hedonist, stop making excuses for your persistent self-indulgence. Like the drug user, for that is what you are, I am convinced that Christ wants to give you back to yourself. Turn to Him for help and deliverance tonight.

Listen: *"Beware lest anyone cheat you through philosophy and empty deceit, according to the tradition of men, according to the basic principles of the world, and not according to Christ. For in Him dwells all the fullness of the Godhead bodily; and you are complete in Him, who is the head of all principality and power." (Colossians 2:8-10 NKJV0*

Pray: Jesus, You are the Way, You are my way. Desperate I come to You, broken, lost, shattered, stained, a shell of festering fragments of what I was once a long, long time ago, an unrecognizable shadow of what I might have been. Redeem O lord, restore O Lord, yes, please redeem me from my sin and from the dark hand of him who has power over me. Stronger than the strong man armed, please, give me back my sweetest friend, yes, please give me back to myself. Amen, and let it be so.

Night-Whisper | **STRENGTH**

Dealing with the different lava flows of both Levite and Leviathan

My friend was driving down the street in a city in South Florida when a man walking along the pavement spotted him. The well bling'd up gangsta, drew back his lips to their full extent, revealing an emblazoned gold grill'd, growling mouth. The message from this gangbanger was clear: "These are my streets, I am in control, so don't mess with me."

Proverbs 15:1

"A soft answer turns away wrath, but a harsh word stirs up anger."
NKJV

Now my friend happened to be a rather large and more than well-armed deputy from the Broward County Sheriff's department, so, in response to this silent but apparently exceptionally aggressive display toward him, he turned around his car and met up with the gangbanger for some genteel conversation, where he then politely informed him of his bad judgment regarding the ownership of the streets and carefully instructing him in both who owned the streets and who was actually in control. Though none of us would have liked to have been involved in that particular genteel conversation, I can inform you that the results of it was that he was never, and I mean never, flashed a growling gold grill again. You see, if the soft answer of our text had been applied in this particular situation, well, it would have got the Deputy killed at some date not long after the gangbanger grilling.

Our verse for tonight speaks of a passionate display of anger. It is better understood maybe, as red-hot displeasure, a most dangerous and violently bubbling pot of molten destruction born from justified rage. God Himself manifests this kind of fearful wrath, which seems wild and intemperate and itching for vengeance. Yes, He does, and it is most clearly seen when Israel, led by Aaron the High Priest, made a molten calf and worshiped and unashamedly cavorted both around it and with it. God wanted to wipe them from the face of the earth over this incident and He wanted to kill Aaron in particular! (See Deuteronomy Chapter 9.) I tell you tonight, if it was not for the calf like eye pleading gentleness of Moses, repeatedly interceding for them through forty days and forty nights, then Israel might have been consumed in God's lava molten wrath on more than one occasion.

When we have been in the wrong, when we have stirred up righteous anger in others, when we have set the scene to justify wrath against us, then there is nothing better than a humble and pleading apology, an open acknowledgement of our wrong doing, seen in calf like tenderness and spoken with both reflective and confessional tones. Undoubtedly, this kind of answer in that kind of situation, will go a long way to halt the flow of all consuming anger from the offended party. Maybe, even recalling that anger, reversing the destruction, refreshing the relationship, restoring the peace that once was there and returning everything to normal. Yes, we need strength, wisdom, honesty and humility to rightly offer soft responses in the face of such righteous and revengeful wrath.

Recalling that anger, reversing the destruction, refreshing the relationship, restoring the peace that once was there and returning everything to normal.

When we have been acting righteously, however, and non-righteous aggression has been directed toward us, you know, if we are suffering directly for righteousness sake, then may God give us the grace to turn the other cheek, to walk the extra mile, to forgive our enemies. No apology is needed here, just courage and the ability to commit ourselves to God.

However, if someone falls in the descriptive parameters of being an obnoxious jerk or a murdering madman, then maybe a visit from my friend, the very big and well-armed Deputy, would mightily help the situation. You see, sometimes, turning the cheek is both dangerous and wrong. You see, the soft answer of our text, is in fact a repentant answer to sin which we must own. When there is no sin, then sometimes, we need to be more like a Leviathan than a Levite in our conversation, our walk and our presence. Think about that and may God grant us wisdom in the outworking of both. Remember though, sometimes friend, you are just going to have to speak tough and be prepared to back it up.

Listen: *"Can you draw out Leviathan with a hook, or snare his tongue with a line which you lower? Can you put a reed through his nose, or pierce his jaw with a hook? Will he make many supplications to you? Will he speak softly to you?" (Job 41:1-3 NKJV)*

Pray: Lord, make me wise tomorrow in both gentleness and in strength, in Jesus name I pray. Amen, and let it be so.

Night-Whisper | **RESCUE**

Of plumbers and 'disrememberment'

Not too long ago, I had a cup of coffee in Starbucks with a descendent of the great abolitionist himself, William Wilberforce. He was a plumber and a very nice chap as well, I am sure William was as well. I mean a nice chap and not a plumber.

Deuteronomy 15:15-18

"You shall remember that you were a slave in the land of Egypt, and the Lord your God redeemed you; therefore I command you this thing today. And if it happens that he says to you, 'I will not go away from you,' because he loves you and your house, since he prospers with you, then you shall take an awl and thrust it through his ear to the door, and he shall be your servant forever. Also to your female servant you shall do likewise." NKJV

I hate plumbing. I can't do it well and so consequently, I avoid it. However, broken, blocked, stinky and overflowing pipes in a functioning kitchen, always demand my immediate attention despite the fact that the almost always bungled attempt at repair, always gets me wet, smelly and flustered, agitated, aggravated and angry! I swear, this mostly happens to me because of the absence of right and necessary tools.

Even so, when the dirty plumbing duty calls, it is with gritted teeth that the cold copper and the dirty ribbed overflow pipe tag team wrestling match begins and from a well learned and safe distance, the wife and family, gazing and listening at the groaning and cursing coming from under some dark tight space, or from a cramped hunched over body, crushed behind some blue lint covered, hard white dryer, simply stare and suck cold air through their own bared teeth, as they look to see if this time, both me and my wrench will for once, just once O Lord, arise victorious from the sodden carpet, instead of damp and defeated with the same pitiful confession on my lips of: "I could do this darling, if only I had the right tools!"

The plumber, when he comes, will always repair the problem calmly and speedily, if albeit, expensively. Maybe, next time I am defeated in the stinky waters, a grand descendent of Wilberforce will descend upon me in my distress and emancipate me from my slavery to gross defeat and embarrassment. I hate plumbing.

Nobel prize-winning American writer, editor, and professor, Toni Morrison dedicated her novel *Beloved* to the estimated sixty million or more black Africans who died as captives in Africa or on slave ships. In her 1998 novel, one of whose themes is the demonic return and embodiment of the mother 'Seth's' child, called *Beloved*. In the story, you see, long time back, mother Seth pursued by hateful slave owners, had cut her own baby *Beloved's* throat with a saw, rather than have her go through her own personal experience of slavery and now, the dead child had returned to wreak her vengeance.

> *Disremembered people and disremembered events, always refuse to stay in the ground*

Beloved, the novel, was later made into a startlingly magnificent film of the same name, starring Oprah Winfrey as Seth, and Thandie Newton as *Beloved*. My favorite scene is the community exorcism of *Beloved* and following that emotionally explosive scene, the release and healing of both the murdering mother Seth, and the local African community. Professor Karen Baker-Fletcher, who refers to the demonic character of *Beloved* as 'an embodiment of vast historical memory,' also remarks that: "The past can be disremembered but never erased." I believe that. Certainly Morrison conveyed most thoroughly that: "Those who die bad won't stay in the ground." I have also found that to be true, for disremembered people and disremembered events, always refuse to stay in the ground and as a testimony to this, the broken truth pipes gurgle loudly in communities, and nasty blockages occur in cultures as the consequent foul brokenness always eventually manifests itself in society.

No one is looking for the disremembered, for they are not lost! No, for conveniences sake, they have been deliberately placed aside. However, be sure of this, that all the disremembered will eventually find us out and come a knocking on our doors, flooding our white ware'd kitchens of community with all kinds of smelly kak. Yes, I hate plumbing, and Pastorally speaking, I hate this kind of plumbing in particular.

When the disremembered manifests itself, manifests themselves even, well, when this happens, we shall all need a Wilberforce.

Nationally, locally and even personally, we shall all need a person of some experience with an appropriate spiritual wrench. So, if you're going to be a political, a theological, a psychological or even a local community plumber, then you had better get some gifting, you had better get some training, and you had better get some desire for the work, for I can promise you this, that you will always have situational and personal, foul, and smelly messes to deal with, both from people and nations, who being deliberately neglectful and hateful of their own plumbing, are never the less, always shocked and surprised by the manifestations of disrememberment, that always eventually rises, through the foul and murky waters of our lives.

Stand out text – Stand Out Text- Stand out text – Stand Out Text-

I hate plumbing for it is always messy, inconvenient and expensive and without the right tools, you will always need a professional in the end, you know, a man with the right tools and training. Let me ask you now, do you have the right tools and training for this kind of spiritual plumbing work? If not my friend, then please keep out of the kitchen.

Listen: *"But you shall remember that you were a slave in Egypt, and the Lord your God redeemed you from there; therefore I command you to do this thing. 'When you reap your harvest in your field, and forget a sheaf in the field, you shall not go back to get it; it shall be for the stranger, the fatherless, and the widow, that the Lord your God may bless you in all the work of your hands. When you beat your olive trees, you shall not go over the boughs again; it shall be for the stranger, the fatherless, and the widow. When you gather the grapes of your vineyard, you shall not glean it afterward; it shall be for the stranger, the fatherless, and the widow. And you shall remember that you were a slave in the land of Egypt; therefore I command you to do this thing.'" (Deuteronomy 24:18-22 NKJV)*

Pray: Lord send us again, a plumber named Wilberforce, remove our blockages and free us for all our spewing garbage, in Jesus name I pray, amen, and let it be so!

Night-Whisper | **WISDOM**

Weeping women

Our text for tonight is both a prophetic and poetic expression, in that it prophetically foretold "the slaying of the Benjamite innocents" by Herod, as recorded in the Gospel according to Matthew. It is also a poetic expression of all the mourning's and moaning's of God's people under their calamitous burdens throughout the ages.

Jeremiah 31:15

"Thus says the Lord: 'A voice was heard in Ramah, lamentation and bitter weeping, Rachel weeping for her children, refusing to be comforted for her children, because they are no more.'"
NKJV

Rachel, cranky, crabby and cross in character, was nevertheless, the best loved wife of Jacob the patriarch. Why? Because Rachel, beautiful in youthful exuberance, fetching in form and adorable in appearance, had captivated Jacob's then momma's boy heart and he fell madly in love with here.

"So Jacob served seven years for Rachel, and they seemed only a few days to him because of the love he had for her." Genesis 29:20 NKJV

Another beautiful woman, a poet and painter herself, better known for being the muse of the Pre-Raphaelite Brotherhood and the wife of Gabriel Charles Dante Rossetti, was today in 1862, despite her own fantastic form and features, found dead from an overdose of Laudanum when her husband and another poet friend returned home from a night out on the town. Around the time of her death there were rumors of suicide and even today, questions are raised about whether Elizabeth Eleanor Siddal was in fact murdered.

Siddal, like her husband Rosseti, was in fact a drug addict. A paragraph can never sum up anyone's life, but it is apparent that Siddal's first pregnancy by Rossetti was in great part, a hopeful security for his continued love, if not fidelity. The still-birth of this security package, so damaged the totality of Siddal's constitution that even whilst pregnant a second time by Rosseti, she overdosed herself to death.

It is reported that Rosseti was inconsolable at the time of Sidal's death and in a reflection of this, took the whole body of his poetic work and placed them in her coffin, binding them in his corpse wife's flowing hair.

Regretting this act, not too much later in life, with his own constitution now displaying all the signs of a slow suicide of the soul, and with his painters eyesight failing, he had his dead wife's body secretly exhumed by night and from the copper hair filled coffin, he removed the poetry from the dark bosom. A single worm had burrowed a bullet hole through the heart of the poetry.

I wonder if this powerful grieving, if not channeled into pleading prayer, will simply bring forth death instead of life?

The exhumed poetic work was edited and published but its "fleshly" content brought the author, both manifest and mighty criticism. This crushing criticism, combined with Rossetti's own drug addiction, his deepening depression and rising delusions, his fear of the secret of the exhumation of his dead love being made public and no doubt the damage done by his own failed attempt at Laudanum suicide, led to a stroke and his eventual and lonely death in 1882.

Rachel had angered Jacob when in her own desperation she had cried:

"Give me children else I die!" Genesis 30:1,2.

Unfortunately this self fulfilling prophecy, was realised just short of the little town of Bethlehem, when Rachel did indeed die whilst giving birth to her second son, whom she named "Son of my pain," whom Jacob, upon her passing, quickly renamed the "Son of My Right Hand."

There are many lessons for us here in both of these poetic stories. From the many, allow me to briefly leave with you a simple consideration and an observation tonight.

First, consider that the grieving's and groaning's of barren women, longing for life to come forth from them, are so powerful, that they seem to resonate through space and time, their echoes being strong enough for many other people to both feel and hang their sadness on. I wonder if this powerful grieving, if not channeled into pleading prayer, will simply bring forth death instead of life? I wonder?

Secondly, observe that there are some old loves and some lost works that really need to remain buried. Therefore, I have to say to some of you tonight: "Let it go. Let them go. Else a worm will burrow a bullet hole through the center of your own heart and soul. Jacob buried his love, erected a pillar of remembrance and then moved on with his life. You need to do the same."

Listen: *"So Rachel died and was buried on the way to Ephrath (that is, Bethlehem). And Jacob set a pillar on her grave, which is the pillar of Rachel's grave to this day." (Genesis 35:19-20 NKJV)*

Pray: Father, deliver me from self-curses, crypt raiding and worms of the heart, in Jesus name I pray, amen, and let it be so.

| Vol 01 | Q1 | NW00042 | February 11th |

Night-Whisper | **WORK**

Of good starts and better endings

I must say, that I do often enjoy some of the unpolished pageantry of postmodern, protestant Christianity. I love the unpracticed symbolism we sometimes employ to mark the end of significant and sometimes damaging events? For example, I recently heard of a small church going through a service of "letting go" of old hurts and wounds, which was symbolized by each member handing a personal and symbolic object to the elders, who in turn took the objects and placed them, symbolically speaking, at the feet of Jesus, at the foot of the cross.

1 Peter 2:6,7

"For in Scripture it says: 'See, I lay a stone in Zion, a chosen and precious cornerstone, and the one who trusts in him will never be put to shame.' Now to you who believe, this stone is precious. But to those who do not believe, 'the stone the builders rejected has become the capstone'." NIV

On another occasion I was involved with a men's retreat, when, at the end of the time away, the men wrote down their sins and bad practices and then together buried them in the red dirt of a Georgia hillside, never to be retrieved nor to be picked up and practiced ever again. It was most excellent, and like I say, I do often enjoy some of the unpolished pageantry of postmodern, protestant Christianity. It's very moving, very helpful. For about a week that is! Or maybe less.

Some of the guys who met in Georgia, did go back for their old buried stuff. The small church I mentioned was still exhibiting open wounds, and was still falling over one another's baggage, and I could recount to you countless other stories as well, of ineffectual protestant pageantry whose significant satisfaction is measured by about the time it takes to get hungry after a Chinese meal and whose power to resist the continuing pressure of sinful habits, supposedly laid to rest by protestant postmodern pageantry, is a strong as an empty coke tin in a large man's hand.

Having examined the very poor results of such postmodern protestant pageantry, I believe the issue of ineffectiveness lies in a false assumption and a misunderstanding. Let me explain.

The false assumption of such linked healing, letting go, stake in the ground, kind of imagery and symbolism, is that we assume that 'that's that!' When in fact, 'that's not 'that' at all! The decision to acknowledge, to let go, to choose life, to be better, to be done with it, are all good and powerful decisions and are worthy to be marked in our memory by powerful imagery. However, the great misunderstanding is that we regard these decisions and images as capstones, rather than cornerstones. In other words, we regard them as completion images rather than starting images, we look at them as endings rather than new beginnings.

> *We regard these decisions and images as capstones, rather than cornerstones.*

When a builder lays the foundation of a new and magnificent edifice, there is often pageantry and celebration, there is imagery and dignitary, there is clapping and signing, there is applauding and singing. However, there is much work ahead. A cornerstone has been laid, an indispensable and fundamental marking stone of measurement, strength and solid direction has been set down as a strong beginning to a certain ending! Now, until the building is complete there is a vast amount of building to be done, an expensive and vast amount mind you! In the end, and usually privately and more often than not in an unseen fashion, the capstone is laid as a protective and often decorative covering stone to mark the completion of the building. It's time now to cut the ribbon, open the doors, move in, rejoice and live out its functionality to the full.

My dear friend, please remember tonight, that there is a lot of work and personal expense in between the cornerstone and the capstone, especially in the personal and unpolished pageantry of postmodern Christianity. So, roll your sleeves up and get on with it. Get to work and complete that sanctified structure which you have started together with God. Do you remember the now abandoned cornerstone which you laid? You thought it was a capstone! It's not too late you know. Go back and start building. The Capstone will come, but not after a lot of hard work.

Listen: *"Therefore, my beloved, as you have always obeyed, not as in my presence only, but now much more in my absence, work out your own salvation with fear and trembling; for it is God who works in you both to will and to do for His good pleasure." (Philippians 2:12-13 NKJV0*

Pray: Lord! I got it wrong! I thought I was done with 'that' when in fact I was only beginning to be done with 'that.' Show me please the architect plans for this new building we have begun, help me clear away the debris, find that cornerstone and joyfully build something magnificent, until we together, can place the capstone on the top and move in and start living productively and powerfully. In Jesus name I ask it, amen, and let it be so!

Night-Whisper | **DISCOVER**

The one necessary root

She said: "Whoever is uprooted himself, uproots others. Whoever is rooted in himself does not doesn't uproot others." So says the 'mad mystic' Simone Weil and of course, I do believe she is quite correct.

Matthew 13:20-21

"But he who received the seed on stony places, this is he who hears the word and immediately receives it with joy; yet he has no root in himself, but endures only for a while. For when tribulation or persecution arises because of the word, immediately he stumbles." NKJV

I do not wish to disparage Simone, this woman of phenomenal intelligence and courageous conviction, but her mysticism was quite, shall we say, 'rooted in a broad spiritual context' rather than Christianity per se. Weil died aged just 34 years, during WWII, where she was working "beyond enthusiasm" for the "free French," allowing herself only to eat what the German imposed food ration on occupied France allowed. Diagnosed already with Tuberculosis she probably ate even less. Upon her death, it was ruled that she had committed suicide by starving herself while the balance of her mind was disturbed. In all probability Simone was severely anorexic.

Weil's last piece of work before her death was called *The Need for Roots*. In this work, Simone, while addressing the past of her defeated and dispossessed country of France both proposes and plans an intricate way ahead for the future of her country after WWII. That is the context from which I have plucked here, her most interesting observation on roots. "Whoever is uprooted himself, uproots others. Whoever is rooted in himself does not doesn't uproot others." I think it somewhat lines up with some of Karl Barth's observations on the love of God, wherein he argues that because "God is rooted in Himself," and therefore, "His love is an overflow of His essence that He turns to us." (*Church Dogmatics*, p273).

Extending these two propositions of Weil and Barth, I wonder if it is correct that people who are rooted in completeness, overflow in giving life, and people who have no root, do not just wither and die themselves, but (forgive the following mix of metaphor) like a drowning man clutching at his rescuer, will from those same panicked, angry, power seeking, self-soul satisfying iron gripped fingers, try and pluck out of the ground those very folks exuding the completeness and wholeness, that they so desperately desire to possess for themselves. I think there is some merit in my thinking, because Jesus alludes to this very fact as not only a natural calamity of growing wheat in this fallen world but as an act of total war from the great enemy of our souls himself, against the church of Christ! What can be said about these things?

First that we need to make sure we have a root within ourselves, which is fixed in the completeness of God and His work for us and in us. The root is within us but the fruit is outside of us, it overflows from us, it hangs down full of righteous seduction, dripping with succulent juices and ready to be plucked from bent branched trees. Always, always dear friend, look at your root and then look at your fruit. Do they match up? Are you rightly rooted?

> *we need to make sure we have a root within ourselves, which is fixed in the completeness of God and His work for us and in us.*

Secondly, that the felt choking from the world and even from mere professors of Christianity in the church, of which there are many, are more indicative of their state than of yours. The strangling tare and the care of the things of this world, will always produce a choking on the fruit bearing trees of God. Be wise in these things, for you will know in your spirit what the personal barrenness of incompleteness feels like and what the coughing choking, life sucking, power hungry, black hole, critical and condemning bad breathed tares feels like as well!

I wonder if it might be better said: "Whoever is uprooted from Christ, uproots others. Whoever is rooted in Christ does not doesn't uproot others." That being the case, it behooves me to ask you tonight does it not? Are you rooted in Christ and in Christ alone? Look at your fruit, does it define your root?

Listen: *"The kingdom of heaven is like a man who sowed good seed in his field; but while men slept, his enemy came and sowed tares among the wheat and went his way. But when the grain had sprouted and produced a crop, then the tares also appeared. So the servants of the owner came and said to him, 'Sir, did you not sow good seed in your field? How then does* *it have tares?' He said to them, 'An enemy has done this.' The servants said to him, 'Do you want us then to go and gather them up?' But he said, 'No, lest while you gather up the tares you also uproot the wheat with them. Let both grow together until the harvest, and at the time of harvest I will say to the reapers, first gather together the tares and bind them in bundles to burn them, but gather the wheat into my barn.'" (Matthew 13:24-30 NKJV)*

Pray: Lord, deliver me from the constant cares of this world and the tares of the enemy. Put soft soil beneath my weakling roots and soft spring showers and the soft, soft sunshine of Your love above my sapling shoots. Root m and fruit me Oh my God! Root me and fruit me. In Jesus name I pray, amen and let it be so.

| Vol 01 | Q1 | NW00044 | February 13th |

Night-Whisper | **TRUTH**

The sound of sharpening knives

I didn't know where I was, so, I went up to the man in the tall black hat and politely explained my situation and asked if he could help? Sniffing through his nose, while tilting his head slightly back, grimacing and arching his lips down, he seemed to chin the air with an affirmative response. Yes, he could help. Thank God. Then, without saying a word, with his left hand he quickly whips out an old butchers sharpening steel and with his right hand, slides out a 12-inch black handled blade! Without saying a word, right in front of my face then mind you, he quickly began sharpening the long shiny knife across the steel. I tell you, I could see the flash of quicksilver shavings shimmer in the late afternoon sunlight as they fell like tiny little welding sparks bouncing on the ground. Just twelve quick strokes up and down the sharpening iron, that's all, but my heart was pounding out of my chest, and like a rabbit in the headlights, I was totally transfixed waiting to see what he would say, waiting to see what he would do! But then, just as quickly, he simply popped the steel and the knife back into his belt, shook his head, turned his back on me and then walked away! I tell you I was so relieved, but I was angry as well. No, I was furious! I was ready for a fight, after all, I only wanted some directions and all he did, was sharpen a nasty looking knife right in front of my face and then walk away.

James 5:12

"But above all, my brethren, do not swear, either by heaven or by earth or with any other oath. But let your 'yes' be 'yes,' and your 'no,' 'no,' lest you fall into judgment." NKJV

Another time, I was bemused by events in my life and approached my 'bestest' of all friends, my dearest wife, asking for her input and direction. Through her nostrils she sucked in a deep breath, tilted her head to the back and slightly off toward her right shoulder and said very slowly, right in front of my face even, "Well, I don't know if I should respond. No, maybe you should speak to someone else. I don't know if you're ready to receive what I have to say. I don't know if you would like it anyway." Just a few quick sharp and shiny words, that's all, but I tell you, my heart was pounding out of my chest and like a rabbit in the headlights I was totally transfixed waiting to see what she would say next. She said nothing! So, I responded in quiet anger to her steel sharpening.

"Go on then," I said. "Fire away, I'm ready, I'm up for it. Say your worst!" Then, nonchalantly like, she tilts her head the other way this time and says, "Nah. It's not a good idea really. Speak to someone else." Then just turns and walks away. I tell you I was so relieved, but I was angry as well. No, I was furious! I was ready for a fight, after all, I only wanted some directions and all she did was sharpen a nasty looking knife right in front of my face.

Like it or not, sometimes, our response to important questions can be rather threatening and very offensive. Our lack of commitment to giving a correct and honest answer can simply make things worse. Our text for tonight is directly related to oath taking and points to the simple necessity of an honest, direct, unambiguous, guileless response to simple questions asked of us. I think it does, and that being the case, some of you need to leave your steels in the kitchen and simply answer the questions asked of you!

> *Our lack of commitment to giving a correct and honest answer can simply make things*

Speak the truth in love my friends but please, do not sharpen truth in someone's face as it's just plain wrong and so very, very provocative. Graciously so, I say graciously so, just let your "Yes" be "Yes" and your "No" be "No."

Listen: *"These are the things you shall do: Speak each man the truth to his neighbour; give judgment in your gates for truth, justice, and peace; let none of you think evil in your heart against your neighbour; and do not love a false oath. For all these are things that I hate,' says the Lord." (Zechariah 8:16-17 NKJV)*

Pray: Deliver me O Lord from the sound of sharpening knives, deliver me into truth and love and gracious answers, in Jesus name I ask it, amen, and let it be so!

Night-Whisper | **LEAD**

The flags of our father's

As far as I am aware, I am a first generation Christian. I have no living blood relative, no blood father especially to model before me how to live the Christian life. I have no spiritual inheritance from my physical line, no spiritual family traits, no family calling and no family prophetic word that I am aware of. On the one hand, this is very sad, but on the other hand, it makes me the leader of the set destiny of my own family line. It makes me the maker of ways, the pronouncer of blessings, and the prophet to all of my line from hereon in who might choose to follow me as I follow Christ.

Numbers 2:1-2

"And the Lord spoke to Moses and Aaron, saying: 'Everyone of the children of Israel shall camp by his own standard, beside the emblems of his father's house; they shall camp some distance from the tabernacle of meeting'." NKJV

Emblems, crests, mottos, seals, standards, flags and nameplates, all are powerful uniting forces to rally soldiers around. The raising of the American flag atop Mount Surribachi on Iwo Jima is testimony to this fact and has united and represented the sacrifice of a nation ever since, and in addition to this, across the world and in another camp, who could ever forget the magnificence of the Motherland Statue, that Sword of Stalingrad, which overlooks the city of the same former name.

From nations to individuals, star spangled banners and personal crests have all been thoroughly influential in people's lives. Indeed, John Calvin himself designed his own personal emblem and seal with the motto: *"Cor meum tibi offero domine prompte et sincere,"* surrounding the image of a heart and hand. Its meaning being: "My heart I offer to you Lord, promptly and sincerely." This motto, this desire and avowed purposes, were not only a focus of Calvin's own life, but all of Calvin's spiritual progeny thereafter, shall we say, have also loved and adopted the very same thought and intent and rallying cry of this most personal and yet now must public emblem.

God the Father organized His redeemed Old Testament people as a marching army under Royal standards around His own Shekinah glory. How about you Father? Can your children point to family emblems and mottoes, to blessings and to prophetic discourse regarding battle honors both previously won and yet to come?

Stand out text – Stand Out Text- Stand out text – Stand Out Text-

The flags of our Fathers will always become the foundational roots of our lives and the lives of children to come. Remember that. It is time for many of you, no, I am sure for most of you men, to raise up a standard for your family to rally around.

Listen: *They said in their hearts, "Let us destroy them altogether." They have burned up all the meeting places of God in the land. We do not see our signs; (Psalms 74:8-9 NKJV)*

"So shall they fear the name of the Lord from the west, and His glory from the rising of the sun; when the enemy comes in like a flood, the Spirit of the Lord will lift up a standard against him." Isaiah 59:19 NKJV

Pray: Rise up O Lord, O Lord my God, rise up within my heart. Set Your seal upon me and my family. Deliver to me, my family's colors, our standard from the ramparts of heaven's walls, that we might march securely under them into Your destiny for us. For Your glory's name I ask it, amen, and let it be so!

| Vol 01 | Q1 | NW00046 | February 15th |

Night-Whisper | **FAITHFUL**

True friendship is eternal

Once upon a time, there was a midget of a man longing to make a difference.

2 Samuel 19:30

"Then Mephibosheth said to the king, 'Rather, let him take it all, inasmuch as my lord the king has come back in peace to his own house.'" NKJV

Not much is known about Johnnie Ring save that he was small, underdeveloped and in many respects, unwanted. Nevertheless, Johnnie's amiable nature led him to be pitied. This pity and the subsequent kind condescension of others toward him, was however, powerful enough to produce a revolving and a fanatical faithfulness, the expression of which, would so turn another man to power the light of change, that this dark world still bathes in the light of it, yes, even to this present day!

John Brown, the enormous abolitionist, had stayed with the Conwell's just weeks before his hanging. Now, eighteen months later, that which Victor Hugo referred to as: "America's uncorrectable sin," Brown's murder, had indeed "created in the Union a latent fissure which was now shaking American democracy to the dire dislocations of civil war."

Just nineteen years of age, Russell Conwell had signed up to fight for the second time, his local militia, this time electing him as their captain and banding together to buy him a shiny sword of ceremonial office. With his new sword, Captain Conwell looked quite the imposing veteran, quite the fighting man.

Johnnie Ring, was such an underdeveloped patriot, however, that he looked like a boy! So much so, that this precluded him signing up himself to fight in the regular forces and so the only way he could get to war, was to plead with Captain Conwell to take him along as his servant. Conwell, neither wanted nor needed a servant, yet pitied his big-hearted little neighbor so much, that he took him along with him anyway! The thankfulness and devotion of Johnnie Ring towards Captain Conwell for this act of kindness was all surpassing in its devotion and all complete in its faithfulness, finding a particular expression in the daily shining and care of that sword of office which had been purchased for Conwell by his comrades.

Johnnie Ring was also a devoted Christian and so when Conwell, a committed atheist, took to laughing at Ring's consistent evening reading of the Bible and his constant praying, he simply took to the reading of his Bible outside of his Captain's tent and then polished his commander's glittering sword, more vigorously every day!

"True Friendship is Eternal.".

A surprise Confederate attack on their position near New Berne led to a hasty retreat across the river by the Captain and his Union soldiers, the covered bridge of which, was lit in fierce and fiery flames behind them, thereby forming a barrier which their pursuing enemies would not and indeed, just could not pass. Through the smoke and flying shot, Johnnie Ring, unlike his comrades and his Captain, had not retreated but had charged back to the Captain's tent and retrieved the glittering sword left hanging on a pole by his comrades in their hasty retreat. Carrying his precious emblem of friendship, Johnny ran toward the burning and blazing bridge. The shooting stopped and both Union and Confederate soldiers watched the little man run headlong into the crackling flames of the frightful furnace. After some time, and to the fearful cheers of all, Johnny Ring emerged out of the other side, all his clothes ablaze.

Johnny ring lingered in this life just a day or two after his roasting and awoke but once from his unconsciousness state to embrace the sword, now laid so respectfully at his side, upon whose steel was etched the words, "True Friendship is Eternal."

Captain Russell Conwell said that it was through Johnnie Ring, giving his life in devotion to him, that he later became a Christian. The Captain, for the rest of his life, hung this inscribed and emblematic sword above his own bed. It is said that each day, the over-diligent Conwell, worked eight hours for himself and eight hours for Johnnie Ring. In doing so, the now Rev. Russell Conwell, became the founder of Temple University, and in his lifetime alone spoke to and influenced well over 10 million people! His legacy in Temple University and his many printed sermons, have influenced millions and millions more since his death.

Yes, once upon a time, there was a midget of a man, longing to make a difference.

Tell me no then my friend, just how big are you?

Listen: *"Now when he had finished speaking to Saul, the soul of Jonathan was knit to the soul of David, and Jonathan loved him as his own soul. Saul took him that day, and would not let him go home to his father's house anymore. Then Jonathan and David made a covenant, because he loved him as his own soul. And Jonathan took off the robe that was on him and gave it to David, with his armour, even to his sword and his bow and his belt." (1 Samuel 18:1-4 NKJV)*

Pray: O Captain O my Captain, I give myself to You in heartfelt dedication and service that my life, even through the flames, would release blessings to the world. Amen, and let it be so.

Night-Whisper | **PROSPER**

The color purple and some big news from Baghdad

Temple University in Philadelphia was founded in 1884 by the Rev. Dr. Russell Conwell. At the time of my writing, it is the 28th largest university in the United States and the sixth largest provider of professional education in that country, being renowned for its specialist courses in: law, education, media, business, and the health sciences.

Mark 8:36

"For what will it profit a man if he gains the whole world, and loses his own soul?" NKJV

As I recounted last night, this 'temple' of learning and blessing, was built through tremendous sacrificial and focused hard work, and of course, lots of money! I suppose, that Conwell could be described as the first great 'prosperity preacher' to come out of America, and his sermon entitled 'Acres of Diamonds' has been estimated to have been preached by him over 6,000 times across a period of 58 years to upwards of 10 million people and above!

The big idea of Conwell's 'Acres of Diamonds' message was that you don't need to look elsewhere for: opportunities, achievements, or fortunes, because the truth is, that all the resources to acquire these good things are in fact already present in your own back yard! In this message, with anecdote upon anecdote, Conwell pummels this theme into the ground of the hearts of his hearers but the first big and Night-Whisper titled blow, relates to a story told to Conwell by an Arab guide he met in Baghdad when he was on his world travels.

The story is about a man who wanted to find diamonds so badly that he sells everything, including his property, and goes off in an unsuccessful and eventually suicidal search for those precious stones. Meanwhile, the new owner of the now dead, diamond-searching Arab's home, discovered that the richest of diamond mines, was actually located right there on his newly and lately acquired property! Conwell then repeatedly beat this same post, deep into the ground of his hearers, through successive examples of American success, American local genius and the sacrificial service of ordinary American men and women throughout the land. Such a message of American self-sufficiency then would have been a very contemporary salve to his very nationalistic listening audience. "Money is power," he says, "and you ought to be reasonably ambitious to have it. You ought because you can do more good with it than you could without it. Money printed your Bibles, money builds your churches, money sends your missionaries, and money pays your preachers, and you would not have many of them, either, if you did not pay them. I am always willing that my church should raise my salary, because the church that pays the largest salary always raises it the easiest. You never knew an exception to it in your life. The man who gets the largest salary can do the most good with the power that is furnished to him. Of course he can if his spirit be right to use it for what it is given to him."

> *The difference between Conwell, this man of millions and millions of dollars and the prosperity preachers of our present day, was that in getting his riches, he chose poverty for himself!*

The difference between Conwell, this man of millions and millions of dollars and the prosperity preachers of our present day, was that in getting his riches, he chose poverty for himself! In 1921, The New York times wrote concerning Conwell that: "Although Dr. Conwell preaches riches, for himself he has chosen poverty, His very earnings of millions have all been given away. He has built a large church. He has founded a University, which now has approximately 7,000 students. He has personally contributed to the support of thousands of students who attended various colleges and universities throughout the country. He is now at 77 engaged in building two hospitals..."

Conwell's Sermon entitled 'Acres of Diamonds' is very American, it is very capitalistic and it is very Republican, and with all that, it is very good indeed! The character of Conwell, the context of his message and all matters concerning his living, coupled with the common sense and practical power of the sermon itself, gird it even today, with a manly virility. I am pleased to tell you tonight that I personally know of a few good men who right now, are intent on making millions with the one purpose of giving them away! How about you? How's the practicality of your giving tonight?

Listen: *"Now a certain woman named Lydia heard us. She was a seller of purple from the city of Thyatira, who worshiped God. The Lord opened her heart to heed the things spoken by Paul." (Acts 16:14-15 NKJV)*

Pray: Lord, make me a purveyor of purple, solid in silver and all glorious in the gold of giving, for Your eternal glory and my temporal health I ask it, amen, ad let it be so.

| Vol 01 | Q1 | NW00048 | February 17ᵗʰ |

Night-Whisper | **GIVE**

The money in God's pocket

It is rumored that the present British Monarch does not carry any cash upon their person. Not that Royalty should have any need to carry money in their pocket mind you! However, I am inclined to believe that God Almighty does in fact carry a few spare coins around with Him, which I am sure in His quieter moments, whilst leaning back against a wall in heaven, with both hands in His pockets, whilst arching His spine and looking out over His creation, He thoughtfully fumbles and jingles through His fingers. Yes, I am pretty sure that God carries at least four coins of remembrance in His own right trouser pocket, those being the widows mite and three cents once belonging to little 'Hattie May Wiatte.' One cent each this time, for the Father, the Son and the Holy Ghost.

Mark 8:17-19

"But Jesus, being aware of it, said to them, 'Why do you reason because you have no bread? Do you not yet perceive nor understand? Is your heart still hardened? Having eyes, do you not see? And having ears, do you not hear? And do you not remember? When I broke the five loaves for the five thousand, how many baskets full of fragments did you take up?" NKJV

The story goes that Russell Conwell, that first great Biblical prosperity preacher, was attending a small but busy church where tickets for the gatherings were obtained weeks in advance of the services! The church was so busy, that eight-year-old Hattie May had problems trying to get into her Sunday school. Conwell comforted her, by saying that: as soon as they obtained funds, they would be building a larger Sunday school for little children. Little Hattie May immediately got behind the project and before her very early death, managed to save some 57 cents. A lot of money for a little girl in those days!

Conwell, moved by the story of Hattie May's money management, utilized the faith and earnest of the dead child and auctioned the 57 pennies to his congregation for $250! This sum was then in turn changed into 25,000 pennies, which, were also sold to raise even more money. Out of the original 57 cents, 54 of them were returned to Conwell, who had them framed and exhibited. The forming of the Hattie May 'Wiatte Mite' society, the vast funding that followed for the realization of future vision, is now history and may I say, a great history at that.

We can learn five important things here:

First, that there was a little girl of vision.

Secondly, that there were parents, who out of great sadness but with tender remembrance, progressed that vision.

> *Enormous mountains were moved into the middle of the sea and great things were accomplished that would not have been accomplished without this complete five fingered, fist-full of faith!*

Thirdly, that there was a man of influence to be moved by that vision and to cast that vision faithfully and fervently before others.

Fourthly, that there were dedicated people willing to expend themselves to expand that cast vision.

Fifthly and above all, when all of this is put together, the vision created such a momentum, such an atmosphere of faith and believing in the people of God, that enormous mountains were moved into the middle of the sea and great things were accomplished that would not have been accomplished without this complete five fingered, fist-full of faith!

By the way, the missing 3cents from the original 57 cents, were never returned...I hear jingling! I say, I hear jingling!

Listen: *"One of His disciples, Andrew, Simon Peter's brother, said to Him, 'There is a lad here who has five barley loaves and two small fish, but what are they among so many?'" (John 6:8,9 NKJV)*

Pray: Lord, give me faith, give me wisdom, give me vision and give me innovation. Yes Lord, give me good ideas and give me guts, that faith may flower and belief would move mountains and make a way for Your people and Your kingdom, in Jesus name I ask it, amen and let it be so.

Night-Whisper | **FOCUS**

The waking of zombies

The Afro-Caribbean spiritual belief system and Hollywood, have given us the scary pictures of reanimated, flesh-eating corpses, or as they are more better known, zombies! I bet you didn't know it but there are in fact two types of zombies in our world. Yes, and this is good to know for I am concerned that I find myself increasingly surrounded by these zombies!

2 Corinthians 4:3, 4

But even if our Gospel is veiled, it is veiled to those who are perishing, whose minds the god of this age has blinded, who do not believe, lest the light of the Gospel of the glory of Christ, who is the image of God, should shine on them. NKJV

The first type is the 'CNC zombie,' that is, the Consumer ridden Non-Christian. They may be "chav" like, or they could be boys from Charter House. They may be shopping at Argos or even at Harrods. They may be lay-abouts or playboys, they may be professionals or stupid! It doesn't matter. The common factor is that these C.N.C. zombies are focused only on what is before them. So, with arms outstretched, vacant eyes and drool dripping from the side of their mouth, they are interested in only consuming, and if the eating is at the expense of someone else, or is someone else, then so be it. The C.N.C. zombie is unaware of their own death and is merry and happy in that the blindness of a sorcerous slavery that binds them in their chains. Yes, the worldwide economic enslavement of the C.N.C. zombies by the enemy of their souls continues apace, but no matter to them, for as long as they are feeding, whether on crêpes or crap, it doesn't matter, not as long as they are simply consuming! As they do this, and this is all they really do, then that full and happy, monosodium glutamate glaze of overfed blindness will continue to be upon them. Zombies! I see these every day.

The second type is the 'F.F.C. zombie,' that is, the Fixed and Focused Christian zombie. I detest these the most, for they are fixed and focused on anything other than the simple love of God in the face of

Christ Jesus. Yes, they are fixed and focused on anything other than the naked revelations of revealed truth. The hammering and beating, the drilling and the banging of the workers of the man of sin constructing his kingdom around their very feet is of no concern to them, for they are fixed on their own churches, focused on their own pet doctrines and their personal pet pastors. Yes, they are fixed on their denominational peccadilloes, they are focused on feeding their own man-made religious machine and keeping it happy, quiet, functioning and controllable. They are focused on wet worship and soft pre-sucked morsels of the word of God, for as long as they can sing well and have some tasty teat to suck from on a Sunday morning, they'll be satisfied with minute microwaved Christianity. They cannot abide strong meat, but only milk, and lukewarm and watery milk at that, which will be poorly digested, and contain only just enough spiritual nutrition to make them feel saved and certainly not enough to make them grow and walk properly! Zombies: nice, well-dressed, well-spoken, well-ordered religious consumer zombies, all joining in the fiddling while the true saints of Christ burn. As long as these zombies are given a free bunny rabbit when they give their lives to Christ and get their hair stroked regularly with a "there, there, there, you poor sweet baby," then they are somewhat happy, but they are zombies never the less! Meanwhile, Satan's New World Order, so enslaves their minds that they refuse to face the smell of the rising stench of Christian decay and see the settling of dust from the crumbling edifice that was once the true church, pouring in on them from un-repented and un-repointed brickwork, letting in the Devil's damp and spreading black death, like a lousy leak from the Hoover Dam all across their 'Praize Factory' focused faces. Good grief it's the entertainment industry that is setting most of their teaching titles and discussion groups. Yes sir, indeed, it's consumer Christianity at its best, but unfortunately the best it can do, is to re-animate a corpse and keep it drooling. In the end, whether 'C.N.C.' or 'F.C.C.' – it doesn't matter, they are both zombies.

> *Christian Zombies are fixed on their own churches, focused on their own pet doctrines and their personal pet pastors.*

When the real Christians arrive on the scene, we won't have questions regarding revival! For the clash of arms, the fall of Kingdoms, the leaping lame, the shouts of happiness breaking out of the open mouths of those delivered from deep gloom and a multitude of other magnificent testimonies to the touchdown of God Almighty, will be unchallenged evidence of God amongst us, which in the end, is all that the real people of God are truly longing for. (No thanks, I don't want to buy that latest soaking CD.)

Meantime, I am keeping the drool from the sides of my own mouth, keeping my arms upstretched to heaven, instead of outstretched to this earth. Keeping my eyes and ears open, my sword unsheathed and my shield well up. Oh, and by the way, I have also bought some old hat pins, they are a mite long mind you, but never the less, they are still sharp, and ready to be sunk deep into a few pink professing buttocks. Tomorrow, I'm off to try to wake up a few zombies. Tonight, I am trying to wake you up. My God! Are you one of these consumer zombies I am talking about? Or are you a real Christian?

Tomorrow, I'm off to try to wake up a few zombies with these sharp hatpins.

Listen: *"I write to you, little children, Because your sins are forgiven you for His name's sake. I write to you, fathers, Because you have known Him who is from the beginning. I write to you, young men, Because you have overcome the wicked one. I write to you, little children, Because you have known the Father. I have written to you, fathers, Because you have known Him who is from the beginning. I have written to you, young men, Because you are strong, and the word of God abides in you, And you have overcome the wicked one." (1 John 2:12-14 NKJV)*

Pray: Lord, break this great witchcraft of the enemy that dulls our ears to the sound of his hammering and blinds us to his wicked machinations. Father, please ram the hatpin of the Holy Spirit's conviction right up our rear end! Wake us up O Lord! In Jesus name I ask it, amen, and let it be so!

Night-Whisper | **CONSIDER**

The trouble with complacent canaries

South African wine-makers are presently growing roses among their vines. If the roses show signs of black spot fungus, the growers can better treat their vines and much, much earlier than they could have done previously. In this case, the rose has become the early warning danger sign of what would have been the certain fungal destruction of the grape crop.

Psalms 40:1-3

I waited patiently for the Lord; and He inclined to me, and heard my cry. He also brought me up out of a horrible pit, out of the miry clay, and set my feet upon a rock, and established my steps. He has put a new song in my mouth — Praise to our God; Many will see it and fear, and will trust in the Lord. NKJV

It was in 1986 when the last 200 canaries were made redundant from British coal mines. For many years, the brightly colored singing birds had been used to test the air quality in mines. Canaries were particularly sensitive to the presence of carbon monoxide and methane, showing noticeably visible signs of distress long before miners were aware of the danger. The canaries might stop singing, sway back and forth on their perch, fall to their small cage bottom and sometimes even die. Thankfully, new digital technology eventually replaced the miner's little feathered friend.

To those who can see and sense, there are always early warning signs to coming destruction. Much can be said about this phenomena, both globally and locally, both materially and spiritually, but tonight I want to speak only personally, for when a Christian stops singing, it is a sure sign that they are about to fall off their perch.

For the Christian, joy is the marker of a healthy atmosphere. When joy is present, hope, faith and love all bloom in their season. However, if you remove joy, then despondency, hopelessness, unbelief and bitterness, like some dread black spot fungus, will blight anything trying to grow both in and around such a Christian.

If the song in your heart has grown silent tonight, then may I say that you are in the greatest of danger! Get out of that place, wherever it is, that is stealing your song and then speedily attend to your own spiritual crop, lest the blight of death come upon you. I have seen too many Christians who have fallen off their perch, and lie there with their little legs stiff and upright in the closing grey. Listen to yourself tonight. How is your singing my friend? Test it! Is your song on your lips and is it joyful. This is important, for you see, the trouble with complacent canaries is that if they don't attend to their lost singing voice, they eventually fall off their perch!

> *If the song in your heart has grown silent tonight, then may I say that you are in the greatest of danger!*

Listen: *"In a year and some days You will be troubled, you complacent women; For the vintage will fail, The gathering will not come. Tremble, you women who are at ease; Be troubled, you complacent ones; Strip yourselves, make yourselves bare, And gird sackcloth on your waists."* (Isaiah 32:10-11 NKJV)

Pray: Lord, forgive my complacency toward the lack of my song and the absence of my joy. Yes, and forgive my love of religious nitrous oxide, that poor substitute for the fruit of the Holy Spirit. Now Lord, send the fresh breeze of Your Holy Spirit into my collapsing lungs and deliver me from all my sin, and this dearth of singing in my soul. Come and put a fresh song in my heart, that I may sing the songs of Zion's comfort and Your Almighty praises once again, in Jesus name I ask it, amen and let it be so!

Night-Whisper | **CLEAN**

Good for gonads

The problem with sin is that it damages the whole man, and tonight, I would like to speak primarily to men and to those prospective fathers who, in their sin, are most certainly not only damaging themselves but their offspring to come, even up to the third and fourth generation! Tonight, I shall not only call your attention to or text but also to a quote from some recent scientific research and shall apply to both, a good old dose of common sense.

Exodus 34:6-7

And the Lord passed before him and proclaimed, "The Lord, the Lord God, merciful and gracious, longsuffering, and abounding in goodness and truth, keeping mercy for thousands, forgiving iniquity and transgression and sin, by no means clearing the guilty, visiting the iniquity of the fathers upon the children and the children's children to the third and the fourth generation." NKJV

A US study recently presented to the American Association for the Advancement of Science (AAAS) suggests that a father's health plays a greater role in the health of future generations than has previously been thought. A team from the University of Idaho in Moscow tested the effects of a hormone-disrupting fungicide chemical called 'vinclozolin' on embryonic male rats and found that the damage caused to them, was also present in rats some four generations down the line! Now a man is not a rat that's for sure, and though some might say that they wish men were as a nice as rats, nevertheless, men are not rats. Even so, science is science and facts are facts. Look, when you put a spanner in the sperm, the repercussions are generational. God has been saying this for thousands of years.

The problem with sin is that it damages the whole man. If I seek satisfaction outside of the boundaries laid down by God, the repercussion are seen in: HIV, gonorrhea, chlamydia and the like, unwanted children, privations, poverty and a billion pitiful existences. Sin damages men:

spiritually, sexually, emotionally, socially, physically and economically. Sin has an holistic infiltration. Indeed, the latest scientific results also affirm the Scriptures, in that not only does sin affect your money sack for generations but it effects your sperm sack for generations as well! Am I being too crude, rude, and lewd? Well, someone needs to be! Yes, someone needs to be telling young men and prospective fathers that "sin puts a spanner in your sperm!" Make no mistake that this is the truth, for even Professor Cynthia Daniels, from Rutgers University in New Jersey, regarding damage to male sperm and seminal fluid says: "We need to open up our eyes and look at the evidence!" Further to this, Professor Neil McClure, a fertility expert at Queen's University Belfast, UK, also acknowledged that once sperm cell DNA was damaged, it had no mechanism by which to effect repairs! He said: "There is no doubt that if you smoke like a chimney or drink vast amounts of alcohol it will result in sperm damage, and probably damage in the DNA of the sperm. My advice to any man trying for a baby would be to lead as healthy a lifestyle as possible." Now there's some good advice!

"Sin puts a spanner in your sperm!"

You might be a sex bomb buddy (or think you are,) but be sure of this, sin is a rampant repercussion bomb, which when not diffused, explodes through the generations of mankind! Your future generations. Don't forget that.

I have no scientific proof, neither do I have scriptural warrant for what I am about to suggest, but I wonder if repentance and faith which receives the mercy and goodness of God might just provide such a deep cleansing, that it could, with time, reach down to the DNA level of sperm and do some fixing? What I am saying is this: I wonder if mercy can mend sperm? What results, I wonder, would tests on the testes of righteous men provide, if done every seven years? Yes, I wonder if God's goodness and I wonder if God's grace is really good for our gonads and a blessing for the a thousand generations to come?

Listen: *"How can a young man cleanse his way? By taking heed according to Your word." (Psalm 119:9)*

Pray: With my whole heart I have sought You; Oh, let me not wander from Your commandments! Your word I have hidden in my heart, that I might not sin against You. Blessed are You, O Lord! Teach me Your statutes. With my lips I have declared all the judgments of Your mouth. I have rejoiced in the way of Your testimonies, as much as in all riches. I will meditate on Your precepts, and contemplate Your ways. I will delight myself in Your statutes; I will not forget Your word. (from Psalms 119:10-16)

| Vol 01 | Q1 | NW00052 | February 21ˢᵗ |

Night-Whisper | **CONSIDER**

All about Eve

Charterhouse public school boy, Peter Gabriel, founder of the hit band Genesis, later continued with his own solo career having his first top ten hit with *'Jeux Sans Frontieres'* or *'Games without Frontiers.'* Gabriel probably based his song lyrics on a popular and lavish Pan European game-show of the same name. The British copied this show and called it *'It's A Knockout.'* It was a funny show and everybody laughed so much at this show that sometimes they cried! In this respect then, Gabriel's repetitive lyric of everyone playing: "games without frontiers and war without tears" was on the one hand quite funnily wrong. 'It's a Knockout' produced tears of laughter.

Colossians 1:16-17

For by Him all things were created that are in heaven and that are on earth, visible and invisible, whether thrones or dominions or principalities or powers. All things were created through Him and for Him. NKJV

Maybe it is just too cold and boring in Iceland, for it was an Icelandic gaming corporation that created a 'player-driven, persistent-world, massive multiplayer online game' called Eve. Set in a science fiction space setting, players can pilot a wide variety of customizable ships through a universe comprising of over, not a few thousand virtual, star gate-connected solar systems! Conquest, cloning, acquisition, economic accrual, manufacturing, trading, alliance building, wars and a multitude of other real time experiences, can all be most thoroughly experienced in this 'New Eden.' Once accessed through the game's fictional wormhole, which, by the way, is called 'Eve.' The game is played in real time and is very, very addictive and at the time of my writing, has over a quarter of a million practicing players and rising! I tell you tonight, that whole worlds have been created in virtual reality where thousands upon thousands of human beings, right now, are hiding themselves and wasting away their time and talents. It is yet another diversion of devilish proportions and there's a multitude of Christians amongst them as well. Why such popularity? Well, I believe Peter

Gabriel, that great angelic messenger of the 1980s, had it right, for there is something attractive about "games without frontiers and war without tears."

On the negative side, has there ever been a time in history where a curer of souls has had to try and pull people out from unreal pits of virtual reality, though the mud of material reality and then up and out through the womb like worm hole into true spirituality? It's ridiculous. On the plus side, has there ever been a time where we can now truly show people how to virtually live, in a spiritual reality, within a thoroughly material world? No, I do not think there has never been a time like this! Ever!

Surely the real possibility of functioning in the spiritual realm, receiving a new name, a new character, a new destiny and participating in: power anointing's, angelic visitations, hyper-travel, intuitive intensity, insight, healing, visions and violence and much, much more, would be a far better draw for the game players of today than the life consuming virtual dreams of a few bored and cold Icelanders? You would think so wouldn't you, but we have a couple of problems to overcome before we can bait this particular 'gaming hook' with these real attractive lures.

Tell me, if we cannot lead the way into living with Christ in the heavenlies, then who can follow?

First of course, is those of us participating in dimensions and worlds unknown to other men, need first to begin to move into those spiritual realms and so much the more. "Higher up and further in," as a brave mouse once declared on reaching the edge of Aslan's land. Yes, we need to go "higher up and further in," indeed. Yet so many of us are still struggling with spiritual mouse clicks on the edge of this vast unknown spiritual realm which lies still so silently set before us. (By the way, the spiritual realm is anything but silent and quiet!) Tell me, if we cannot lead the way into living with Christ in the heavenlies, then who can follow?

Secondly of course, despite our ignorance of it, we need to realize that there nevertheless lies before us a world of waiting wonder and also of most dreadful danger. This is no game without frontiers we are spiritually inhabiting and engaging with here, this is no war without tears either! This is the really real world, the solid world of set spiritual density, and if you're not careful, then it will wound you like a knife, burn you like fire, consume you like quicksand, cower you like a whipped dog and haunt you like following shadows, cast along the damp and silent, frost ridden lanes of your life. This is the spiritual realm of which we are the rulers and the takers. Yes, this is the realm of the shining ones but of the shadow creatures as well. Beware, all of you who consciously enter in here.

You see, there is a spiritual reality that far outstrips any player-driven, persistent-world, massive multiplayer online game. One day, as we fall headlong into its limitless and starry depths, it shall be revealed to us in all its fullness. For now though, the spiritual realm is only truly open only to those who have the time and the inclination to gain the skills and the gifts to function in it.

For now though, the spiritual realm is only truly open only to those who have the time and the inclination to gain the skills and the gifts to function in it.

I say again, beware all who enter here into the spiritual realm! For this is no online game and you are no avatars in that game. It's all real! Real flesh, real blood, real soul, real spirit. Tell me tonight then O Gameboy guru: are you wise enough to let go of 'virtual unreality?' Yes, let me shout and ask you: "are you brave enough to enter into the fullness of spiritual reality?"

Listen: *"For we do not wrestle against flesh and blood, but against principalities, against powers, against the rulers of the darkness of this age, against spiritual hosts of wickedness in the heavenly places." Ephesians 6:12-13 NKJV*

Pray: While I draw this fleeting breath, when mine eyes shall close in death, when I soar to worlds unknown, see Thee on Thy judgment throne, Rock of Ages, cleft for me, let me hide myself in Thee. Amen, and let it be so.

| Vol 01 | Q1 | NW00053 | February 22ⁿᵈ |

Night-Whisper | **DANGER**

The disappearance of a duck's quack

I very much dislike the simple and watery old picture of a life depicted as: "a stone thrown the into the still water of the universe, the ripples from its insertional impact, slowly spreading out in ever wider and increasing circles, caressing in gentle undulation, everyone else waiting patiently on the surface of the deep." Oh please! Pass me a sick bag.

2 Kings 3:1-3

"Now Jehoram the son of Ahab became king over Israel at Samaria in the eighteenth year of Jehoshaphat king of Judah, and reigned twelve years. And he did evil in the sight of the Lord, but not like his father and mother; for he put away the sacred pillar of Baal that his father had made. Nevertheless he persisted in the sins of Jeroboam the son of Nebat, who had made Israel sin; he did not depart from them." NKJV.

Even so, in living and especially in the way we die, we all have a peculiar ripple effect on life and the universe, but I think much more importantly than that, we each have a voice which echoes throughout time and eternity! In other words our actions, our words, those outworked intentions of our heart, our 'voice,' if you will, does most definitely repeat itself and not necessarily in dissipation either, but rather, with an expanding effect in focus, in strength, and in spreading fervor! Unless that is, you are a duck.

It has been an 'urban legend' for some time, that a duck's quack has no echo. Well, of course it does have an echo, the only problem is, that you cannot hear the echo because the quiet elongation of the noise of the initial quack, cancels out the incoming and reflected sound waves. There, knowing that, you can now sleep easier tonight for believe it or not, a lot of money has been spent on investigating the seeming disappearance of a ducks quacking echo!

We all know of the beautiful iridescent qualities of the Opal, reflecting and refracting wavelengths of light, even at times, seemingly absorbing them completely. Building on this natural photonic crystal effect which seems to absorb light, there is no doubt that manmade and mass produced photonic crystals may well lead to a new wave of powerful light driven computers. Now then, in the same way a photonic crystal can absorb certain frequencies of light and reflect others, so sonic crystals can do the same. Manifestations of this sonic phenomena might be heard in the strange acoustic properties of the Whispering Gallery in St. Paul's Cathedral in London, where a whisper can be heard 42 meters away on the other side of the Gallery or maybe, even in the Mayan Pyramid of Kukulkan at Chichén Itzá, in the jungles of the Yucután Peninsula of Mexico, where if you stand at the foot of any of the stairways that climb the outer walls and then clap your hands, the resultant echo will sound like the chirp of their sacred quetzal bird, the spirit of the Maya, incarnated in Quetzalcóatl, their plumed serpent god. Interesting eh?

> *Our life and especially our voice, ripples its own unique wavelength signature out into both space, time and the spiritual dimension.*

The rediscovery of this strange acoustical physics, where the varying wavelength of sounds essentially interfere with themselves and cancel themselves out, might not only lead to a more peaceful urban environment but be utilized in military stealth technology such as the coating of submarines with sound absorbing paint, or used even in the protecting of our cities against seismic shock waves. It's all wonderful stuff for sure but for tonight, my key point concerning this physical phenomenon, is the fact that ripples of echoes can and do, cancel themselves out!

Our life and especially our voice, ripples its own unique wavelength signature out into both space, time and the spiritual dimension. Like the physical properties of sound waves, not only can our unique expression of life, our own distinct voice, cause ripples, but more importantly, it can and does, cause deep echoes! Oh, the stir of echoes from ages past that undulate across our cold waters even today! Oh, the past voices that though dead, still speak to us today, loud and long! Yet I tell you, many of those mighty echoes we should have been hearing today, have become silent 'might-have-beens' for they have, unfortunately, been well and truly cancelled out by themselves.

In our text for tonight we see the bad king Jehoram, meaning 'Exaltation of the Lord,' the ninth king of Israel, who also happened to do some good. Yes, befriended and then rightly influenced and chastised, even by Elisha himself, Jehoram produced a little goodness in his voice. Yet, this voice was lost, and was most clearly cancelled out, by his ongoing and continuing evil.

There is a great lesson in this for us tonight, for in my life, I have heard some great voices, even some of the greatest, become turned into the sound of a quacking duck, a sad cartoon caricature orange beaked voice, with no seeming echo. This has happened because the echo of their voice has been cancelled out, usually at the end of their journey, by sin. Yes, silly, stupid, sorry, shameful, sonic crystals of sin, have absorbed their once most glorious echoes. Now, they shall pass unheard into eternity. Now, they shall lie silent in the grave. It's all very sad.

Yes, silly, stupid, sorry, shameful, sonic crystals of sin, have absorbed their once most glorious echoes. Now, they shall pass unheard into eternity. Now, they shall lie silent in the grave. It's all very sad.

So what about you tonight? What about your voice? Shall it grow more focused, fervent and strong, or through the sonic crystals of sin, shall it be turned into the simple sound of a sorry duck's quack? Yes, remember tonight, that your voice echoes! Please then, I beg you, don't let sin and all its attendant stupidity cancel its goodness out forever, especially as you come to the end of your road or your rope!

To some of you I say: "Whatever you are considering doing that you know is sin, stop even the consideration of it!" To others I say: "What you have started to do, stop immediately! Repent and stop immediately. For why should your life become nothing but a ducks quack?"

Listen: *"By faith Abel offered to God a more excellent sacrifice than Cain, through which he obtained witness that he was righteous, God testifying of his gifts; and through it he being dead still speaks."* (Hebrews 11:4 NKJV)

Pray: Lord, haunt me with echoes of Your people's voices now long gone. Let me hear their powerful voices speak so powerfully still. May I be lifted and encouraged by their sound waves of faith. As for me O Lord, may my voice become more focused, firmer, stronger, stouter and may its echoes be heard when I too am long since gone. In Jesus name I pray it, amen, an let it be so.

| Vol 01 | Q1 | NW00054 | February 23rd |

Night-Whisper | **CLEAN**

Jalousie strudel

I love food, and pastry in particular. The thin elastic qualities of apple strudel pastry is an especial delight to me, especially when it's home cooked, for then, more often than not, it is cooked so wonderfully that the thinness of the pastry sometimes opens up like a 'jammy' womb, revealing all the steaming seductive goodness inside! And I tell you, when apple strudel is cooked correctly, it incites a green jealousness to seep from the curled lips of lesser chefs, especially if they are French! Indeed, a famous French pastry style is named after such 'green feelings,' in that it is call 'Jalousie!' This particular pastry is openly slatted in such a way that it intentionally exposes the yummy goodness of the bubbling and enticing fragrant offering which waits so obviously wantonly inside. Don't tell me that food isn't sexy!

Song of Solomon 2:9

"My beloved is like a gazelle or a young stag. Behold, he stands behind our wall; He is looking through the windows, Gazing through the lattice." NKJV.

Who'd have thought that this Jalousie pastry style would go on to inspire Mr. Van Ellis Huff, graduate of Florida University, to invent the parallel-angled, glass slatted shutter, world famous 'Jalousie Window.' Admittedly, Mr. Huff got his idea from wooden slatted windows which he observed in British Barbados but the name and inspiration for his windows he got from pastry! Wasn't it Elisha, who when in need of inspiration, cried out in 2 Kings 3:15: "Bring me a confectioner!" I'm sure it was.

Yes, this Jealous Jalousie window style, reminds me of the time I lived in South Florida, where most of the older squat, flat, anti-hurricane designed Florida homes, still sported the old style Jalousie windows, which were in turn, markers of an age now long gone, when the only air conditioning available was to open the windows and let through a directed breeze whilst minimizing the access of hot sunlight.

In Bible times, of course, windows were mostly small and completely open. Yet many, especially those higher up and facing outwards, were larger and latticed. People falling out of these to their deaths was a particular problem in both the Old and the New Testament, never the less, the latticed windows of old, those old windows of a jealous kind, could be used to foster privacy whilst at the same time giving both access to cool breezes and allowing the quiet, unseen observation of approaching people.

In our text for tonight it is the beloved, the bride, who speaks of her lover gazing at her through the lattice. If eyes are the windows of the soul, then they are shuttered with Jalousie eyelids. Our God has jealous eyes for us and we should have jealous eyes for Him!

> *Our God has jealous eyes for us and we should have jealous eyes for Him!*

This verse tonight speaks to me of desire, of righteous voyeurism, of jealous protectiveness and my friends, some of you need to make better use of your jealous eyes tonight, observing only Him, allowing only the cool breeze of the Holy Spirit to blow across and make cool the marbled floor of your own most private soul.

Pastry is seductive. So are our eyes. Let us therefore make a most thorough use of these Jalousie windows which God has given us. He who has eyes to see, let him be very careful of both what he sees and what he allows to blow through the open windows of his soul.

Tell me then, what are you looking at tonight? What have you been watching?

Listen: *"For at the window of my house I looked through my lattice, And saw among the simple, I perceived among the youths, A young man devoid of understanding, Passing along the street near her corner; And he took the path to her house In the twilight, in the evening, In the black and dark night. And there a woman met him, With the attire of a harlot, and a crafty heart." (Proverbs 7:6-10 NKJV)*

Pray: O my jealous God! I am betrothed to You. God the Holy Spirit, I open my jealous eyes to You, come and blow across my soul, in cooling and enticing, comforting and exciting breezes. O God the Holy Son, my gaze is fixed on You and in all my secret places, from the corners of my soul I gaze out and wait for You. O Holy Father God, the doors of my inner courtyard and the steps to all my inner chambers are open only to

You and for You. Yes, Triune triumphant God, my eyes are turned to You alone. Amen, and let it be so.

Night-Whisper | **FAITHFUL**

Rings of gold on beds of fulfilment

Vows are voluntary promises made with God. Vows are considered Biblically to be both sacred and binding duties, which if righteous when made, both scarily and majestically change their form from voluntary to compulsory and must then, at all costs, be put into practice!

Numbers 30:1

If a man makes a vow to the Lord, or swears an oath to bind himself by some agreement, he shall not break his word; he shall do according to all that proceeds out of his mouth.

Biblically, vows were often born out of mostly distress or desire and they were expressed as pledges toward God in return for favor. The favor required was various but the pledge then given, whether it was expressed in terms of devotion, abstinence or destruction, was never the less, always sacrificial in nature.

Marriage vows are also voluntary promises, which when made, turn into compulsory, sacred and binding duties! In the end, these marriage vows involve the devotion of one man to one woman, of one woman to one man, with the mutual abstinence of anything and anyone that may mar that devotion or might become, the destruction of the fulfilment of that devotion. Though often delightful and desirous, the continual completion of this marital devotion, the fulfilment of these vows is always, I say again, is always sacrificial.

Marriage vows are made only between a man and a woman before God. These voluntary promises made before God are then mightily and mysteriously turned into a binding covenant of oaths and pledges called marriage. The marriage is performed and carried out by the man and the woman being wed. Did you get that! The man and woman marry themselves with the vows which they take before Almighty God. It is simply the privilege of any minister, and that is all it is, a privilege and not a power, to make a pronouncement on the correctness of such vows when made before God. At the time of my writing, I am counselling a couple tonight, who are in the process of getting married and I shall later, on a beach in south Florida, have the privilege of pronouncing the correctness of their marriage which they shall make with one another. Husband and wife, you marry yourselves in both the beginning and the continuance! Remember that.

Today is the day of my own wedding anniversary. Currently, I have been married over 35 years. Like all husbands, I have an obligation, today especially, to examine my own marriage and make some pronouncements of either correctness or dysfunction. All us married folk have a mixture of both these things in our relationship and though the balance of one against the other may positively change throughout the years, yet with the years, comes the danger of a settling and a setting. A settling for less than the best and a setting of the less than the best, in unchanging stone!

With years of marriage comes the danger of a settling and a setting. A settling for less than the best and a setting of the less than the best, in unchanging stone!

Vows however, never go hard or moldy before God. They are as a fresh and as binding, as breathtaking and as beautiful as the day they were made. The relationship they are attached to therefore, needs must be the same. There is always then in any relationship, more work yet to be done.

I remind myself tonight and in the so doing also remind many of you and warn I hope, many, many more, that the achieving of the breathtaking and the beautiful, always takes commitment and sacrifice and both of these are a continual feast. Let us married folk and soon to be married men and women, commit ourselves then tonight, that on the morrow and long times thereafter, we shall achieve these vows with joy, so that all our settlings may be of diamonds of light and all our settings, may be rings of gold on beds of fulfilment. For when the judge of the whole earth looks down on our marriage beds, He does not wear a black cap and gown, but rather sports a paper party hat and a smiling face, always looking on with longing and laughing, whilst holding a party blower in one hand and several party poppers in the other. Rejoice therefore in the wife of your youth and the husband of increasing age. Rejoice! It's party time, for the marriage and its bed are both holy and undefiled.

Listen: *"Then Moses spoke to the heads of the tribes concerning the children of Israel, saying, "This is the thing which the Lord has commanded: If a man makes a vow to the Lord, or swears an oath to* *bind himself by some agreement, he shall not break his word; he shall do according to all that proceeds out of his mouth." (Numbers 30:1-2 NKJV)*

Pray: Hear my cry, O God; Attend to my prayer. From the end of the earth I will cry to You. When my heart is overwhelmed; Lead me to the rock that is higher than I, for You have been a shelter for me, a strong tower from the enemy. I will abide in Your tabernacle forever; I will trust in the shelter of Your wings. Remember that! For You, O God, have heard my vows; You have given me the heritage of those who fear Your name. You will prolong the my life, my years as many generations, yes, I shall abide before God forever! So then, prepare mercy and truth, which in turn, may preserve me! Then I will sing praise to Your name forever, that I may daily perform my vows. (from Psalm 61)

Night-Whisper | **REPENT**

The Borsalino back step

The Bible is the scariest book I have ever read, for the aspects it presents us with regarding our Holy and loving God, are sometimes both punishingly perplexing and terribly troubling!

Numbers 16:1-3

Now Korah the son of Izhar, the son of Kohath, the son of Levi, with Dathan and Abiram the sons of Eliab, and On the son of Peleth, sons of Reuben, took men; and they rose up before Moses with some of the children of Israel, two hundred and fifty leaders of the congregation, representatives of the congregation, men of renown. They gathered together against Moses and Aaron, and said to them, "You take too much upon yourselves, for all the congregation is holy, every one of them, and the Lord is among them. Why then do you exalt yourselves above the assembly of the Lord?" NKJV

In Numbers chapter 16, to say that the Lord got a little annoyed at His people is so much an understatement that it verges on reefer madness! Let's face it, let's man up about this friends, for it is in the plain reading of the text, God lost it here! Yes, God's wrath was so kindled by these conniving and ungrateful, power hungry and arrogant bunch of bananas that His righteous anger knew no bounds. Twice he says to Moses here, whilst rolling up his sleeves mind you, *"Get out the way mate, cause once and for all I'm gonna whack the lot of 'em!"* Numbers 16 (my translation). The Hebrew 'Wa'akaleh,' translated here as *"that I may consume them"* means very simply that: *"He's going to take away the garbage and throw the trash in the impacter and good riddance to the lot of it!"* God is very, very angry here.

On the first occasion of 'God losing it' in this chapter, (Yes I do hope that little phrase troubles you. It should,) it was only the intervention of Moses that saved the congregation as a whole. Yet, still God burns alive in Holy pan fire, frying consummation, the 250 incense swinging usurpers who stood before Him, and then turned on Dathan and Abiram, their goods, their animals and their whole family, including the lickly, little ones, and swallows them alive into the mouth of a burning hell! Again, it was only the intervention of Moses on this occasion that saved the congregation as a whole. Through the prayers of Moses, God held back His wrath. Are you troubled yet? You should be.

On the second occasion of 'God losing it' in this chapter, (Yes I do hope that little phrase troubles you even a little more now. It should,) it was only the intervention of Moses again that saved the congregation as a whole. Yet still, God sent a quickly consuming plague, killing 14,700 of his people before Moses and Aaron could do their work of supplication and propitiation, standing between the dead and the living, until the wrathful plague was halted. Only then did God hold back His wrath. Are you troubled yet? You should be.

Borsalino is the name of a hat company known particularly for its fedoras (felt hats). This Borsalino hat, is a wide-brimmed black felt fedora which today is commonly worn by Orthodox and Hasidic Jewish sects.

Moses and Aaron saved Israel over those few days and maybe, one other woman saved one other man and their whole family as well! Let me explain:

If you closely look at our text for tonight, you will see not only the names of Korah, Dathan and Abiram but also of 'On,' the son of Peleth. Yet 'On' and his family do not appear as names of the dead in any of the related Scriptural texts? It would appear that on the part of 'On,' some wise and speedy repentance had come upon him, and after his little foray into the land of 'Usurption,' he had speedily detached himself from his partners in crime. Rabbinical oral history, tells us that it was 'On's' wife who mightily advised him to get his act together, put his Borsalino on his head and back out of the business deal, post haste! It is not unreasonable to believe that she did just that, and that her husband 'On' hearkened unto the wisdom of his "what the heck do you think you're doing!" wife. I'm pretty sure the conversation that went on in the tent of 'On' would have made a Hollywood producer blush! Yes sir, these were deceitful times and desperate times for sure and we all know what animated language the heat of desperation produces in us. Blood and fire were at stake here and 'On's' wife was by no means cooking, no sir, she had no intention whatsoever of 'frying tonight!'

Tonight, there are no doubt some not-so-wholesome deals that some of you have gotten yourselves into. Maybe, even some of you have been fortunate to have some loving people close to you, express their deep concern for the transactional outcome of your choices but you've thus far ignored them. Well, if the ground is beginning to shake before your feet, if people are dropping like flies around you, if your good wife is still bleeding your ears and God is feeling like an enemy rather than a friend, then maybe it's time to start listening, to put your Borsalino on and back on out there right quickly now, doing the dance of the 'Borsalino back step' as you go! I believe you know better than to align yourself with rebellion and unrighteousness, with un-holiness and unwholesomeness. C'mon, you do know better than that. Don't you?

If the ground is beginning to shake before your feet, if people are dropping like flies around you, if your good wife is and God is feeling like an enemy rather than a friend, then maybe it's time to start listening, to put your Borsalino on and back on out there right quickly now, doing the dance of the 'Borsalino back step' as you go!

Listen: *"And the king of Israel said to Jehoshaphat, 'I will disguise myself and go into battle; but you put on your robes.' So the king of Israel disguised himself, and they went into battle. Now the king of Syria had commanded the captains of the chariots who were with him, saying, 'Fight with no one small or great, but only with the king of Israel.' So it was, when the captains of the chariots saw Jehoshaphat, that they said, 'It is the king of Israel!' Therefore they surrounded him to attack; but Jehoshaphat cried out, and the Lord helped him, and God diverted them from him." (2 Chronicles 18:30,31 NKJV)*

Pray: Lord, it is so scary to have our eyes opened to the terrible predicament we, our family or our friends, have gotten ourselves into. As we put our Borsolino hat on our banana shaped heads and back out of the dreadful predicament we have put ourselves into, we, along with Jehoshaphat and the wife of 'On,' cry out to You for help. Aarggghghghghgh...HELP Lord!!!!! Amen, and please come quickly to our aid!

Night-Whisper | **DESTINY**

The making, the breaking, and the branding of mavericks

Even though they are rarely wanted by the rest of the herd, there has always been a need for the unorthodox, the unconventional and the non-conformist.

Exodus 3:1-2

"Now Moses kept the flock of Jethro his father in law, the priest of Midian: and he led the flock to the backside of the desert, and came to the mountain of God, even to Horeb." KJV.

The banding together of cattle in herd mentality, might for many, lead to: safety, acceptance, corporate fellowship and copulation. However, for the unbranded bull, all those mooing hides, the hoofed up dust and the half eaten grass by those muddy and well trampled waters, offers little consolation for their pioneer spirit. So, they leave the herd or are ejected from it because of all their 'over the horizon' whining, and plough their own trails on the roads less travelled, through the high sierras and down the rocky crags.

It's a lonely life being a maverick, but it is only the mavericks that forge the newer tracks amongst God's green and rolling hills. Yes, it is only the mavericks that find the mount of the Most High God and return to the herd with a message. All true prophets are of necessity, mavericks.

I have often wondered whether mavericks are made or born? I believe it can be either. I believe it can be both. Pity the born maverick then, penned in by the herd, the deep furrows of the track, the fences, the tall tales of fearful giants and the taller tales of safer days 'herd-side,' for I tell you, that such a bull shall die on his frustrated feet, long, long before his horns shall ever hit the dust. Pity the self-made maverick as well then, who, while longing not to be so unacceptable, and seeking earnestly some respectable conformity, nevertheless, when exhibiting the signs of some seeming mad cow disease, is rejected and derided, excluded and divided from those he longs to be with. Forgive me for mixing my animals, but mavericks bulls are often the scapegoats that are sent away into the desert with a flea in their ear, carrying the sins of the people.

Yes, mavericks are both born and made but both must, one way or another, embrace the loneliness of the backside of the desert. Moses was such a man, born and made a maverick. John the Baptizer was such a man, born and made a maverick. Hosea was such a man, as was Jeremiah, Amos, Paul, and tens of thousands of others, named and unnamed, who were all mavericks, each of them returning to the herd with a burning message from Horeb, that only a maverick man might get!

A maverick with a message is hated by the enemy as well as his family, and the enemy will always try and break him.

A maverick with a message is hated by the enemy as well as his family, and the enemy will always try and break him. Remember, that there was once a maverick Levite, (Judges 17:7 onwards) who left the herd at Bethlehem only later to sell his maverick soul for ten shekels and a shirt. Once the transaction was done, he found it easier to sell it again and then again, and for a little more money each time. The consequences of this breaking of a maverick bull, was that the man and his message was marred beyond recovery. Yes, there are two things that break a maverick and ruin his message once he gets it. First money and secondly the need for herd respectability. Yes, money and the need for affirmation from the other animals in the herd are the two siren scimitars which might slice the maverick man in two. Demas was cut in two by the former (2 Tim 4:10) and God help us, Peter and Barnabas were both sliced and diced a little by the latter. (Galatians 2:11-21)

The original and popular use of the word maverick referred to "wayward calves and cattle, who wandered the range, unbranded." Such cattle when found, hardy and well-fed, became the property of the first person to put their own brand upon them. Broken Mavericks are always branded in the end, for Mavericks always disturb the herd. Yes, often times then, many religious leaders throughout the ages, even popes and protestant senior pastors all, have all discovered that the best way to deal with a boisterous bull in a church, is to brand him first and then cut his balls off.

Mavericks in the making, wandering in the backside of the desert before they arrive at the Mount of God, before the fire of the burning bush is given into their bosom, might be some of the loneliest, frustrated and disconsolate people I have ever met, but oh my God, oh dear Lord deliver us, those now branded bulls, those former mavericks of old, now wandering around without their balls but accepted by the herd, are the some of the saddest animals in the world, sporting both bad meat for the butcher and polluted manure for the ground, for once the branding took the light from their eyes, they also lost their flavor, their singing salty savor and became respectful, ruined and absolutely rotten. There is no recovery from this.

May God grant His flock, many a mighty maverick, both born and made and may such mavericks, avoid both the branding iron and the plush pliers of the caring castrators. In all their wide and windswept wanderings, may they find the Mount of God, see the burning bush, receive the majestic message in their hearts and from such burning and lonely furnaces of affliction, deal death to Pharaoh's everywhere and reveal the safe paths of deliverance to all the flock of God. Amen.

Popes and protestant senior pastors all, have all discovered that the best way to deal with a boisterous bull in a church, is to brand him first and then cut his balls off.

Listen: *"Before I formed you in the womb I knew you; Before you were born I sanctified you; I ordained you a prophet to the nations." Jeremiah 1:5 NKJV*

"Then the Lord put forth His hand and touched my mouth, and the Lord said to me: 'Behold, I have put My words in your mouth. See, I have this day set you over the nations and over the kingdoms, To root out and to pull down, To destroy and to throw down, To build and to plant.'" Jeremiah 1:9-10 NKJV

"For behold, I have made you this day A fortified city and an iron pillar, And bronze walls against the whole land — Against the kings of Judah, Against its princes, Against its priests, And against the people of the land. They will fight against you, But they shall not prevail against you. "For I am with you," says the Lord, "to deliver you.'" Jeremiah 1:18-19 NKJV

Pray: Help us O Lord, to arm our mavericks and not to harm them. May they find new paths, hidden trails, fresh waters, and for their own hearts sake and for this our holy herd's continued deliverance, may they find both The Mount and The Message, in Jesus name we pray, amen, and let it be so.

Night-Whisper | **DESTINY**

A consideration of destiny or saving and shaping

The current commercials on television tell me that with the cost of one cup of coffee per month, I can help save the lives of ten million children each year. That's pretty dramatic? That's pretty wonderful. It got me thinking though, I mean what would those poor countries do with ten million more children per year? Maybe the global elite have got it right in culling down the global population. For the sake of the planet of course.

Lamentations 1:9

"Her uncleanness is in her skirts; She did not consider her destiny; Therefore her collapse was awesome; She had no comforter. 'O Lord, behold my affliction, For the enemy is exalted!'" NKJV

I don't buy it.

Even if it is the most expensive thing in the world, there is no question that life should be saved, but especially if it can be saved so cheaply. However, it is just not enough to stop there, for the challenges that saved lives present to us all are enormous.

I helped my wife set up and run a crisis pregnancy center and was involved in counselling some of the exceptionally young fathers, so I know that lives saved from an abortionist's knife, though being precious and wonderful in themselves, nevertheless, present the parents, the wider family and the even the state, with some remarkable challenges of support, mentoring, training and releasing! Yes, of course we should save lives of all people created in the image of God, but it doesn't stop there, it can't stop there! It is easy to string a straight line from a starting point to an end point, but if all you have is a starting point, then all you have in your hand is a string that goes nowhere. We need to have an end game.

We have the same problem in the church. We sometimes are privileged to be involved in seeing people saved among us but we don't really have an end game for them. Yes, I tell you, if having Christ formed in us is simply a matter of getting folks to read their Bible a few minutes in a morning, then turn up at all our meetings, sit up and listen, shut up and pay up, then we do not have an end game, we do not have a destination to pin our line upon.

This happens in the church, mostly because we as individuals do not have a destination ourselves. If you will, we have no real knowledge of our personal destiny, therefore we ourselves are not travelling along a straight line from good beginnings to directed destiny. If that is the case for most of us, and I think it is, then just how can we assist others in finding and pursuing their own manifest destiny in Jesus? We can't.

It seems to me that if you save a life, you also have the duty to shape a life. I think that's imperative and therefore in light of that, I shall leave you with these challenging thoughts tonight: Where are you going? How are you going to get there? How is your shaping of your own life, as well as the lives of other people you are somewhat responsible for? C'mon, be honest, how is it going? Consider your destiny and the destiny of those you have helped bring into life, for if you do not, the dizzy and meandering collapse of both you and those individuals you have birthed, will be awful and only the enemy shall be exalted when that happens. So, just what is your manifest destiny in life? Find it friend, seek it out, and then when you find it, pursue with all of your passionate might! **The Bible calls this: Discipleship.**

> *It seems to me that if you save a life, you also have the duty to shape a life.*

Listen: *"See, O Lord, and consider! To whom have You done this? Should the women eat their offspring, The children they have cuddled?" (Lamentations 2:20a NKJV)*

Pray: Lord, help us to have such a possessed destiny for ourselves and for those we give life to, that we would pray and plan, sow and reap, step and keep, on Your chosen and directed path of growth for us. Help us to be wise in this, that we might never have to end up consuming ourselves in irrelevance and eating our own offspring with directionless and unfruitful living. In Jesus name I pray: Oh God help us to make disciples! Amen, and let it be so.

| Vol 01 | Q1 | NW00059 | February 28th |

Night-Whisper | **ACTION**

Trading for the Transjordan-pondering the Ponderosa principle

The tribes of Reuben and Gad and the half tribe of Manasseh were cattlemen with lots of cattle. I mean herd upon herd of moo-cowing beasts, I mean, good grief batman! They had more cattle between them than the Ponderosa ranch could ever cope with.

Deuteronomy 3:19

"But your wives, your little ones, and your livestock (I know that you have much livestock) shall stay in your cities which I have given you."

Now, this penchant for collecting cows, was aided and abetted by the fact the land they were presently loitering in, the land on the wrong side of Jordan, if you want, was in fact the best of the best of land for cattle. In terms of product and possession, they were exactly where they needed to be, especially since they had cleared out the last of the giants, and his bedstead!

The bravest of these tribesmen had at that time approached Moses with a trading proposition, which simply said: "Let us stay here, let us settle here and store our wives and cattle right here, then we shall go over the Jordan with our brethren, fully armed into the promised land and fight alongside them until they get their possession."

Now, I say they were brave men and they were, and this comforted Moses who had already seen a whole generation fall in the desert over the last forty years and knew that their tottering heart of frail belief had been previously far too easily toppled into unbelief causing a curse from an angry God to fall upon the congregation. Moses was well aware of the need for strong hearts and would not put up with anyone who might weaken into a cursing of all the corporate heart of Israel. Yes, despite the comfort of their bravery, Moses took some convincing and the Transjordan took some trading, but eventually, their wish was granted to them.

Here in our text, after forty years of desert wandering the Promised Land is open for the people of God to possess, or rather should I say, the people of God are now open to possessing the Promised Land given to them! Now then, God here is reminding these settled 2½ cattlemen tribes of their previous commitment to go and fight and in the reminding, makes mention of the foundation of their initial main bargaining chip! It's quite funny really, for I think God is saying "Let's not go over your bargaining position again, please! I know, you have a lot of cattle! Oy vey! Ok, I get it, it has been agreed, now please don't go on about it, just get on with it!"

Tonight, maybe you also have some legitimate reasons to ask God for something that was not initially promised to you and maybe is also 'up for grabs?' If so, then maybe it is time to get to the bargaining table of God and start presuming on His ears?

Now apart from this verse giving me a giggle tonight, there are three very important things to remember here.

First, that these 2½ tribes were not condemned in their choice of land possession. It wasn't what was originally on offer, but they wanted it, had legitimate reason for wanting it, asked for it, bargained for it and got it! God did not condemn them for this.

Secondly, that other land had been allocated to other descendants of Abraham, for example, even the descendants of Lot had spiritual titles that resulted in material possession, which were non-negotiable. However, this former land of the giants, this good cattle land, was spiritually speaking, 'up for grabs' and therefore grab it they did.

Thirdly, that there is some play in the promises of God. I don't know if this was the best choice for the 2½ tribes, or, if it was a better choice for themselves than God's initial choice? However, I do know their bargaining chip of having much cattle, was legitimate, well used in the bargaining banter and well-remembered by God Himself!

Tonight, maybe you also have some legitimate reasons to ask God for something that was not initially promised to you and maybe is also 'up for grabs?' If so, then maybe it is time to get to the bargaining table of God and start presuming on His ears? Who knows, you might just get what you ask for, and it could be a very good thing indeed!

Listen: *"Then the Lord said to me, 'Do not harass Moab, nor contend with them in battle, for I will not give you any of their land as a possession, because I have given Ar to the descendants of Lot as a possession'." (Deuteronomy 2:9 NKJV)*

Pray: Lord, deliver me from unholy pragmatism. However Lord, when two and two make four, help me to be wise enough and brave enough, to make You a most considerate, settlement offer. Yes Lord, help me not settle for less but help me to know the best and ask for some more, in Jesus name I pray, amen and let it be so!

Night-Whisper | **PREPARE**

Coming out from behind the coward's castle

I was watching an old video of that great Yorkshire giant, Leonard Ravenhill. He was recounting a story which took place in the early 20th Century on the streets of his home city of Leeds in England, where an atheist was verbally accosting church attendees, laughing and shouting and scorning them with words like: "Why are you going to hear a man speaking from behind a coward's castle, a pulpit! You can't talk to him or challenge a coward like that, come and listen to me!"

Acts 17:17-18

"Therefore he reasoned in the synagogue with the Jews and with the Gentile worshipers, and in the marketplace daily with those who happened to be there. Then certain Epicurean and Stoic philosophers encountered him. And some said, 'What does this babbler want to say?'" NKJV

In one church where I once pastored, each month we held a 'shoot the Preacher session,' where I set myself up as a target, having to give an account of my previous months teaching. That meant answering questions, clarifying positions, and putting some concrete down the side of some post holes previously dug but obviously not dug deep enough! This is a good practice for the church and for the teachers in and of the church for no one should be allowed to be six feet above contradiction. Nobody should be allowed to turn the pulpit into a coward's castle.

There a few notable exceptions in some churches today, where some selected questions are answered by some of the teachers. Sometimes this is done publicly and sometimes this is done over the internet. I think this is most commendable. However, in the vast majority of gatherings this does not happen and where it does, it's still not good enough! Nobody should be allowed to turn the pulpit into a coward's castle.

In the past, I have boxed badly at an amateur level and I have gone on to be and A.B.A. coach in the sporting field of boxing. I have spent too many hours pounding a bag, pummeling pads or even beating the air. It's all important stuff for the boxer in training but it pails into insignificance against actual ring work. Getting into a ring, especially a ring in another club and sparring round after round, going toe to toe with boxers of differing styles and abilities is really the only way to vastly improve on your own game. Nobody should be allowed to turn the pulpit into a coward's castle.

It is the same in teaching and in preaching. You need to be able to stand toe to toe and give a reason for the hope that is within you. Whitefield and Wesley did it regularly, they had to do it, because they regularly boxed in someone else's ring, and it usually was on enemy ground. I am afraid we still have far too many sissies in cowards' castles around our land and some of you preachers tonight may well have adopted their most pitiful style. Nobody should be allowed to turn the pulpit into a coward's castle.

> *Nobody should be allowed to turn the pulpit into a coward's castle*

Friend, it's time to take the Gospel into the market place again. This means you need to be prepared, and no, I am not talking about seminary. If there is any place on the planet, that will advocate the making and placing of sissies into cowardly castles today then God help us, it is our seminaries, which major on the subtleties of good churchmanship rather than pungent preaching and jaw cracking punches. Nobody should be allowed to turn the pulpit into a coward's castle, especially not seminary professors.

The only way to get properly prepared for verbal combat is to go and seek out the fighting journeymen of times gone by. Make them your mentors. Even if they are dead and with the Lord, make them your mentors still. Listen to them, mark their methods, take it and bring it with all prayer and the power of the Holy Spirit into your generation and into your day. Travel far to be with such men and if you can, go a few rounds with them yourself if you dare! I tell you what, one of my other churches had a monthly preachers get together called 'Fight Club,' for nobody should be allowed to turn the pulpit into a coward's castle.

I have a pair of old leather boxing gloves hanging in my study. They are dirty, stink of old spit, sweat and testosterone and are spattered with old blood. They are my gloves and it's my blood that is on them. They are a testimony to me of all my training, of all my sweat equity which having once paid, allowed me to be able to stand toe to toe with someone and trade blow for blow. They are also a picture of who I am in Christ, a fighter and someone who is more than a conqueror. They are a challenge to me today, to train in such way as to fearlessly and with great confidence, take the Gospel to this angry old world.

> *Either get in training or get out of the ministry. Yes, go somewhere and get a job stroking bunny rabbits. It will be better for everyone.*

What about you preacher? Are you ready to fight in the market place or are you content only to remain the sissified occupier of a coward's castle? If it is the latter, may I encourage you to do two things. Either get in training or get out of the ministry. Yes, go somewhere and get a job stroking bunny rabbits. It will be better for everyone.

Nobody should be allowed to turn the pulpit into a coward's castle.

Listen: *"And he spoke boldly in the name of the Lord Jesus and disputed against the Hellenists, but they attempted to kill him. When the brethren found out, they brought him down to Caesarea and sent him out to Tarsus." (Acts 9:29-30 NKJV)*

Pray: Lord, as you did with your people of old, matching them up with a few fights with "Orrible Og" and "Slippery Sihon" before they properly entered the promised land, so match me up O Lord and give me so much ring experience that when it comes to the main event, I will prove to be more than a conqueror through Him who loved me and gave Himself for me. Amen, and let it be so!

It's time to order your next Quarter of

Night-Whispers

& maybe order one for a friend as well!

To do this today, go to

www.Night-Whispers.com

---------------------------*0*---------------------------

Night-Whispers is written by Victor Robert Farrell, produced by WhisperingWord Ltd. and licenced for the sole use of:

The 66 Books Ministry

A modern day,

Back to the whole Bible,

Boots on The Ground,

Proclamation Movement.

www.66Books.tv

Night-Whisper | **CONSIDER**

Of black cocks and mad March misconceptions

The fastest land animal in these Islands of mine, in this now quite, quite, post Christian and ever darkening mad and not so United Kingdom, is of course, the brown hare.

Ecclesiastes 10:12-13

"The words of a wise man's mouth are gracious, but the lips of a fool shall swallow him up; the words of his mouth begin with foolishness, and the end of his talk is raving madness." NKJV

Brown hares are larger than rabbits, with longer limbs, and a loping gait. They have black-tipped ears which are equal in length to their head and in the month of March, they seem to go stark, staring mad!

The observed seeming madness of 'March hares,' is in fact the panic actions of unreceptive females 'boxing off' the unwanted attentions of males, who are in turn, bouncing mad with the usual spring fever! Yes, misconception can always lead to seeming madness. Especially in these islands of mine.

For me though, it is the West Country and that majestic county of Cornwall which seems to have become the central repository for all the folklore mysteries and madness of this England. Yes, Cornwall for me, has always been a magical but mad place, full of misunderstanding and misconception. For example, it is recorded that just fifty years ago from the time of my writing, a Cornish woman was observed in her window, making a sacrifice as her husband was dying. She did this by taking a black cock and wringing its neck. The cock was killed so as to accompany her husband's soul to the gates of heaven so that when St Peter saw the black cock, it would remind him of his own denial of Christ and move him to mercy so that he would allow her husband through the pearly heavenly gates. How about that for a multitude of mad March misconceptions!

Oh and by the way, if you think the West Country is not just as insane with mad March misconception today as it was over fifty years ago, then just go and visit Glastonbury for a taste of madness on a stick, 'New Age' style.

Winter is passing and the arrival of March marks for all of us, a season of new conceptions, a season of life and a season of new beginnings. All of nature will shortly fill itself up with the ebullient flowers of exuberance, for winter has passed and spring is almost upon us and sunshine and fresh sharpness, follows quickly on! How wonderful. How exciting! Oh how I love Spring.

However, I have observed in these times, that always, such a spring release does bring with it a kind of madness and for those wise enough, for those who can for just a few moments each day, stand outside of themselves and listen, stand outside of themselves and look, they will both hear and see, often for the first time, often because only March and the gushing of spring time allow it to spring forth, yes, they will both see and hear, the mild March madness of their very own misconceptions. None of us are exempt from this seasonal insanity, no not one.

Spring fever breads madness but if we are wise, we will see our insanity and sacrifice it for wisdom.

Let me encourage you then this coming month especially, to go with the seasonal flow and to let the sap rise within you, then, when you get your ears boxed, as you most surely will (for we are all a little raving mad sometimes, yes, we have all got it wrong somewhere,) take time to take hold of those mad March misconceptions of yours and once and for all, in your own rising light, ring their black and feathered necks. If you do this, then I tell you, they shall never bother you again!

I tell you, now is a great time to ask God to show you where you are 'getting it wrong!'

Listen: *"There is a man in your kingdom in whom is the Spirit of the Holy God. And in the days of your father, light and understanding and wisdom, like the wisdom of the gods, were found in him." (Daniel 5:11a NKJV)*

"The entrance of Your words gives light; it gives understanding to the simple." (Psalms 119:130 NKJV)

Pray: Blessed be the name of God forever and ever, for wisdom and might are Yours and You change the times and the seasons; You remove kings and raise up kings; You give wisdom to the wise and knowledge to those who have understanding. You reveal deep and secret things; You know what is in the darkness, for light dwells with You. This month of March O God, let those controlling misconceptions of mine be seen in Your light and then my God, let us rings their black necks together. In these things, I ask for a hunter's patience and I ask for a butcher's strength, in Jesus' mighty name, amen. (From Daniel 2:20-22 NKJV)

Night-Whisper | **MONEY**

Dealing with the Reverend William Fold

The Levites had no inheritance in the land of promise! It can be truly said that the Levites served the spiritual needs of the people of God. This was their commission and their destiny.

Deuteronomy 12:19

"Take heed to yourself that you do not forsake the Levite as long as you live in your land." NKJV

Bow then, to help the Levites fulfil that commission and achieve that destiny, God almighty made it incumbent upon the people they ministered to, that they not forget the material support of the Levites. If that were to happen, maybe some Levites would starve to death but I tell you, most would go and find jobs with good incomes elsewhere, long before that happened. In other words, because of material necessity, they would desert their calling and their destiny.

Allow me then please tonight, to now turn my attention to New Testament ministers, where I believe there are two types of employed ministers.

First the contractual minister.

There are those ministers who have been employed by congregations that can afford them and they have entered into a vocational and financial contract of employment with one another. This is always a precarious position and I know of many a minister, who, once they stopped tickling the ears of their employers, have been financially starved by such congregations and to such an extent, that they became wrecks for many years thereafter both financially and otherwise. Churches, if you are employing a minister and you want to dismiss them, you want to move them on, you want to replace them, then just tell them! Don't starve them and ruin them, tell them! Come to some financial arrangement with them if needs be, yes, dismiss them if you must, but don't ruin them. Talk to them and at least give them some time to find a job elsewhere to contractually express their vocational callings. Yes, if there is a mismatch, tell them. If however, it is the faithfully preached word of God that's getting to you, if you can't stand the heat from the prophetic kitchen then please, next time go looking for a minister down at the cats protection league for there's many a pussy cat out there simply looking for a bowl of milk. I assure you, you will not have to look far. No, if you are wise, give the one that's bothering you with the Word of God a pay rise.

Second, the relational minister.

If you can't stand the heat from the prophetic kitchen then please, next time go looking for a minister down at the cats protection league for there's many a pussy cat out there simply looking for a bowl of milk. I assure you, you will not have to look far.

There are other ministers who have not entered into contract with any congregation or ministerial or denominational affiliation, yet believe God has called them to a life of ministry, in which they have to trust God for their material provision.

You may enter into private verbal contracts of support with such folk and if you do, then stick to it. In addition, those of us who actually seek out and benefit from the ministry of such folk should, when we can, give to their ministry and give to them. Remember to do this as you seek and utilize their ministry, not as they seek to impose their ministry and financial obligations upon you! However, this giving you enter into is not contractual or obligatory, but rather, it is Holy Spirit and conscience driven. Even so, beware here, that your conscience is not manipulated by strong arm giving tactics of any kind. You are under no contractual obligation to support such folk. If God has called them to a life of financial faith living, then God shall provide for them. The Holy Spirit and conscience may direct you, but you are under no legal contractual obligation at all!

There is now one other minister which I must refer to, who is most prevalent in our times. These are not New Testament ministers for sure, yet they do abound in and around the church. These are: the Hucksters, the Hawkers, the Peddlers and the Sellers of various brands of good, old fashioned snake oil. You shall recognize them easily, because they always have 'a new move of God,' an 'anointing,' an 'insight,' a 'product,' at hand which they will make you feel good about buying, especially if that product will do you no good at all! These folks are usually dressed in green suited dollar bills and go by the name of Reverend William Fold. Unless you revel in plastic spirituality, avoid them like the plague and steer well clear, for strange fire is always swallowed up by God in the end. Always!

Concerning your giving then and your own bill fold tonight, may I encourage you to 'man up' about it! Get wise, keep generous but become intensely practical. Oh and remember, Tithing is a Biblical principle, but it is not a New Testament practice. Think about that. (Now, that HAS put the cat among the financial pigeons!)

Listen: *"You shall not forsake the Levite who is within your gates, for he has no part nor inheritance with you." (Deuteronomy 14:27 NKJV)*

Pray: Lord, help me to give generously and practically to those I have entered into contract with. For all the rest O Lord, guide and direct me, in my giving. Finally Lord, concerning Rev. Bill Fold, help me see that he is already fat enough to burst and die and that I have far too much useless snake oil already lining up my bookshelves to even think of buying more! In Jesus name I pray, amen, and let it be so.

Night-Whisper | **PERSEVERE**

Of magic fairies and velveteen rabbits

God wants you to be a fairy! Now there's a sermon you won't hear too often. However, I do believe it to be the truth. Yes, God wants you to be a fairy!

1 Thessalonians 2:6-9

"Nor did we seek glory from men, either from you or from others, when we might have made demands as apostles of Christ. But we were gentle among you, just as a nursing mother cherishes her own children. So, affectionately longing for you, we were well pleased to impart to you not only the Gospel of God, but also our own lives, because you had become dear to us. For you remember, brethren, our labour and toil; for labouring night and day, that we might not be a burden to any of you, we preached to you the Gospel of God." NKJV.

It was famous children's author, London born American, Margery Williams Bianco, who penned the famous book entitled, *The Velveteen Rabbit*. The story tells of how a young boy receives a velveteen (cotton imitation velvet – not the real thing) rabbit for Christmas and how this new toy, what with the loss of his favorite china dog, eventually becomes the little boy's most well-loved and constant companion. The story goes of how the velveteen rabbit finally meets up with very well made toys, which have no seems in them at all, and then discovers that these well-made toys are not toys at all but are in fact, real live rabbits!

The boy, as happens not only in stories, becomes very sick with scarlet fever and while sent to recuperate at the seaside, is given a brand new rabbit with shiny glass eyes. The reason for this seemingly callous substitution, was the practice in those days of destroying by fire, all the scarlet fevered, germ-laden items, so as to ensure the infection stopped. How very Biblical!

So now, the old velveteen rabbit, while awaiting the burning flames in which he would perish forever, cries a real tear and this very real tear, brings forth the nursery's magic fairy! Although the rabbit thinks he was real before, the fairy tells him that he was only actually real to the boy. In the end, the nursery fairy flies him to beneath the waiting trees, where the old velveteen toy finds himself translated at last, into a very real rabbit and runs speedily away, to join all the other hopping little bunnies in the wild and wonderful woods. How lovely.

Scarlet fever appears to be have become less aggressive than its previous expressions in the children of the past, where once upon a time, the rampant and red disease, left children with scars often far worse than death. It was this red fever that left a young Norwegian girl called 'Kaata Ragnhild Tollefsdatter,' at a very early age, both deaf and blind. In the mid 1800's, the isolation of this young girl was most profound and pitiable.

Yes, just how many isolated, lie believing, ragged little rabbits, are you saving from the burning?

A Norwegian teacher called 'Elias Hansen Hofgaard,' took on the care and education of this scarlet fevered damaged young woman and with great dedication, utilized the 'oral method' of teaching with Kaata, to reveal to the society, the first well known speaking deaf-blind person in the history of the world. I am sure you have heard of her and of Hofgaard, her nursery magic fairy. No?

It was an American, Caroline Yale, a teacher of blind students that somehow developed this Hofgaardian method of instruction of deaf blind people. Further, it was one of her own students, Miss Sophie Alcorn, who practiced this method on two young children, *Tad* Chapman and *Oma* Simpson, producing the *'Tadoma'* method of instruction, where the deaf blind person could feel the very life of words, by placing their thumb on the speaker's lips and their fingers along their jaw line, with the middle three fingers falling along the speaker's cheeks and the little pinky finger, positioned effectively now to pick up the vibrations of the speaker's throat. Sophie taught her 'Tadoma Method' real good, and later one of her own students, Miss Anne Sullivan, today in 1887, for the very time, came into the life of a very scarlet fevered damaged, velveteen rabbit of a little girl aged just 6 years of age. Her name was Helen Keller.

Now then, do you see that Anne Sullivan, this nursery magic fairy, actually came from a long line of miracle workers! With love, sacrifice, strength and determination, she invaded the high walled bastion of isolation in which young Helen Keller had lost herself and slowly and determinedly released her! Keller became the first deaf blind person to receive a degree, becoming a writer, an active political mover, a world-famous speaker, and a friend, both of the famous and of Presidents, having personally met with all of them, from Grover Cleveland to Lyndon B. Johnson! All of this was able to come about, simply because a miracle worker, a magic fairy from a long line of other magic fairies, came into her life, allowed the deaf and the blind to touch her and to learn from her, and to such a phenomenal extent, that a scarlet fever damaged, ragged little velveteen rabbit of a girl, could be released into the wild, wild woods of humanity, to touch and to train, to change and to release many another toy, which was simply waiting for the bonfire.

> *How is your missionary work among the spiritually deaf and the blind going tonight?*

How is your missionary work among the spiritually deaf and the blind going tonight? How is your discipleing of others going tonight? How is your dedication tonight? Yes, just how many isolated, lie believing, ragged little rabbits, are you saving from the burning?

God wants you to be a fairy! Now there's a sermon you won't hear too often. However, I do believe it to be the truth. God wants you to be a fairy!

Listen: *"Jesus answered and said to them, 'Go and tell John the things you have seen and heard: that the blind see, the lame walk, the lepers are cleansed, the deaf hear, the dead are raised, the poor have the Gospel preached to them.'" (Luke 7:22-23 NKJV)*

Pray: Lord, fulfil the words of Your good news! Then help me Lord, to be focused and dedicated in my discipleing of others. Amen and let it be so.

Night-Whisper | **HONOR**

Rough and ready

Driving along the Brownsboro road from Louisville to the city of Goshen Kentucky, I would pass the Zachary Taylor National Cemetery and always gaze at the regimented white gravestones all neatly lined in rows.

Malachi 1:6a

"A son honours his father, and a servant his master. If then I am the Father, where is My honour? And if I am a Master, where is My reverence? Says the Lord of hosts." NKJV.

Of course it is here, where Virginia born but Kentucky bred and prospered, former President of the United States lies interned on his own plot of land in his own mausoleum. Just a few miles down the road on the left hand side, still part of an old farm lay another old mausoleum, a white wooden church, which I am sure a heavy sneeze would have brought crashing down around it's ears. This old church is the remains of a former slave church. I do not know where its original occupiers are interred.

Zachary Taylor, 'old rough and ready,' descended from Edward 1st, and having not a few near relatives of the same by blood and marriage still around, as an high ranking Confederate officer, had a military career in the US Army himself, spanning some 40 years. Nevertheless, he and his family were still the proud owners of 10,000 acres of slave plantation in Kentucky.

It was the slavery issue which dominated Taylor's short term in office and I wonder, if the assassination theories are correct, (Taylor's family had his body exhumed in the 1990's to check for arsenic poisoning) that it was that which also got him killed? You see, although President Taylor owned slaves, he took a moderate stance on the territorial expansion of slavery and this angered fellow Southerners. Indeed, in answer to their sabre rattling, he told them that if necessary, to enforce the laws, he personally would lead the Army and "Any persons taken in rebellion against the Union, he would hang... with less reluctance than he had hanged deserters and spies in Mexico." President Taylor died in mysterious circumstances whilst the Henry Clay Compromise of 1850 was being debated. The compromise failed.

I am focusing on this story tonight, not to indulge in the conspiracy theory musings of the majority of United States citizens but to acknowledge both a different age and a different perspective. An age where today in 1849, Zachary Taylor, an elected slave owning President of the United States would not be sworn into office because his inauguration was on a Sunday! This old Episcopalian did not wish to violate the Lord's day and thus for one whole day the nation was forced to proceed without a President. The nation, it's young bureaucratic wheels, the emissaries of foreign powers, dignitaries and paying customers one and all, all had to wait while 'old rough and ready' gave God the honor He so rightly deserves.

> *Zachary Taylor, President of the United States would not be sworn into office because his inauguration was on a Sunday! This old Episcopalian did not wish to violate the Lord's day and thus for one whole day the nation was forced to proceed without a President.*

Times have, in many respects, unquestionably changed for the better, but my how in many more respects maybe, times have also changed for the far, far worse.

In the human condition, times are rarely optimal and people, nations, societies and communities are all, in one way or another, in a constant mess of change. The same will, to some extent, be true of your community today, whether it be nation, city, church, work or family. The lesson from 'old rough and ready' President Zachary Taylor is very simple tonight: No matter how rough the situation is, always be ready to give God the honor and the glory He so richly deserves. Even if it means closing down the country for a day!

Listen: *"Then it shall be to Me a name of joy, a praise, and an honour before all nations of the earth, who shall hear all the good that I do to them; they shall fear and tremble for all the goodness and all the prosperity that I provide for it." (Jeremiah 33:9 NKJV)*

Pray: Lord tonight we pray for our leaders and ourselves as leaders. We are pulled down and broken Lord, heaped up to the hilt in death and swill. In Your anger O Lord, remember mercy. In Your fury, do not forget

Your goodness. In Your hostility, no longer hide Your face from us. Rather, by the blood bought grace of Jesus, bring us health and healing; and reveal to us the abundance of peace and truth. Cause our captivity to cease and rebuild those places we have pulled down and cleanse us from all our iniquity by which they have sinned against You, in Jesus name we pray, amen, and let it be so. (Adapted from Jeremiah 33:4-8)

Night-Whisper | **FIGHT**

'The Big E' - her stars and His scars

John 20:27-28

"Then He said to Thomas, 'Reach your finger here, and look at My hands; and reach your hand here, and put it into My side. Do not be unbelieving, but believing.' And Thomas answered and said to Him, 'My Lord and my God!'" NKJV

Having rejected his Southern Baptist roots, the former decorated army flyer and WWII veteran, embarked on a screenwriting career in Las Vegas, the end of which was the creation of a vast cultural consciousness spanning several generations. After a tumultuous life, he became the first person to be buried in space, the genesis of his ideas and the birth place of an imagery ship with the registry entry of 'NCC 1701,' which has sailed into the minds of thousands of millions of *Star Trek* fans. I am of course talking about Gene Rodenberry's constitutional class heavy cruiser, which is better known to most of us as The United States Star Ship, USS Enterprise.

The real 'Big E' was the Seventh US Navy ship to bear that name, and the Yorktown Class Carrier launched in 1936 would survive WWII and become the most highly decorated ship in the history of the American Navy, her crew earning her some twenty distinct and bloody battle stars. Indeed, she was the most decorated ship of the whole of WWII and even received the most prestigious decoration her Majesty's Royal Navy could offer in the form of the British Admiralty Pennant.

Our great Commander in Chief Himself, Jesus, Eternal King of Kings, the eternal 'Big E,' if you will, and Lord of Lords, occupies all of these, that is, His vast and varied all unbounded seas, which are surrounded by a trillion bright and shining stars and He does so with ease, all the while bearing those most precious of all eternal scars, those wounds of winning, gained at the most crushing defeat of our great enemy at Calvary's cross. Yes, our Jesus, bears the marks of His victory on His real and resurrected body.

It is my belief that there will be scars received on earth, which shall be borne in heaven. Scars which are grotesque in deformity here, but which in heaven, are turned into bejeweled and emblazoned touchable tattoos. I believe that scars gained here in the wars of the Lord, are the only thing that shall be carried into heaven and they along with their bearers shall be remembered, honored and most well-loved.

Brethren, where then are the mighty men of the greater David today? Where are the Christians whose names shall sail with glory through the gates of Heaven into heaven's victorious seas? Where are the men bearing battle scars?

This poverty ridden and most pitiable condition of the present Western Church cannot continue, for in the West, darkness is making fast its plans, and is ready to rise up quickly against this sleepy church of ours, who like Jonah of old, sleeps in the bowels of the ship in the most vicious of rising storms. Trouble is coming and I am not glad for it but as an observer of the weather of time, I tell you tonight, that trouble is coming and it is more than we have ever seen thus far.

Trouble is coming and I am not glad for it but as an observer of the weather of time, I tell you tonight, that trouble is coming and it is more than we have ever seen thus far.

Who knows, maybe from our own, quickly coming Pearl Harbor, some ships of renown shall come to sail the seas once more, for I tell you, battle scars from the wars of the Lord, are the only things you shall take into heaven with you.

Listen: *"Proclaim this among the nations: 'Prepare for war! Wake up the mighty men, Let all the men of war draw near, let them come up. Beat your plowshares into swords and your pruning hooks into spears; let the weak say, 'I am strong.' Assemble and come, all you nations, and gather together all around. Cause Your mighty ones to go down there, O Lord. Let the nations be wakened, and come up to the Valley of Jehoshaphat; for there I will sit to judge all the surrounding nations. Put in the sickle, for the harvest is ripe. Come, go down; for the winepress is full, the vats overflow - for their wickedness is great. Multitudes, multitudes in the valley of decision! For the day of the Lord is near in the valley of decision." (Joel 3:9-14 NKJV)*

Pray: Heaven knows that getting scars only makes us who we are and no matter how much our heart is aching, there is always beauty in the breaking? Beauty in the breaking Lord and blessing in the making, of wounds and scars and battle stars strewn along our windswept pennant. Give us strength and courage Lord and we shall give You our glory, Yes, all glory to God in the Highest and praise to our great King who from the lips of angels makes sweet hosannas sing. Lord, the people of the Hebrews with palms before Thee went; Our prayer and praise and anthems before Thee we present. To Thee, before Thy passion, they sang their hymns of praise; to Thee, now high exalted, Our melody we raise. Thou didst accept their praises; accept the prayers we bring, who in all good delightest, Thou good and gracious King.

(Some words, adapted from the song 'Broken,' by Lyndsey Horn and from Theodulph of Orleans, who praised God in prison and died in that same place of his praising.)

Night-Whisper | **DESIRE**

How's your sex life?

Do you pray when you get up in the morning? Yes, afore ye face the coming day, do you take the time to kneel and pray?

In a morning, though I do pray for others, I mostly pray for myself, and mostly for me and mine. So, with such seeming familial selfishness, I thought it would be good to examine all of my personal prayers made over the mornings now long since gone. Having done that, I have found that I can group them under less than a handful of four major headings. Here they are: I first pray for power, then I pray for provision followed by protection and finally, for presence.

Isaiah 26:9a

"With my soul I have desired You in the night, yes, by my spirit within me I will seek You early." NKJV

I pray for power! Power to be healed of my infirmities that seem to increase exponentially as I get older! Power to be delivered from my demons and my long besetting sins. Power for God to come and change relationships, maybe even me, maybe. Occasionally I pray for power, that I might, in all my daily circumstances, display the Father's glory. Oh yes, I like a bit of justifying grandeur to be mixed with my all my personal ponderings. *I, you see, pray for power!*

I pray for provision. I pray for my daily bread and a whole lot more to put in my large refrigerator and freezer. I pray for chunks of money to feed the barking bills. I pray for postal miracles, yes, I pray for money in the mail. My wife prays for the same! For sure, I pray for strength for the coming day but mostly I pray for money, materials and manpower. *I, you see, pray for provision.*

I pray for protection. For after all, if God does answer my increasingly necessary but ever boring prayers, I don't want these good answers stolen from me at the last, I don't want to receive them with trouble added on the end. I need to at least cover all my bases of possible loss. Yes, I pray for protection. Panic prayer insurance is surely a very good thing to have? *Yes, I, you see, pray for provision.*

Finally, **I pray for presence** and believe it or not, this brings me onto the question of my sex life, indeed, to the question of your sex life as well.

You see, on those occasions when I have been thoroughly examined by my local doctor, even just verbally so, he has always questioned me about my libido, or rather, if there is any lack of it. When this question has been asked of me over a visit to him regarding anything other than my genitals, it has always left me with a stunned look on my face. "Eh? What on earth did you ask that for?" In addition to the stunned look, I have to be honest that my response has never been the whole truth. "Yeah fine Doc! No problems in that department, no siree. Phew praise God!"

The doctor of course, in questioning my prowess in the bedroom is looking at sexual desire as a sign of physical health.

The doctor of course, in questioning my prowess in the bedroom is looking at sexual desire as a sign of physical health. If I am ill, then the power of my desire is often re-routed into fighting disease, overcoming anxiety, or repairing the body. From a doctors point of view, him questioning the function of my libido is simply a fault finding question to discover indicators of failing health. Which believe it or not, brings me back to spiritual desire and especially to my prayers of presence.

It is too easy to begin the day with God and then forget Him for the rest of it. When my prayers for His manifest presence in my day are nothing but a quick tag line hooked onto the other guff, then my desire for Him is low, my desire for Him is waning, my spiritual libido, if you will, is not functioning as it should, indeed, I am spiritually sick.

So, let me ask you tonight my dear friend, how is your spiritual sex life? Is everything OK in the spiritual bedroom department my friend? Oh really? Do you desire Him during your day? If everything else was stripped away, would you still want Him? Do you long for Him tonight? Will you seek Him all your day tomorrow? Indeed, will you count your day an utter failure if you cannot feel His kind caress, enjoy His presence over a cup of coffee, or see His face amongst the milling crowd? How's your spiritual sex life then tonight?

If you are too tired for desire and frankly, that's the usual cause amongst us Christians, simple hard pressed tiredness, even exhaustion, then you need to refocus the use of your time, change your diet and get to bed earlier. It's as profound and as practical as that. If however, you have no desire for Him whatsoever and frankly never really had, then you are very simply, a user and an abuser of God. Your prayers have been prayers of provision, protection, power and prostitution. Nothing else. There has been no relationship in them whatsoever.

> *Your prayers have been prayers of provision, protection, power and prostitution.*

Let us change our ways. Let us re-order our prayer patterns and on the morrow, let us choose to desire His presence. Let us begin, to court our God once more, in pursuing, desiring and dedicated, adoring relationship.

Listen: *"I have not spoken in secret, In a dark place of the earth; I did not say to the seed of Jacob, 'seek Me in vain'." (Isaiah 45:19a NKJV)*

Pray: Lord, You have said, "Seek me and live!" Lord, You have said "You will find Me when you seek me with all your heart." So with all my heart and mind and will, I decide to desire You. In the coming days O Lord, surprise my choice by adding the glow of passionate fires! Amen, and let it be so.

| Vol 01 | Q1 | NW00067 | March 07th |

Night-Whisper | **CARE**

Oh, for such slippy feet!

What amazing things to say! What prophetic affirmation and additional and palpable power, does Moses now give to all the long laid blessings once received from beneath the departing hands of Jacob of old, which long time past now, were also once laid in wonder upon all his waiting sons!

Deuteronomy 33:24-25

"And of Asher he said: 'Asher is most blessed of sons; let him be favoured by his brothers, and let him dip his foot in oil. Your sandals shall be iron and bronze; as your days, so shall your strength be'." NKJV

Asher, the eighth son of Jacob, here becomes the symbol of the summation of all the hand laid blessings of Israel. Here, 'happy' Asher, for that is what his name means, the most favored in the blessings given to his brethren, is blessed both above and below the ground of promise. Blessed above, with so much oil, that his descendants would wade through its oily effulgence, anointing their feet in the flowing fatness of all the dripping trees laid up in olive groves and planted without number! Blessed below with so much mineral wealth, that both the possession and export of the same would provide them with every material blessing that their full fat hearts could ever desire! I tell you, what a blessing this was from Father Jacob. I tell you, what a blessing this was from Father Moses as well! Oh to receive such a personal and powerful, prophetic blessing from a blessed and powerful, God honored departing father.

The last time I remember holding my father, he was lying on the couch. Made dumb and immobile by a stroke, all he could do was stare at me pitifully through his blank and glassy eyes. All the upside down lies which he had told in his life and laid up in his high bombastic belfry, though quiet for so long, like insane black bats had finally been chased from their long sleep by the sound of the hunched back blood clot now tolling the bells in his head, and now, these lying bats swarmed the air in derision around his old sick brow. It was me, just in my early twenties at the time, who held my old father to myself, blessing him in his brokenness, telling him that I loved him no matter what. It was all wrong. I mean, it was all the wrong way around! The elder, should be blessing the younger, but like a parent attending their children's funeral, I held my dying earthly father one last time and blessed him. These things, should not be so. He should have been blessing me.

It is my personal goal, to so spiritually prosper, that it will demand such an expectant and respectful honor from my children, that at the time of all my departures, they will run to seek a blessing from me, because they know that not only do I have it to give them, but that the receiving of such a fatherly blessing, will be of inestimable value to the one who might possess it, because God has been so evidently with me.

> *If you have missed the blessing of an earthly Father, then go and privately seek out a particular blessing from your heavenly Father.*

May I encourage you tonight then in two things?

First, that if you have missed the blessing of an earthly Father, that you would privately seek out a particular blessing from your heavenly Father.

Second, that once being in receipt of such mighty blessings from above, you would thoroughly commit yourself to grow spiritually and in such a way, that when the time of all your departures are at hand, you too might have the authority and the respect, to place a prophetic blessing upon the bowed and waiting heads of all your eager children. Especially upon those whom you have helped both to birth and grow into the Kingdom of Christ our Lord and particularly on those of your most well-loved blood line.

Remember, death may be your final departure, but is it is only one in a thousand of others which you shall make upon your long journey home. Yes, make sure, that in all your departures, you have both a blessing to leave and a blessing that is wanted!

Listen: *"When Esau heard the words of his father, he cried with an exceedingly great and bitter cry, and said to his father, 'Bless me - me also, O my father!' And Esau said to his father, 'Have you only one blessing, my father? Bless me - me also, O my father!' And Esau lifted up his voice and wept. Then Isaac his father answered and said to him: 'Behold'...." (Genesis 27:35 & 38-39 NKJV)*

Pray: Bless me Oh my Father. Bless me with the tri-fold fatness of the land beneath my feet, the ground on which I walk and all the heavens above. Bless me especially, with a great and particular, personal and prophetic chariot, upon which I might ride the heights of all the land which You have apportioned to me. In Jesus name I pray, amen, and let it be so.

Night-Whisper | **HAPPY**

The House of Fun

Jeshurun is a hypocorism, a pet name, a term of endearment, a poetical name, if you will, for the people of Israel. Jeshurun means: 'the dear upright people.' Look at that! Jacob, received the God changed name of Israel, and then goes on to dearly refer to him as Jeshurun.

Deuteronomy 32:15

"But Jeshurun grew fat and kicked; you grew fat, you grew thick, you are obese! Then he forsook God who made him, and scornfully esteemed the rock of his salvation." NKJV

I love that one commentator says: "With the new name goes a new chance in life, to live up to its meaning." I like that! Jeshurun is God's nickname for the people He loves, yet even this nickname carries with it a deep aspirational desire. "Jeshurun: My dearest and upright one." I know that my heavenly Father calls me 'Robert.' I wonder if he has a nickname for me as well? I'm going to ask Him! He might just let me in on it!

Now, imagine you have married a beautiful woman, hot to the heart, gentle on the mind, and pleasing to the eyes and to top it all, she can't keep her hands off you. Steady now tiger, calm down! What a joy that would be, I mean, wouldn't it? I know you'd sign up for that particular blessing and I am sure that both in your joy and in your delight you would also call her "Darling; My beloved; Dearest heart; or even Pookie (maybe); and a whole lot more loveliness besides!" Pet names, you see, spring from hearts of love, racing hearts if you will. So tell me, is your heart racing for God? It is obvious that God's heart was racing for Jacob, for Israel, for His Jeshurun. Is His heart racing for you?

Now to help you calm down from my hot wife analogy, will you imagine another picture, that in a short time, this same woman who once caused your heart to race, has fed her face so much and sat on her butt for so long, that her ankles have swollen, her neck has sprouted folded rolls of stinky pink flesh all spotted with little grey stubby hairs, and she has, overall, moved beyond the voluptuous, even way past the outer solar system of fatness and travelled into the deep realms of 'orrible obesity and to top it all, she can't stand you. Indeed, whenever you draw close to her, in either comfort or rescue, she kicks you in the shins, knees you on the outside of the thigh, thumps you on the chest and spits in your face. She is troublesome, worrisome, embarrassing and hateful. That dream of your youth, has now turned into a nightmare and a big fat kicking nightmare at that!

> *That dream of your youth, has now turned into a nightmare and a big fat kicking nightmare at that!*

Our text for tonight, tells of a far worse disaster. It tells of chosen and indulgent adultery and I tell you, there is nothing beautiful in that. Nothing whatsoever. It's fat with sin and God's response to such sinful adulterous obesity is black looks, green jealousy and red-hot anger! You see, losing the fun of fellowship leads to the sad over indulgence in the tempting but unsatisfying, heart festering, food-fest of sin.

I have seen the Christian Jeshuruns lose the fun of fellowship and fall. Yes, I could make mention of many a famous name, that fell and became fat, that became fat and fell, oh hell, let's not judge them though, for it could be me, it could be you, that loses the fun O Jeshurun. Yes, I have seen many an unsinkable marriage, sink! Joyless, fat and fun-less. I have seen many an unbreakable relationship, break, for goodness sake, but remember, don't lets judge, for it could be me, it could be you, that loses the fun, O Jeshurun.

In case you missed it, here is my only point for tonight: Don't lose the fun of following Jesus. Don't flirt with foreign Gods, and don't forget who fathered you, because if you do, then in His anger, He might just turn his face away from fat old you. O Jeshurun, don't become a filthy bum.

Listen: *"They provoked Him to jealousy with foreign Gods; with abominations they provoked Him to anger. They sacrificed to demons, not to God, to Gods they did not know, to new Gods, new arrivals that your fathers did not fear. Of the rock who begot you, you are unmindful, and have forgotten the God who fathered you. And when the Lord saw it, He spurned them, because of the provocation of His sons and His daughters. And He said: 'I will hide My face from them, I will see what their end will be, for they are a perverse generation, children in whom is no faith."* (Deuteronomy 32:16-20 NKJV)

Pray: Lord, I love You! What do you want to do tonight? What do you want to do tomorrow? Where do You want to go? What shall we do together? Let me hear You call my name, let me hear You call me son, your heart's delight, most dearest child, even Your son of fun, Your beloved faithful Jeshurun. Amen and let it be so.

| Vol 01 | Q1 | NW00069 | March 09th |

Night-Whisper | **FOCUS**

Singleness of heart

Q:- Why can a Pirate intending to celebrate,
Never proceed on a life that is totally celibate?

A:- Because there is no 'ahRrrrrrr' in Celibate.

From 1 Corinthians 7:2-6, the gifted single, the apostle Paul himself, by His wisdom in the Holy Spirit, gives God's view on the Holy service of sex in marriage.

1 Corinthians 7:1a

"Now concerning the things of which you wrote to me." NKJV

If I didn't believe this book was God's revelation to us, as a married person I would be somewhat 'miffed' at a single bloke trying to give me some advice. However, this book is the Word of God and therefore I sit up and take notice.

It's worth remembering that in writing this book, God did not take folks and turn them into human automatons or fleshly dictating machines, just to string together a few letters of the alphabet. No, rather, the breathed out word of God came to us through the full personality, character, life situation, geographical and historical context, of all the various writers, including the apostle Paul. That being the case, Paul here places for us at verse 1 and verse 7 of this passage, his own personal book ends for the context of the central verses of 2-6. Here they are:

Verse 1- "It is good for a man not to touch a woman." NKJV

Verse 7- " For I wish that all men were even as I myself." NKJV

The apostle Paul, that gifted, single minded, single person, was most definitely placing a personal preference of the single lifestyle above marriage. In the context of his laser like focused apostleship, although marriage was good, for him being single was even better. It was better for him because he had free range over the gigantic ranch of his time, yes, he had all the time in the world to focus on one thing, and that was pleasing his heavenly Father and pursuing His calling on his life. To that end, he regarded his singleness as a precious gift, a gift of value and everyone must agree, that it was indeed a gift well spent. Whether the great apostle was a widower is irrelevant here, for in terms of his calling, he intended to be single and he called this being single, 'a good thing.'

I have been a single man and should my wife depart to glory afore me, then I shall be a single man again. I write therefore out of some experience and much observation. In light of this I have observed that there are four states of singleness, defined as: looking, waiting, resigned and chosen.

There are four states of singleness, defined as: looking, waiting, resigned and chosen.-

You can be single and looking for a future spouse. The majority of younger folk are in this hunting mode. Prayerfully of course! Be sure that you keep in the God ordained hunting grounds though, that is, if you are a Christian, then be sure to find a Christian spouse. Hunting outside of the parameters will get you into trouble and cause untold problems among family, friends and the fellowship of the local church. If you marry a non-Christian you are in for a world of hurt. It's hard enough being married to a Christian. Be sure of this!

You can be single but in a relationship where you are waiting to take those oaths of commitment in the context of community and faithfulness. You better be saving your money at this point. Be faithful and watchful in all your waiting. Oh, and keep your hands to yourself! Remember, you get to take the wrapping off on the wedding night. You never unwrap the gifts until Christmas. Never.

You can be single and reluctantly resigned to that state, daily struggling to give God the glory no matter what. Your singleness may be a result of death, catastrophe, illness, ugliness, both internally or externally, the decision of others, or, what we glibly call the providence of God. In any event, you didn't want to be single, but there you are. Oh hard condition. May God grant you change in it soon. Meanwhile, well done in seeking God's greater glory. You shall not go unrewarded.

Finally, you might be single because you have chosen to be so. Yes, there is a small rise (very small) in postmodern Christianity of the appearance of 'the young celibate.' Healthy, young folks, choosing to dedicate themselves to the service of God in prayer and the service of God in the service of others. I must admit that this troubles me, for unlike

Roman Catholic celibate lifestyles, (which by the way, have nevertheless harbored the worst of sexual perverts, mostly homosexuals) we Protestants have no structure, no community, no mentoring accountability, with which to maybe properly express the celibate lifestyle.

Now then, those are all statements for further consideration and questioning for sure, yet here are two equations which I believe to be certain:

Singleness + Purposelessness = Idleness

Idleness + Indirection = Personal Disaster!

In other words, if you choose singleness and, despite the contradiction in my words, I do believe this is a chosen gift, then you had better have a singleness of heart toward your own laser like focused calling. For if your singleness is not poured out in the service of God and others, then it shall find a festering fistula of fulfilment of sinful and selfish indulgence and I tell you, that an unfocused single life indulging in sin can only spell utter disaster.

For if your singleness is not poured out in the service of God and others, then it shall find a festering fistula of fulfilment of sinful and selfish indulgence and I tell you, that an unfocused single life indulging in sin can only spell utter disaster.

On reflection, I suppose the advice of the last paragraph applies to each and every one of us, single or otherwise: **Know your calling and follow it with singleness of heart.**

Listen: *"Do you not know that those who run in a race all run, but one receives the prize? Run in such a way that you may obtain it. And everyone who competes for the prize is temperate in all things. Now they do it to obtain a perishable crown, but we for an imperishable crown. Therefore I run thus: not with uncertainty. Thus I fight: not as one who beats the air. But I discipline my body and bring it into subjection, lest, when I have preached to others, I myself should become disqualified."*
(1 Corinthians 9:24-27 NKJV)

Pray: Lord, with singleness of heart, I pull back the bow of my anointing and let loose the arrow of my calling into the target of Your desire and Your destiny for me. I ask for a bulls eye! So give me a steady arm, a focused eyes and a singleness of heart, in Jesus name I pray, amen, and let it be so!

| Vol 01 | Q1 | NW00070 | March 10ᵗʰ |

Night-Whisper | **BE**

God is still a poet and He's wearing a construction hat!

Is the core of the Father, is God the Father's heart, scientific or artistic? Well, tonight I have the answer for you and I am pleased to tell you that in His essence, at His heart, God is indeed an artist and a very particular one at that! I know, what a statement! It's astounding isn't it?!

Nevertheless, the Scriptures are quite clear, for in our text for tonight the 'workmanship' of God which we read, could also be translated as the 'poem' of God. Indeed, the only other place this word is used is in Romans 1:20, where God says:

Ephesians 2:10

"For we are His workmanship, created in Christ Jesus for good works, which God prepared beforehand that we should walk in them." NKJV

"For since the creation of the world His invisible attributes are clearly seen, being understood by the things that are made, even His eternal power and Godhead, so that they are without excuse."

In other words, the creation of the world is His science on the move but "the things that are made," are His poetry, if you will, His science fashioned in His loving artistic, poetical and mighty hands. Yes, that is the meaning of "the things that are made!" So, a better translation might be this:

"For since the creation of the world His invisible attributes are clearly seen, being understood by the poetry, or by the poem, or by His full poetic works!"

Let me say this now then, that both science and sanctification are the chariots of God in which the poetry of the Father both rides and resides. Hallelujah!

A poem is very simply, a fabrication of powerful words that forms itself into an emotional reality, it is a living entity even, a moving being, if you will, a shining sun in in the center of bright spiral star systems, all whirling around the plug hole of an invisible, all sucking blackness. A poem is centipede; a millipede; a bumblebee that should not fly, feeding on the nectar, hidden down the fluted shutes of flowers, bathed in showers of rain, where the wine stain of crushed blueberries drips on the thigh of sighing women in the arms of their muscular lovers, panting over them in hungry desire; A poem is the essence of fire, of wind, of reflections in water and the squelching sounds of wet, wet earth; It is the laughter heard in mirth and seen in smiling faces; it is the taste of chocolate and the touch of chocolate colored puppies that chase their tails, it is the leather wonder of whales, spurting blow holes; and the velvet sheen of blind moles burrowing beneath the ground, and in the singing of a billion olfactory sensors in blood hound's brown and crinkled nose, and the perfume of the rich and red and ragged, all unfolding rose, yes, in all these things, God's workmanship performs its poetic prose; yes a poem is even in our sighs, for even under the sour-ness of all our grey and fallen skies, God is still a poet.

> *Both science and sanctification are the chariots of God in which the poetry of the Father both rides and resides.*

I want to tell you tonight that you are the poem of God, even a constructed and dancing piece of prose Divine, all ready to be spoken on the heavenly stage and I tell you, what a performance that could be!

Be sure to find your voice.

Listen: *"My heart is overflowing with a good theme; I recite my composition concerning the King; my tongue is the pen of a ready writer." (Psalms 45:1 NKJV0*

Pray: Jesus! You are fairer than the sons of men; Grace is poured upon Your lips; Therefore God has blessed You forever. Gird Your sword upon Your thigh, O Mighty One, with Your glory and Your majesty, and in Your majesty ride prosperously because of truth, humility, and righteousness; and Your right hand shall teach You awesome things. Your arrows are sharp in the heart of the King's enemies; the peoples fall under You. Your throne, O God, is forever and ever; a sceptre of righteousness is the sceptre of Your kingdom. You love righteousness and hate wickedness; Therefore God, Your God, has anointed You with the oil of gladness more than Your companions. All Your garments are scented with myrrh and aloes and cassia, Out of the ivory palaces, by which they have made You glad. Lord help me hear Your voice and Oh my God, let me find and never lose the voice you have given me. Amen and let it be so. (Psalms 45:2-8 NKJV)

| Vol 01 | Q1 | NW00071 | March 11ᵗʰ |

Night-Whisper | **WISDOM**

Cut loose

In his play *The Phoenician Women,* Euripides writes that: "A man is known by the company he keeps." This saying may be at least 2,500 years old but it has nevertheless, stood the test of time and is still as true today as it was then.

Luke 7:36-37

"Then one of the Pharisees asked Him to eat with him. And He went to the Pharisee's house, and sat down to eat." NKJV

"A Man is known by the company he keeps." Now our Jesus was known by the religious folk as: "A glutton and a drunkard! A friend of tax collectors and sinners!" Indeed, our Jesus was the friend of all harlots and ne'er-do-wells, and openly showed this to the watching world by allotting to them, as one old commentator so delightfully puts it: "table fellowship." Yes indeed, "this was the most emphatic way of Jesus declaring His unity with sinners." By offering them 'table fellowship'

Jesus accepted the dinner invitations of the most disreputable of folk but He did so with the Divine intention of offering them an invitation Himself to the Father's own great table of forgiveness. The association of Jesus with the most disreputable of folk always led to their healing, their repentance and their transformation. Let me ask you tonight then, does your association with openly disreputable folk lead to their same transformation? Or rather, and most horribly dear Christian, are they transforming you? (1 Corinthians 15:33)

"A Man is known by the company he keeps." Now, Jesus was rarely seen with the hypocrites. Not in 'table fellowship' so much anyway, though our text for tonight is one notable exception. Yet, even this 'table fellowship' with hypocrites was for the sole purpose of revelation and demonstration. Revelation of their hearts and demonstration of the Father's heart, even His forgiveness. Tell me again then, just why are you associating with hypocrites?

"A Man is known by the company he keeps." Good books and good men are always good things to have around, good things to be associated with, good things to even let write on you. Yes, let write on you. Be aware though, that there are some wolves out there, yes, there are some wandering stars that we need to disassociate ourselves from. There are some little mouths speaking great things, there are some fools that delight in grabbing dogs by the ears, there are some silly women and some stupid men of not too good repute, that we had better steer clear of and even cut loose from! When you do, and do you must, be sure to tell them why. Who knows? It may even cause them to change their ways. Why not see this truth telling, as our tip on leaving this kind of 'table fellowship.' Leave a big one. Then never go back. Some of you have the graffiti of bad company written on your faces. End that kind of bad table fellowship today.

Good books and good men are always good things to have around.

Listen: *"These are spots in your love feasts, while they feast with you without fear, serving only themselves. They are clouds without water, carried about by the winds; late autumn trees without fruit, twice dead, pulled up by the roots; raging waves of the sea, foaming up their own shame; wandering stars for whom is reserved the blackness of darkness forever." (Jude 12-13 NKJV)*

Pray: Lord, give me a nose for wolves and from the corner of my open eyes, allow me to see their hidden teeth. Lord, give me an eye for big clouds that bear no moisture and an ear for crashing waves. Lord, give me a voice and courage to speak to fruitless trees and a wariness for untethered stars that streak across my sky, in Jesus name I cry. Oh and last of all, yes most of all I pray, give me an axe, a straight eye, and a big swing to cut away the creeping blackness. Amen, and let it be so!

Night-Whisper | **CARE**

Resurrection always follows the last supper

It is no doubt somewhat apocryphally that Justus Liebig was expelled from his German grammar school after causing an explosion in his chemistry class! Even so, Leibig's love of chemistry set him on course for a very successful teaching career and a life of discovery.

Lamentations 5:1-4

"Remember, O Lord, what has come upon us; Look, and behold our reproach! Our inheritance has been turned over to aliens, and our houses to foreigners. We have become orphans and waifs, our mothers are like widows. We pay for the water we drink, and our wood comes at a price." NKJV.

It was this same chemist, this "father of fertilizer," who developed a method of extracting meat from the carcasses of animals primarily slaughtered for their hide. This same concentrated meat extract, was invented by around 1840 and then commercialized by the 'Liebig Extract of Meat Company' starting around 1866.

The company's original product was a viscous liquid, containing only meat extract and 4% salt, but for the masses, a cheaper, dried bouillon cube was invented which the company trademarked as OXO. From the early 20th century, OXO began to thoroughly embed itself into the British and Commonwealth psyche. Indeed, in 1908, OXO became the first commercial sponsor of the Olympic Games which were then being held in London.

I write tonight's whisper from the 8th floor of the OXO Tower, overlooking the city of London and the river Thames. The building was originally constructed as a power station for the Post Office but was subsequently acquired by the Liebig Extract of Meat Company for conversion into a cold store.

Rebuilding this old power station to an Art Deco design, the Thames river-facing facade was retained and extended. A tower was added upon which Leibig wanted to feature illuminated signs advertising the name of their OXO product. Permission for the said advertisements was refused. So, instead, the tower was built with four sets of three vertically-aligned windows, each of which happened to be in the shape of a circle, a cross and another circle! This design both then and now, reads "OXO," thus proving the old saying that: "Where there is a will, there is a way!"

> *After the last supper, mothers continue to weep all the more over their own lost calling and all their lost children. Listen! Do you hear the weeping?*

In the latter part of the 20th century, there was in the UK, a famous OXO campaign featuring "the OXO Family," which simply depicted blue collar, working class folks eating a meal together. During the course of the years it tracked this same homely, gravy boat focused OXO family growing up, which in turn, reflected all the vast social changes of the time, especially depicting the decline and collapse of family values. In 1999, after 23 years on television, the advertisers believed that the home-cooked family dinner, with all the clan sat around the table, was outdated and frankly, because so many women were now working outside of the home, their fictitious advertising family, together with real "old fashioned" families depicted there, were in fact, well and truly dead. As is the actress who played the mother. (Cancer. Aged just 66)

The outcome of this death of family and old fashioned family values, was the airing of their final commercial which they entitled, "The last supper." Here, after 23 years living in the same house, the OXO kids have grown up and flown the coop, whilst the world outside has turned and moved on unrecognizably. The final scenes depict the grieving mother crying in her empty kitchen being comforted by her old husband one last time. He whispers in her ear: "Time to go," and so, the OXO family, together with real family values disappeared from British homes forever. This factual and fictional history brings many important things to mind this evening, however, for sake of brevity let me leave your dreams with but two.

First I need to remind you that although the Last Supper of Jesus was followed by death, just three days later it was followed by a glorious resurrection! While there is life, there is always hope you see, and though women may be well on the move, it is still true that mothers continue to weep all the more over their own lost calling and all their lost children. Listen! Do you hear the weeping? For mothers, the loss of family strikes at their very heart, their very being and for society to resurrect itself, motherhood, in the context of a valued family, yes of the Biblical family, must be resurrected. Without the family, and the Biblical values of family, society is dying and mothers are still weeping over this loss. Do you hear them?

One thing we all must do, is show mothers the practical hope of our innovative love. This is true love, this is heroic love, this is the rough 'fight of love,' of which Spurgeon says: "No featherbed warrior can get involved with!" Yes, in our day, to resurrect family values we need true loving innovation of Biblical proportions.

> *Without the family, and the Biblical values of family, society is dying and mothers are still weeping over this loss. Do you hear them?*

Secondly, that although our Godless and politically correct, morally corrupt and degenerately sick society, will not allow planning permission for such an innovative resurrection of Biblical family values to occur, it is up to us Christians to ensure that the cross of Christ, once again becomes the touching center of the circles of male and female, of man and wife. Me thinks that we Christians in our day, need to build another OXO Tower.

Listen: *"But know this, that in the last days perilous times will come: For men will be lovers of themselves, lovers of money, boasters, proud, blasphemers, disobedient to parents, unthankful, unholy, unloving unforgiving, slanderers, without self-control, brutal, despisers of good, traitors, headstrong, haughty, lovers of pleasure rather than lovers of God, having a form of godliness but denying its power. And from such people turn away!" (2 Timothy 3:1-6 NKJV)*

Pray: Lord, the joy of our heart has ceased; Our dance has turned into mourning. The crown has fallen from our head. Yes, woe to us, for we have sinned! Yet, You, O Lord, remain forever; Your throne from generation to generation. Why do You forget us forever, and forsake us for so long a time? Turn us back to You, O Lord, and we will be restored; Renew our days as of old, unless You have utterly rejected us, and are very angry with us. Father, we are done with the bride of Frankenstein and need real resurrection from the dead. Please forgive us, and restore to us our real mothers, as we, in new and innovative loving ways, restore their value to our broken and monstrous society! Amen, and it be so!

(adapted from Lamentations 5:15-22)

| Vol 01 | Q1 | NW00073 | March 13th |

Night-Whisper | **WISDOM**

The wisdom of not doing the dirty on your own doorstep

Proverbs 11:29

"He who troubles his own house will inherit the wind, and the fool will be servant to the wise of heart." NKJV

For the 'Nth' time, I shall be flying across the pond once more in a couple of days. I tend to fly the cheapest way, which usually means flying at the most unusual of times. Becoming mostly then cramped and cranky, I suppose, the only thing I look forward to in these journeys are the in-flight movies. Interestingly, it just so happens that the first in-flight movie ever shown, had its title based upon our text for tonight. In 1960, the first class passengers of Trans-World Airlines viewed the very first ever in-flight movie, and it was of course called: *Inherit The Wind*.

Inherit the Wind was the movie of the Broadway play based on the famous watershed event of the creation and evolution debate called the 'Scopes Trial,' the beginnings of which was the challenge of the Butler Act, which, it just so happened, was today in 1925 debated in the Tennessee Senate. The Butler Act proposed a law, "forbidding public school teachers to deny the literal Biblical account of man's origin and to teach in its place the evolution of man from lower orders of animals." Both the play and film grossly misrepresented the facts and the character of the people it portrayed, but triumphed primarily in its attack against the 'fascism of McCarthyism.'

Our text for tonight says: "the wise of heart does not trouble his own house, and those that do are fools, who in turn shall see their inheritance dissolve into nothing, only to then feed on air and become a servant to the wise and generous non-troublers!" Be sure, if you bring trouble into your house where once there was peace, you shall be degraded by that trouble! Whether that trouble is financial fiddling, relational unfaithfulness, physical violence, dishonor of mouth and action, unsociable-ness, a lack of affability, a niggardly withholding of necessities, or of any other withholding of that which is due, or any other kind of duplicitous dealings, this is true household mismanagement, and it is trouble with a capital 'T' and it shall disinherit you and reduce you to the position of a poverty stricken servant. Be careful then that you never defecate on your own doorstep.

The Bible is full of people who defected on their own doorstep. Simeon and Levi, for example, roiled the waters of Jacob's family when they murdered the men of Shechem. Then again, Achan also troubled the house of Israel, even to the death of many others, when taking the forbidden and the accursed thing. And did not Saul trouble the land, with his misplaced and fleshly zeal? And friends, mustn't we all beware of the misplaced zeal for our own selves, of the theft and the degrading of others, all of which will castigate those who should be blessed by us and who one day might well have been a blessing to us?

> *Be careful then that you never defecate on your own doorstep.*

Father are you troubling your children? Wife, are you troubling your husband? Brother, are you troubling your sister? Son, are you troubling your father? If you are, then beware! For I hear the sound of a clanging mission bell and see the future race of tumbleweeds, rolling through your deserted streets.

The Butler Act roiled a nation's waters and it's still reeling from it today and should Christ tarry, should the waters settle, the bottom of the pond will no doubt look a very poorer place. Be careful then, family, community or nation, that you never defecate on your own doorstep.

Listen: *"But when he came to himself, he said, 'How many of my father's hired servants have bread enough and to spare, and I perish with hunger! I will arise and go to my father, and will say to him, "Father, I have sinned against heaven and before you, and I am no longer worthy to be called your son. Make me like one of your hired servants."'" (Luke 15:17-19 NKJV)*

Pray: Lord, I have troubled my own spiritual house and my own family house. Rightly O Lord I should inherit the wind, and yet Lord I cry to You tonight that You would make me a greater son and restore both to me and to mine, those years which I have allowed the Locusts to eat. In Jesus name I pray, amen and let it be so.

| Vol 01 | Q1 | NW00074 | March 14ᵗʰ |

Night-Whisper | **ASK**

Progenitor proceedings, pious ingenuity and permissible percussion

There is nothing wrong about stretching the skin of truth over the drum of human understanding and then beating out the Gospel upon it. As long we don't break that skin of truth and as long as we do not beat the drum for nothing else but His glory, then such pounding percussion, I suppose, is quite permissible. Let me explain.

Numbers 27:1

"Then came the daughters of Zelophehad the son of Hepher, the son of Gilead, the son of Machir, the son of Manasseh, from the families of Manasseh the son of Joseph; and these were the names of his daughters: Mahlah, Noah, Hoglah, Milcah, and Tirzah."

We live and move in a library of immeasurable proportion and stories in their billions are piled high up to this most lofty of ceilings, especially the stories of redemption, which in their multitudes also lay strewn all around our feet, waiting to be seen, picked up, read and enjoyed. I believe this, and that is why I go a-seeking pictures of redemption in the stories of our day, even if the hellish side of Hollywood is producing them! You see, God is still painting His pictures of redemption and for now, it is still His blood red period. For the moment, for the moment I say, it is still His blood red period.

I say this because our text for tonight tells the story of five virgins appearing before Moses, all seeking the inheritance usually reserved for sons. It is the great and somewhat controversial Methodist theologian Adam Clarke, who with some tongue in cheek, recounts as "pious ingenuity" the "Mystery of the Five Virgins!" I retell his account however, without my own tongue in my own cheek and in the so doing, I am blessed by yet another redemptive picture.

These five virgins act like the five wise virgins of Matthew 25:1-10, in that, whilst waiting for the bridegroom, they took oil to keep their lamps burning. Yes indeed, in this way the virgins of our text, are types of those who make a wise provision for their eternal state. In the same way, their actions should encourage all weak and destitute believers, who, though they are orphans in this world, shall not be deprived of their heavenly inheritance. Therefore, whatever you need, indeed, whatever you want, if it is righteous, then go and ask God for it now!

Therefore, whatever you need, indeed, whatever you want, if it is righteous, then go

The name of the dead father and his five virgin daughters are mysteriously instructive; for the now dead father's name, Zelophehad, means: 'the shadow of fear or dread.' The first daughter, Mahlah, means: 'infirmity.' The Second daughter, Noah, means: 'wandering.' The third, Hoglah, means: 'dancing for joy.' The fourth, Milcah, means: 'queen,' and the final virgin, Tirzah, means: 'well pleasing!'

So the story of the five wise virgins could very easily mean that: "Because we are all born of the shadow of fear, (Zelophehad,) we are birthed in sin and dipped in death, and through this fear of death, all our life we are subject to bondage, which in turn begets (Mahlah) infirmity. Thus, being so infirm, being so bent and warped, being even a picture of a 'sick at heart' society, we (Noah) wander about for help and comfort, which, by God's grace, we then find in Christ, who in turn, changes our sorrow into joy (Hoglah,) bestowing His royalty (Milcah) upon us, making us kings and priests unto God and His Father, so we shall at last, be presented to Him, glorious and without blemish, being (Tirzah) well-pleasing and acceptable in His sight."

Methinks this is more than a pious ingenuity! I think it is a remarkable redemptive story, laid within a much larger redemptive narrative.

Looking at this story from a wholly human perspective I would go further and say, like these five virgins, we need to be as bold as brass in taking the 'Kingdom of God' by storm. Grace is there for the taking and yes sir indeedy, we need to go looking and we need to go asking for it!

Let's get ingenious about this, I mean, let's take the roof off someone's home to get to Jesus; let's put a ladder against His wall and, even if it's late at night, let's throw rocks up at His window. Yes! Let us ask for bread from His bakery even if it's way past closing time and the fire has gone out. Then, when we have that bread of life, that real bread which comes down from heaven, let's wake the rest of our sleeping neighbors up with a whole load of different kinds of drumming and shout, "Hey! Come and share this bread of God! Come dine with me on everlasting life"!

See the picture? Good. Now go out and beat that drum my friend. He who has ears to hear, let him hear.

Listen: *"So Moses brought their case before the Lord. And the Lord spoke to Moses, saying: 'The daughters of Zelophehad speak what is right; you shall surely give them a possession of inheritance among their father's brothers, and cause the inheritance of their father to pass to them.'" (Numbers 27:5-8 NKJV)*

Pray: Lord, may I always been seen at Your throne, claiming that which is in myself, not even mine to mention, and that in the so doing, all the blood bought blessings of Your Son and my Savior, Jesus Christ the Lord, may be poured upon this expectant, bold and waiting head of mine, in His great name I ask it, amen, and let it be so!

Night-Whisper | **GRACE**

Refuge! Refuge! Refuge!

Blood. From Genesis onwards, from the time Cain slew able, when 'innocent' blood was first spilt upon the ground, that outraged human hemoglobin which ignited in spontaneous combustion, is even now is continuing to burn like a red emergency flare shot up into the very center of the pupils of God! Heaven looks down upon this spreading purple wine stain on the green carpet of life, for you see, God always has His attention drawn to the spilling of innocent blood, for blood is the emblem and carrier of a person's life, and innocent blood, especially stains the land upon which it is spilt.

Deuteronomy 19:10-13

"Lest innocent blood be shed in the midst of your land which the Lord your God is giving you as an inheritance, and thus guilt of bloodshed be upon you. "But if anyone hates his neighbour, lies in wait for him, rises against him and strikes him mortally, so that he dies, and he flees to one of these cities, then the elders of his city shall send and bring him from there, and deliver him over to the hand of the avenger of blood, that he may die. Your eye shall not pity him, but you shall put away the guilt of innocent blood from Israel, that it may go well with you." NKJV

I wonder if there is left just one clean spot on the planet, you know, a place where this staining scream of innocent blood has not spread its burning arms to heaven?

The problem with this kind of red and noisy, power packed pollution, this shedding of innocent blood, is that it causes a consequential reaction in the God of justice, for when the land is polluted by such blood, it calls forth His furious anger upon it, and only righteous retribution can expiate the shedding of such innocent blood, whose rich red flare burns in the watching eyeball of the Almighty. You see, spilt innocent blood demands a cleanup operation of almost catastrophic proportions and that my friends holds a very expensive price tag.

Only when punishment falls upon the originator of the offence or their substitute, can the puss of this pollution be pierced out from the putrid boil of injustice, thus allowing the land to be healed of its hideous infection. Yes, when retribution is visited upon the offender or their substitute, then and only then, can reconciliation with God occur. Did you get that? It is God, who is ultimately alerted and offended at the shedding of innocent blood! It is God that has to be propitiated. It is God, that is to be thoroughly satisfied with the retribution being poured either upon the head of the offended or their innocent substitute. You might be offended here because you have forgotten that deeper law, that law: "which is written in letters deep as a spear is long on the fire-stones on the Secret Hill. That is engraved on the scepter of the Emperor-Beyond-the-Sea" – that law which speaks of a reckoning upon the earth for all the innocent blood which has been shed, thus causing the whole land to be overturned and perish in fire and water.

It is as though God has made a silent covenant with the planet that allows the blood and the red stained earth to continually scream, until all the innocent blood shed upon its soil is finally expiated.

It is as though God has made a silent covenant with the planet that allows the blood and the red stained earth to continually scream, until all the innocent blood shed upon its soil is finally expiated. Quieted.

Yes, think not that this bright blue orb of ours hangs silently in the cold blackness of this night, no, the earth weeps profusely, and joins innocent blood in a dirge duet as she traverses her lost ellipses among the hot stars all hung in the seeming silent and but listening space, whilst and all the waiting watchers hear all their broken hearts and await God's coming judgment. Selah.

Yet the ears of all the living have been plugged by Satan and his sick society of selfishness and death. For our nations are awash with the spilt blood of the innocent. For blood by a billion bucket loads, all full of human abortions, the off scouring of Satanic selfishness, have been thrown like old offal into the pigsty of pride, and have spattered the walls of God's universe with red, and caused the very stars to stink! Yes, space is not silent, but full of the shrieks of crying babies, all ripped from the womb, limb by limb, or salted to death, or sucked into oblivion, even millions upon millions of them all united in life-robbed anger, with all their screaming accusations and shouts for vengeance continuing to echo through the eons, all being amplified through the red and sodden soil, of a sad and singing, shocked and reeling, offended mother earth. Earth does not thank you for such selfish 'population control.' She curses you for it.

Our verse tonight finds itself in the context of the three major Levitical cities of refuge. At least one would be within a day's journey of anywhere within Israel, and have the roads of refuge being built to them, being both straight and true. These roads were also thoroughly maintained and kept clear each and every spring. Indeed, when signs were needed to point the way, some say that upon these roads, over every bridge that crossed a ravine, that the signs would be pointed in the right direction and read very simply: 'Refuge! Refuge! Refuge!'

Yes, the Holiness of the Office of High Priest, even then, meant that their death was enough to cleanse the land of innocent blood and pronounce the guilty free to go.

These cities of refuge, were built primarily as a place of protection for those folk guilty of manslaughter. Here they would stay, the city becoming for them an open prison, where they would be protected from the tribal avenger of blood, until either they were acquitted by their trial, or the death of the High Priest instigated their immediate release. Yes, the Holiness of the Office of High Priest, even then, meant that their death was enough to cleanse the land of innocent blood and pronounce the guilty free to go.

Manslayers made it to the city of refuge. Murderers never did. This capital crime was dealt with by the avenger of blood out in the field, or by the Levitical court held at the city gate.

Christ however, in His own innocent shed blood forgiveness, makes no such distinction between murder and manslaughter. For the great and ever-holy, glorious and gracious High Priest of the universe, is become a city of refuge for both the manslayer and the murderer! You see, His death cleanses all. His life justifies both the weakest and the worst. Yes, all roads of the Gospel lead to His overwhelming forgiveness and each turn, bridge and crossroads of your life has been marked with these three lit and neon words, all pointing to Jesus and saying: 'Refuge! Refuge! Refuge!'

If you are a murdering mother tonight or a complicit father, then I beg you to flee to Jesus, for the land cries against you, no, not only that, but the very voice of your children which you have murdered cries out against you and seeks the judgment of God upon your very wicked heads. Flee to Jesus now and let Him your refuge be.

Listen: *"And this is the case of the manslayer who flees there, that he may live" (Deuteronomy 19:4 NKJV)*

Pray: Lord, the land cries out against us. O God stay your hand that Your people might have the time to proclaim Your city Jesus, as the great and only refuge of the sinner, even a sinner like me. Be satisfied with the blood of the great High priest, who we take now as our Savior and who He takes even now as His blood bought children. So in Your anger remember mercy, and in your great and rich red grace, justify both the manslayer and the murderer together. We ask You this in Jesus name, amen and let it be so.

| Vol 01 | Q1 | NW00076 | March 16th |

Night-Whisper | **CONSIDER**

Grace has its dangers

In our text for tonight, general Joshua, on being aware of the day of his departure from this life, has called Israel together to remind them, to gently reprimand them, and also to refresh them concerning their continuing conquest of the promised land.

Joshua 24:13

"I have given you a land for which you did not labour, and cities which you did not build, and you dwell in them; you eat of the vineyards and olive groves which you did not plant."

Sure, Joshua was old and advanced in age but this day, this particular day, he is made aware of his own particular departure time. He's been looking upward at the flight departure board and sure enough, his name has just flicked over and appeared on the call board.

"Behold, this day I am going the way of all the earth." Joshua 23:14 NKJV

After a completed life, I too would like to be so close to the Lord, that I might hear Him rub His hands and say:, "Robert, it's today. 14:30hrs. Can't wait!"

I think Joshua's knowledge of his departure was not a general summary of the outcome of advancing years, but rather, a certainness of knowing, when all the "No, and, the "No not yets'" were turned into "Yes!" and "Today!'" I do believe that some people with listening ears, do get the opportunity to hear their name called over the eternal Tannoy. I think we all do. If we want to.

Joshua, his eternal bags all packed, first reminds them of God's grace, and our text for tonight is testimony to that fact. This land was a gloriously great and gracious gift to them, but the danger with that grace, is that it is often received with such a quiet and diminishing unthankfulness, that it results in the cascading and catastrophic lackadaisicalness of an inattentive worship, (is there really any such thing as inattentive worship?) and quickly following on that state, is a lecherous idolatry, which will result in the response of the jealous judgment of God, in an all-consuming anger. In other words, if grace is expected but in the receiving is treated as something that was almost deserved, then it does not produce thankfulness, and that lack of thankfulness in turn diminishes our spiritual stature and to such an extent, that we no longer reach up to God, but rather stoop down to idols, causing us, the now abusers and rapists of His grace, to be most severely judged by God the giver.

> *The abusers and rapists of His grace, will be most severely judged by God the giver.*

Now, the scary thing is, that Joshua in his departure discourse goes on to force his listeners into a position of choice. He does it by saying in effect, "I don't know who you 'numpties' are gonna serve, but as for me and my house, we are going to serve the Lord." Israel's reply at Shechem, is with a shocked agreement! "Oh no," they say, "We are gonna serve the Lord as well. Honest!" And in response Joshua warns them, rebukes them ,and goads them even farther saying: "No you can't serve Him because He is Holy and Jealous and if you mess with Him, He will turn on You and consume you!"

Friends, Joshua could not have been clearer.

So, Israel then, with great clarity and confirmation, enter into the Covenant of Shechem, the recorder and witness thereto, being a large stone which was set up under an even larger oak tree, it becoming a silent sentinel, if you will, to Israel's word which would in just a few generations also give witness to the breaking of that covenant by them, again and again and again, until God did finally turn on them and utterly consume them from His gracious land. All this, after previously doing them the greatest of good.

There is some reminding, there is some reprimanding, and there is some refreshing for some of you who read this tonight. Whatever you do, do not stoop to adulterous idolatry and force God to turn on you, after He has done you so much good already! I think even grace, yes, especially God's greater grace in Jesus, is still written on a page bearing the watermark of Shechem. Don't abuse God's grace. Don't lose it. Don't fake it. Don't rape it. For methinks that such free grace, when so dreadfully shamed, might bear an ever greater retributive consequence than the law.

Listen: *"For it is impossible for those who were once enlightened, and have tasted the heavenly gift, and have become partakers of the Holy Spirit, and have tasted the good word of God and the powers of the age* *to come, if they fall away, to renew them again to repentance, since they crucify again for themselves the Son of God, and put Him to an open shame. For the earth which drinks in the rain that often comes upon it, and bears herbs useful for those by whom it is cultivated, receives blessing from God; but if it bears thorns and briers, it is rejected and near to being cursed, whose end is to be burned. But, beloved, we are confident of better things concerning you, yes, things that accompany salvation, though we speak in this manner." (Hebrews 6:4-10 NKJV)*

Pray: Our exclamation to you great King is this: "As for me and my house we too will serve the Lord!" This is our desire, to honor You, and so to this end we give You both our heart and our soul. Those of us who are the heads of our families, give them all to You and plead with You tonight, to break open the closed rock once more and let the rivers of life pour through each of our generational ravines, that the spirits of Your chosen and elect, would be graciously washed away to waiting heaven's shore. In thankfulness, and by remembrance, we shall not shame Your grace. In this we make to You, both our proclamation of intent, and our prayer of much needed aid, Yes, in Jesus name we ask it, amen, and let it be so.

Night-Whisper | **HOPE**

The last man standing

After the death of general Joshua, a whole new generation of Israel is left to conquer the Promised Land. All of the previous generation that lived in Egypt as slaves, that left there under the victorious and redemptive hand of God were now dead! All that is except one, and he is literally the last man standing and his name is 'Dog.'

Judges 1:1

"Now after the death of Joshua it came to pass that the children of Israel asked the Lord, saying, 'Who shall be first to go up for us against the Canaanites to fight against them?'" NKJV

I am a dog lover and I mean real dogs, I mean working dogs, yes, I mean of course, Border Collies! These kind of dogs are truly man's best friend, and are chiefly marked by their companionship, by their strength and by their humble faithfulness. So was Caleb, son of Jephunne of the tribe of Judah. He was a real dog!

This last man standing is of a remarkable spirit. He shines among Israel, his strength being rooted both in a personal relationship with the Most High and in his committed and personal holiness to the Most High. There is life in this old 'dog' and lots of it. I look at him now, old but straining at the leash, his grey haired muzzle straight and true, his eyes focused and fixed on the prize, his feet ready for action, his body taut in waiting and watching expectancy. Revered head of his family, chief of his clan and renowned among his tribe of Judah, when the prayer of direction is offered up to God, the answer from the Father's lips is swift and sure. Listen:

Now after the death of Joshua it came to pass that the children of Israel asked the Lord, saying, "Who shall be first to go up for us against the Canaanites to fight against them?" And the Lord said, "Judah shall go up. Indeed I have delivered the land into his hand." Judges 1:1-2

God has not forgotten this old 'dog' and rewards Caleb's strength and courage, nay, watches with smiling glee as the younger hounds hold back against the foe whilst this old 'dog' fearlessly chases the biggest and the baddest, up the lofty mountain top and takes it for his own! Yes indeed, "Judah shall go up!"

Caleb might be old, Caleb might be the last man standing, but he has been feeding on the word and friends, that means even at a good old age, he's as fit as a butcher's 'dog.' How are you planning to spend your latter years? In a rest home by the sea, sucking humbugs and sipping tea? Or charging up some mountain somewhere, slaying giants and singing nearer my God to thee?

How are you planning to spend your latter years? In a rest home by the sea, sucking humbugs and sipping tea? Or charging up some mountain somewhere, slaying giants and singing nearer my God to thee?

Some think that the name Caleb means 'Dog.' I think he was quite the spiritual bounty hunter. How about you old boy? How about you?

Listen: *"As yet I am as strong this day as on the day that Moses sent me; just as my strength was then, so now is my strength for war, both for going out and for coming in. Now therefore, give me this mountain of which the Lord spoke in that day; for you heard in that day how the Anakim were there, and that the cities were great and fortified. It may be that the Lord will be with me, and I shall be able to drive them out as the Lord said. And Joshua blessed him, and gave Hebron to Caleb the son of Jephunneh as an inheritance." (Joshua 14:11-13 NKJV)*

Pray: Lord, I would be an old dog, the mouth of my spirit full of chomping teeth! Not gumsy and limping along crippled with rheumatoid arthritis and maybe bow legged with nutrient deficient rickets. No. not me Lord. So, let me not get fat and have my belly drag the ground, nor allow my breath to labor or my open mouth to drool over my fur of motley grey, hardly covering the flee eaten flesh which I have long been far too tired to scratch. No, I would rather be an old dog like Caleb Lord ! Ready, fit and strong, still straining at the leash even in my later years. Lord give me this special difference of spirit right now and so prepare me in my younger days to be an old dog fighting still. Yes, even restore to me the health of those years which the Locusts have eaten. In Jesus name I bark it, Woof and Woof again!

| Vol 01 | Q1 | NW00078 | March 18th |

Night-Whisper | **RESCUE**

The marketing of God

We in the Laodicean church age have but one major problem in our Evangelistic method. God is not with us. I know that is an astonishing statement to make yet not I think, an unreasonable one.

John 16:7-11

"Nevertheless I tell you the truth. It is to your advantage that I go away; for if I do not go away, the Helper will not come to you; but if I depart, I will send Him to you. And when He has come, He will convict the world of sin, and of righteousness, and of judgement: of sin, because they do not believe in Me; of righteousness, because I go to My Father and you see Me no more; of judgment, because the ruler of this world is judged." NKJV

When a person is convicted of sin, they are convinced deep in their being that they are sinners and sinners against God in particular. They are full of a sense of their own undone-ness, their own menstrual-stinking filthy raggedness, the embarrassed stench of which they know has found itself lodged in the nostrils of a Holy and pure God. They are convinced of their own nakedness before the whole host of a holy heaven, revealing the hanging and rolling, undulating shaking belly-fat of their sin. Indeed, they feel themselves grossly obese with their sin. They are undone, and they know it, feeling the weight of the long shadow of a coming and righteous judgment made ready to fall with blunt force trauma on their screaming little heads, to then smash them all to pieces. They feel they deserve this. In this convicted state, for the first time ever, they see their complicit alignment with both darkness and the devil and they are greatly alarmed, knowing they can do nothing to rectify the rot, and thus, being so desperate, they seek the services of a mighty and merciful Savior.

Now if that's conviction on sin, and I think it is, then you will agree with me surely, that this is a rare as rocking horse poop in our Evangelical churches. Yes, we in the Laodicean church age, have but one major problem in our Evangelistic method. God is not with us. I know that is an astonishing statement to make yet not I think, an unreasonable one.

> *Most of the folks in our churches are lost. We have sold them a pup and they have simply been converted to cultural Christianity.*

Most of the folks in our churches are lost. We have sold them a pup and they have simply been converted to cultural Christianity. Many of those unsaved folk with some bravery and integrity, even with authenticity and anger, shall leave our ranks. Even now, thousands upon thousands of them do so, each and every year, carrying with them both distrust and disappointment in abundance, and frankly, who can blame them for they were conned into a false Kingdom instead of being convicted and converted into the true Kingdom of Christ.

If we are going to rightly market the message, then we had better first answer the door, face the 'Fella' whose been knocking for a long, long time now and buy some of His goods! Yes, amazingly, Jesus still loves us His church and despite His impending vomiting, is, through the greatness of His gagging, still inviting us to buy the cure. Yes, there is a cost attached to it but I believe it is well worth the paying. How about you? How's your eyesight friend?

Listen: *"And to the angel of the church of the Laodiceans write, 'These things says the Amen, the faithful and true witness, the beginning of the creation of God: "I know your works, that you are neither cold nor hot. I could wish you were cold or hot. So then, because you are lukewarm, and neither cold nor hot, I will vomit you out of My mouth. Because you say, 'I am rich, have become wealthy, and have need of nothing' - and do not know that you are wretched, miserable, poor, blind, and naked - I counsel you to buy from Me gold refined in the fire, that you may be rich; and white garments, that you may be clothed, that the shame of your nakedness may not be revealed; and anoint your eyes with eye salve, that you may see." (Revelation 3:14-19 NKJV)*

Pray: Lord sell us this gold, sell us these garments and then O Great Ophthalmologist, go to work on our eyes that we might truly begin to see. Clothe us please, even with those so distinct, washed and wonderfully white, other worldly garments. Fulfil that prayer of Moses and make all Your people prophets, even the true proclaimers of the Gospel in its fullness, and then with it, O Lord have mercy upon us, with that mercy, if needs be, send us fiery persecution to try us and bring us forth like gold refined in such a flame. Finally, tonight then O God, though we squint and squirm though we might pull away from You, please grab us and stretch open the sockets of our eyes, while smearing in Your all seeing salve, that clarity might come at last, yes, that clarity and conviction might come to us at last before it is all too late. Amen and let it be so.

Night-Whisper | **HOPE**

If I could turn back time

Before the destruction of Sennacherib's army, in the 14th year of his reign, Hezekiah is sick and dying. His prayers no doubt called forth an answer from God and it came upon the lips of the sent and true prophet Isaiah, who says:

"Thus says the Lord: 'Set your house in order, for you shall die, and not live'." 2 Kings 20:1 NKJV

These words of Isaiah, may have been delivered in absolute and seeming, mind-unchangeable form but it made no difference to Hezekiah, who with great tears weeps his reasons for the gift of more years. Hezekiah's weeping request is granted, and it is Isaiah again, who though by now is some distance away, either in the middle of the court or maybe even the middle of the city, is turned around by God with a message, some medical information and a miracle. Nice.

The message was clear:

"Thus says the Lord, the God of David your father: 'I have heard your prayer, I have seen your tears; surely I will heal you. On the third day you shall go up to the house of the Lord. And I will add to your days fifteen years. I will deliver you and this city from the hand of the king of Assyria; and I will defend this city for My own sake, and for the sake of My servant David.'" 2 Kings 20:5-6.

The medical information was also clear:

"Take a lump of figs." So they took and laid it on the boil, and he recovered. 2 Kings 20:7 NKJV

2 Kings 20:9-11
Then Isaiah said, "This is the sign to you from the Lord, that the Lord will do the thing which He has spoken: shall the shadow go forward ten degrees or go backward ten degrees?" And Hezekiah answered, "It is an easy thing for the shadow to go down ten degrees; no, but let the shadow go backward ten degrees." So Isaiah the prophet cried out to the Lord, and He brought the shadow ten degrees backward, by which it had gone down on the sundial of Ahaz. NKJV

In its application over a 3 day period, this prophetic poultice proved to be the perfect cure. A natural cure at that as well! Note, that Hezekiah was going to die for want of a natural cure. Note, that God told him he was going to die without at first telling him of this simple natural three day cleansing cure. The only conclusion I can come to here is that God was testing Hezekiah's faith muscles. I hope He doesn't test mine this way! God is a very tough 'Life coach' that's for sure. In any event, whatever Hezekiah's most miserable of maladies was, it called forth believing and desperate pleading prayer, and the seeming initial and absolute declaration of God regarding his forthcoming death, is revealed in our text for tonight, to be both changeable and conditional. However, Hezekiah did not know that! We however, must remember that, for friends, things can change, situations can be reversed. cancers can be cured, even in the final seconds! So, I say to you: "Keep praying until God unequivocally calls you to stop praying."

> *As the initial and certain word regarding Hezekiah's most imminent death went forth from the true prophet Isaiah, time had to be reversed to cancel out the certainty of it, so that a new prophetic word might then be spoken?*

Hezekiah, receiving a natural cure in the natural world wanted a supernatural sign as a sure stamp of God's real intervention, especially as it was a three-day cure. So, God most graciously grants this request. Indeed, Hezekiah is induced into testing God most thoroughly, even in effect, is invited to have time move speedily forward or speedily backwards. Of course, Hezekiah opts for what he considers to be the harder option for God and a more certain sign for himself. So he says, "Move time backwards!"

For sure then, the shadow of Hezekiah's sundial now moved from sunset to sunrise. Yes, without minimizing the mighty miracle and turning into one of light refraction, couldn't God, wouldn't God, stop and turn back time for those he loved? Indeed, didn't God make the sun and the moon to stand still in the Valley of Aijalon? Yes, He did! Indeed, another preacher has commented that as the initial and certain word regarding Hezekiah's most imminent death went forth from the true prophet Isaiah, time had to be reversed to cancel out the certainty of it, so that a new prophetic word might then be spoken? Who knows? Who can explain this thing?

Although God gives us no scientific explanation for this mighty miracle, it is of great encouragement as one commentator put it, to take note that "God controls all the shadows in our life." Yes, He does, and friends for us tonight, as the dial of our life moves into darkness, let us pray hard to our Father, for who knows that if we won't be allowed to arise in the sunshine of the morning and stand again to find that maybe God will have turned back time for us as well. Why shouldn't He? Therefore my brother, therefore my sister, keep on believing and do keep on asking.

Listen: *"So Isaiah the prophet cried out to the Lord, and He brought the shadow ten degrees backward, by which it had gone down on the sundial of Ahaz." (2 Kings 20:11 NKJV)*

Pray: It seems it was good for me to go through all those troubles. Throughout them all you held tight to my lifeline. You never let me tumble over the edge into nothing. But my sins you let go of, threw them over your shoulder - good riddance! The dead don't thank you, and choirs don't sing praises from the morgue. Those buried six feet under don't witness to your faithful ways. It's the living - live men, live women - who thank you, just as I'm doing right now. Parents give their children full reports on your faithful ways. God saves and will save me. As fiddles and mandolins strike up the tunes, we'll sing, oh we'll sing, sing, for the rest of our lives in the sanctuary of God. Isaiah 38:17-20 (from The Message)

| Vol 01 | Q1 | NW00080 | March 20th |

Night-Whisper | **CONSIDER**

The manufacture of the spiritually retarded and crippled clowns

The shepherds of Christ wash the feet of fellow travelers, all journeying together across this dirty world, moving ever closer to both the heart and the city of Jesus.

Jeremiah 3:15

"And I will give you shepherds according to My heart, who will feed you with knowledge and understanding." NKJV.

The shepherds of Christ, in healthy discipleship, might retool these same journeymen, re-arm them, re-orient them, re-educate them, and most certainly reinforce them in the faith once delivered to the saints. Once they have done this, the shepherds of Christ shall always return these travelers to their destiny and their journey, until the next and necessary pit stop in the teaching circuit, when they shall have the privilege once again to now deal with a bigger, leaner, ever onward, and ever upward looking disciple than they previously had the privilege to service. For now, having thus been so well fed, their disciple's personal journey, through both challenge and change, has brought to them an increase in spiritual musculature, and with it, increased personal strength and increased personal maturity, and they have moved on, manned up, and grown in both grace and truth!

Those who have been well discipled by the servants of Christ, always grow in their appetite as journeying men themselves, and have embarked on that path in such a way, that the sight of the heavenly city is clearer, the smell of the green, green grass of their eternal home is that much more acute, their ears are more full of the sound of singing angels, their skin is more sensitive to the feeling and the flowing of the wind of the Spirit, their arms are stronger and more lifted up in prayer, and their feet are full of peace, being more certain, more sure and more directed in the way that ever before. And though their armor may carry a few more dents, it is brighter; and though their sword is bloodied, it is yet sharper; the loins of their mind now being more lifted and focused; the belt of truth, tighter and more secure around the chiseled core of their being! Yes indeed, the shepherds of Christ, that is the pastors and leaders of the church of the living God, shall happily and with great thankfulness, always stoop to wash the feet of such travelling and growing disciples.

Now, this picture of growing and journeying strength, of maturing in grace and truth, I believe is a Biblical expectancy. However, and unfortunately, this picture is in fact, to our Laodicean lot anyways, an unwanted and unsought for fantasy! Ashamedly, for I speak as a shepherd and a foot washer for regarding the absence of such journeying men: it is the shepherds who are mostly to blame for this most sorry state of affairs.

In my journeying around Christendom and in my ministry to the people of God trapped in the same, I am tired of seeing many gigantic staff led churches, doing everything for their congregations to simply justify their often too well paid existence. In doing this, they have been enabling thousands of kindergarten kiddies to simply continue to languish on the breast, that have, in the so doing, created vast churches of sucklers and suckers, even baby Christian clowns. It's just pitiful.

I am tired of seeing many gigantic staff led churches, doing everything for their congregations to simply justify their often too well paid existence. In doing this, they have been enabling thousands of kindergarten kiddies to simply continue to languish on the breast, that have, in the so doing, created vast churches of sucklers and suckers, even baby Christian clowns. It's just pitiful.

All teachers must ensure that at some point, and the sooner the better by the way, that their pupils overtake them. Yes, all teachers must pull back the bow for eventual release. However, when teachers have students who never move on, and in North America especially these stunted students attend churches in their tens of thousands, then two strange things will happen to the church.

Watch this now, for first of all, the teachers themselves will turn into smiling imbeciles, toting suitcases full of well-worn platitudes and the odd blunt instrument, and secondly, their students will turn into spiritual cripples, even retarded Christians, who of necessity, have to have their backside wiped for them and be personally spoon fed with poorly, pre-chewed rubbish.

Such sad shepherding is not releasing strong disciples onto their journey, but rather, it is producing imbecilic imitations of Christ, who ride around the children's race track, pulling into the same old pit stop for the same old problems, which will be dealt with by people in the same old inept, low octane, low expectation kind of way. There is, you see, no expectation or plan, no daring demand, no challenging necessity, for people to grow in grace and truth! There is no urgent necessity to make disciples, to program of expectation for people to become like Jesus.

I do not envy the shepherd, who has sold himself into such dismal drudgery and I pity the sheep that still suck on these strange, fat staff-titties that such churches alluringly dangle before them, for neither the smiling and imbecilic teachers nor the crippled disciples they produce, will stand in the fires which are to surely come upon us.

There is, you see, no expectation or plan, no daring demand, no challenging necessity, for people to grow in grace and truth!

It is out of such a great concern that I speak so harshly and so jarringly tonight. For presently the church of God cannot stand, is not standing, and will not stand, in the trouble that is to come upon us. That my friends is an abominable shame, a joke formed in the pit, and I am afraid, is most assuredly fostered from the pulpit, via spoon fed bite size nonsense and skinny irrelevancies. Cool or not so cool, senior or otherwise, I pity the pastor that has to stand before Jesus and account for every empty, energy absent, wimp of a word which he has spoken. It will not bode well for such makers of retards.

Yes, if you are not changing and growing, then you are spiritually retarded. If you are not being re-armed, re-orientated, renewed, refreshed, re-educated and re-enforced in your faith to then be released upon your destined journey, then you are being short changed, slowly killed, and are going nowhere. Indeed, you are purposefully being kept in your wheelchair and paying through the nose for the privilege. You are a spiritual retard and you have been fed and bred for it from what some other imbeciles have termed 'the finest emergent pulpits in the land.'

I must confess, that at the moment, I can find no hope in my heart for such lost shepherds, locked into such a good looking and grossly debilitating system. However, I do believe there is some hope for those lost sheep who are sick of mommies milk and wanting at last, to take care of their own rear end. Yes, there is hope for those sheep if they want it.

The beginning of the answer is simple. Find some hard looking men and some greener pastures. Find some scarred and sun burnt shepherds, molded by the heart of Hosea and sporting the look of Amos the iron man about them, and if they and the greener grass they provide are over the hill and far away, then move there! Time is running out. For the sake of your poor retarded spirit, find a good restaurant that serves whole food, that makes you eat your greens, that measures your B.M.I. and coaches and cajoles you into becoming a muscular man of God, a man of the Word and the Spirit, a man that can survive in the field, form families and feed himself and them, teaching them to do the same. Find such a church and go to it.

Find a good restaurant that serves whole food, that makes you eat your greens, that measures your B.M.I. and coaches and cajoles you into becoming a muscular man of God, a man of the Word and the Spirit, a man that can survive in the field, form families and feed himself and them, teaching them to do the same.

The servants of Christ wash the feet of travelling men, journeying across this dirty world ever closer to both the heart and the city of Jesus. Tell me. Do you have big spiritual muscles? Do you have a full belly? Clean feet? Are you on your journey? Are you on the move?

Listen: *"Therefore, beloved, looking forward to these things, be diligent to be found by Him in peace, without spot and blameless; and consider that the longsuffering of our Lord is salvation - as also our beloved brother Paul, according to the wisdom given to him, has written to you, as also in all his epistles, speaking in them of these things, in which are some things hard to understand, which untaught and unstable people twist to their own destruction, as they do also the rest of the Scriptures. You therefore, beloved, since you know this beforehand, beware lest you also fall from your own steadfastness, being led away with the error of the wicked; but grow in the grace and knowledge of our Lord and Saviour Jesus Christ." (2 Peter 3:14-18a)*

Pray: In my life Lord, be glorified today. In Your church Lord, be glorified today. In this world Lord, be glorified today. Ruin this retarded Laodicean church Lord, by raising up men like You, full of grace and truth, full of the Word and the Holy Spirit, wholesome, healthy, hard and happy. Then Lord, make me one of them, in Your great name I pray. Amen and let it be so.

Night-Whisper | **PREPARE**

Turning aliens into citizens

It was just four Night-Whispers ago in which I made mention of that mighty old warrior called Caleb, who together with the rest of His tribe, was, after the death of General Joshua, given the single honor of being the first tribe to go up and possess the rest of the land. That tribe of course was the tribe of the Lion, it was the Messianic tribe, it was the tribe of Judah. Looking at our text for tonight we have to say that: "My oh my, how things have changed and that, right quickly." A thousand men of Judah, all with full and smelly pants, are now bewailing Samson's might and fervour. Imagine that! What a stink.

Judges 15:11

Then three thousand men of Judah went down to the cleft of the rock of Etam, and said to Samson, "Do you not know that the Philistines rule over us? What is this you have done to us?" NKJV.

When I think of North America and of Britain and Europe, it is evident that in the names of multiculturalism, humanism, liberalism and political correctness, all our gates have been opened wide to everything that is non-Christian, even anti-Christian. Lest I be misunderstood tonight, lest I be accused of playing the race card, it behooves me then to clearly state, that I do not believe that God is a white Englishman and that yes, I totally rejoice that my brethren in the church in which I serve, are made up of peoples from every tribe, of every nation and of every tongue. How wonderful is that!

However, the multitude of peoples now inside our gates are not Christian, no indeed, they often carry with them an anti-Christian message, and whilst we, the most present indigenous peoples of both these islands and the great North American continent are busy deserting our roots and following the way of Baal, even slaughtering our unborn in their tens of millions, (may God forgive us), yes while we are doing this, in short, yes very short time, these present Philistines shall thoroughly rule over us. The rising demographic line and the speedily changing city sky-line, even the most popular fist name chosen for babies, are both clear testimonies to that fact. "My oh my, how things have changed and that, right quickly."

The choices to this challenge are threefold: We either continue to turn tale, turn them out, or turn them into.

Remember, like I said before, God is neither white nor does He hold a British, American, or any other earthly passport. So, I am not so interested in turning any one into model earthly citizens of any earthly country, but rather, I am interested in the proclaiming of the Gospel of repentance from dead works to faith in Jesus Christ the Lord, to all the people both within our gates and outside of them, so that heaven shall be fuller still with the best of eternal citizens from every tribe and tongue, all together occupying that great city above, even the heavenly Jerusalem, which is the mother of us all.

> *God is neither white nor does He hold a British, American, or any other earthly passport.*

In our once English speaking lands, one chief advantage of our present earthly heritage has been the freedom of this Gospel expression. Because this is most assuredly and slowly, being taken away from us now, we need to act immediately and sacrificially in the proclamation of this Gospel to all these tribes and tongues now occupying the centers of all our cities. If we don't, then as sure as eggs is eggs, we soon to be, totally defeated Judeans, with our pants full of a cowardly smell, shall find ourselves handing over all our remaining Samson's into the hands of the offended Philistines. This always happens and then when they are murdered we shall declare them martyrs and call them heroes.

Now, let me lastly turn from this national problem to a very personal one and ask you, just what internal spiritual territory is it that you have given over to the enemy? What is it that you have failed to thoroughly conquer? Have all your personally, Spirit honey sweetened strengths, also been bound and blinded by the Philistines in the gates of your own soulish city? I tell you: "Unless you want to be swallowed up in all their desires, you too must either turn them out, or, turn them into."

Oh and by the way, don't trust in your compromising Christian cowards, they will turn you over to the enemy in an instant.

Listen: *"Tell me, you who desire to be under the law, do you not hear the law? For it is written that Abraham had two sons: the one by a bondwoman, the other by a freewoman. But he who was of the bondwoman was born according to the flesh, and he of the freewoman through promise, which things are symbolic. For these are the two covenants: the one from Mount Sinai which gives birth to bondage, which is Hagar - for this Hagar is Mount Sinai in Arabia, and corresponds to Jerusalem which now is, and is in bondage with her children - but the Jerusalem above is free, which is the mother of us all. For it is written: 'Rejoice, O barren, You who do not bear! Break forth and shout, You who are not in labour! For the desolate has many more children than she who has a husband.' Now we, brethren, as Isaac was, are children of promise. But, as he who was born according to the flesh then persecuted him who was born according to the Spirit, even so it is now. Nevertheless what does the Scripture say? 'Cast out the bondwoman and her son, for the son of the bondwoman shall not be heir with the son of the freewoman.' So then, brethren, we are not children of the bondwoman but of the free." (Galatians 4:21-31 NKJV)*

Pray: In the spiritual realms O God, come and fight for us, that those things righted in heaven, might be made fully manifested upon the earth. In Jesus name we pray, amen and let it be so.

Night-Whisper | **INTEGRITY**

Food for thought by the mining of memory

It was writer Davis Grub, reflecting on his art, who recalling a conversation around the subject says: "A young writer once came to me years ago and said, 'Why write anything? It's all been said.' And I said, 'Yes, but not by you.' And I think unless you believe in the sacred individuality of everyone, then you don't believe in writing at all. Because no metaphor can have any real meaning unless, having originated in the mind of the poet, it finds soil to make its resurrection in the mind of somebody else." How wonderful.

Leviticus 25:22

"And you shall sow in the eighth year, and eat old produce until the ninth year; until its produce comes in, you shall eat of the old harvest." NKJV

I visited a younger church last night. Just planted five years ago it was at that easily recognized stage of growth, where younger, single folks, had banded together, married, mated and brought forth offspring. Like attracts like you see. It's got very little to do with God. Very soon, the kids will grow, more married couples with younger children will arrive, a professional and instructional children's program will of necessity be instigated and heavily subsidized, a children's minister and later a youth pastor will be added to the staff and behold! The arrival of yet another S.A.C. A 'Standard American Church.' The inevitability of it all can sometimes get quite depressing, but that is not my point for tonight. No, my point is that tens of thousands of these new churches planted across America and planted across the world, most readily express the generation gap, by the absence of more mature folk in their ranks. Mature in years, mature in warfare, and mature in words especially. Wise leaders of these younger church plants will pray for such additions to their church communities. Wise leaders won't listen to the demographic target rubbish so easily regurgitated by that purpose driven church propaganda which has become as damaging in the short term as humanism has been in the long term.

The first, and I feel most famous of David Grub's novels, is *Night of The Hunter,* which was, again in my opinion, made into one of the best movies ever produced. I want to tell you tonight though, that the fruit of this story, revolving around the actor Robert Mitchum playing one of *the* great movie monsters of our time as he portrayed a serial killer preacher, who turns one of Elisha Hoffman's hymns entitled, "Leaning On The Everlasting Arms," into probably the most malevolent sound of evil ever heard, grew mostly out of his own aged mother's recounting of very real incidents she had encountered when she was working as a social worker during the great depression in its particular manifestation in and around the town of Moundsville West Virginia. From the quality of the movie, it is evident that Grub mined his mother's memories very well indeed.

Older individuals living amongst us should have great stories of the past to recount to us, indeed, have often participated in these great stories themselves and if we are very fortunate, have become the product of those great stories of the past, now told before us on two legs. Older folks should be individuals of life and lip, full of tales yet to be mined by younger folk, and deep mines they should be as well, full of treasure, laid down over the years in golden seams, which, if found by younger sojourners, can be used to pay the expense of all the encounters of life yet to come upon those of us still 'wet behind the ears.' Their stories may be dead and gone, ah but the seeds of these stories when once laid in fertile hearts can find their life giving resurrection in the mind of many others and produce bushels of instructive fruit.

> *Older folks should be individuals of life and lip, full of tales yet to be mined by younger folk, and deep mines they should be as well, full of treasure, laid down over the years in golden seams, which, if found by younger sojourners, can be used to pay the expense of all the encounters of life yet to come upon those of us still 'wet behind the ears.'*

Let us then honor the elderly warriors among us and let us, the warriors of today, make sure our stories are set to seed, ready to be planted in younger hearts, so that they can blossom and open in flower upon the fertile minds of the always arriving young.

As for those S.A.C.'s? Well, I think they are so full of unbiblical ferment, that they might all eventually explode.

Listen: *"Now Herod the tetrarch heard of all that was done by Him; and he was perplexed, because it was said by some that John had risen from the dead, and by some that Elijah had appeared, and by others that one of the old prophets had risen again." (Luke 9:7-9 NKJV0*

Pray: Father, may Jesus so manifest Himself amongst our aged, that even despot Kings would acknowledge the presence of ancient prophets among us. Father, so fit our own lives with wisdom, that we would mine the memories of the aged and eat of their rich fruit, so that resurrection life would spread its roots deeper in our own minds and our hearts. Finally, tonight O Lord, fit us for our own journeys end with retentive memory banks and stories of the wonders of the Lord to fill them to the full. Amen, and let it be so.

Night-Whisper | **DANGER**

Nabel wasn't able to be bound in the bundle of the living

The new mother gazed lovingly into the eyes of her beloved newborn.

Isaiah 32:6-8

"For the foolish person will speak foolishness, and his heart will work iniquity: To practice ungodliness, to utter error against the Lord, to keep the hungry unsatisfied, and he will cause the drink of the thirsty to fail. Also the schemes of the schemer are evil; He devises wicked plans to destroy the poor with lying words, even when the needy speaks justice. But a generous man devises generous things, and by generosity he shall stand." NKJV

Also, read:- 1 Samuel 25.

"Oh darling" she said to her happy husband,
"Oh darling what shall we call him?"

"My love," he responded, "Our first born. My firstborn and a son at that! Hallelujah! How about we call him 'Idiot?'"

"A little harsh." She replied, "A little harsh my darling, my heart. How about we call him 'Stupid?'"

"Hmmm" he says, happy but unsure. "That's only two syllables compared to three. Let's get back on track, how about we call him Simpleton?"

"Three syllables," says she, "Oi vey! What's all this thing about three? Tell you what," says she, "Let's cut to the chase with this child and give him a one syllable summary."

"What do you suggest?" says he expectantly,

"Fool!" she exclaims, " Let's call the little darling: 'Fool!'"

And so the son was named Fool, or, as we know him tonight: Nabel.

Nabal was a descendent of that great man of renown, the last man standing of his whole generation, Caleb. Our story for tonight goes to show a few important things, the primary one being that the fruit of the loins, very often does fall very far from the tree. Nabal, most certainly did.

Now Nabal was a rich man. I can only assume this is why he happened to get hooked up with a wise and beautiful and well righteous young woman called Abigail. I am always amazed at what rich fools can buy for themselves. Nevertheless, make no mistake about it, Nabal was a rich fool. Some doctors examining the full story of Nabal's unhappy demise, looking in 1 Samuel 25, surmise that he suffered from a "Circulatory Disease which in the end, probably gave him a cerebral hemorrhage. The cause of this disorder," they suggest, "is that 'Nabal was probably a confirmed alcoholic who had arteriosclerosis and associated hypertension with the lesion which killed him, probably being located in one of the atheromatous patches in the brain, and it was that which accounted for the ten day of coma prior to his eventual death.'" So there you go!

I am always amazed at what rich fools can buy for themselves.

Anyone who drinks himself to death is indeed a fool. Are you this kind of fool? Make no mistake about it. I have met many folks calling themselves Christians, who have been sent home from hospital to die because the doctors know the cause of their illness is alcoholism and nothing else. I ask you again: Are you this kind of fool? Are you a secret drinker a private alcoholic?

Nabal is, very simply, emblematic of the fool who rejects God and His anointed. He is drunk on his own goods and his own power. He is a brute, an abuser of men, a miser of his personal riches, a fool who regards his personal relations as cattle to be branded and used even as he so desires. Nevertheless, David privately protected this man's goods and his standing, indeed, it was David's presence in the wilderness that allowed Nabal's continued and increased prosperity. Imagine that.

At the time of sheep shearing, in an area then dominated by the wool trade, it was the presently proclaimed and future coming King, David son of Jesse, who himself instructed his followers to go and politely, calmly, gently, and with great respect, ask for some recognition of his protection and consequently, just a very small part in Nabal's prosperity, so that

David's troops might be fed and might be allowed to rejoice along with him at the celebrations. Nabal, was well able, to provide all this.

However, Nabal the fool, feigns ignorance of David, and then questions both his lineage and his anointing. His troops politely leave and when David receives this particular slap in the face, he straps on his sword and instructs his followers to do the same. David angrily mounts his steed with the sole purpose of covering its flanks with Nabal's blood.

It was wise Abigail, who leaving her husband in a drunken stupor, rides to meet David in the way, to try and avert his righteous vengeance. She is successful in the so doing and when, in the mid-morning of the morrow, she then recounts in the ears of her head thumping, husband, the great escape she has engineered for him, he has a heart attack, a brain seizure even, and enters into a ten-day coma, a coma from which he will never recover. David rejoices in Nabal's death and then marries the street-wise, sweet wise Abigail.

> *David rejoices in Nabal's death and then marries the street-wise, sweet wise Abigail.*

All born fools who, in their drunken pride reject the gentle approaches of King Jesus, shall in the end be killed by God Almighty. All faithful wives bound to such fools, whether by blood or marriage, (listen well now) shall be saved at last and shall be joined to Jesus as His bride.

God paints us a simple picture tonight, a picture that even a fool can understand. If you are one of those fools tonight, you had better wise up.

Listen: *"So it was, in the morning, when the wine had gone from Nabal, and his wife had told him these things, that his heart died within him, and he became like a stone. Then it happened, after about ten days, that the Lord struck Nabal, and he died." (1 Samuel 25:37-38 NKJV)*

Pray: Please, let not my Lord regard this scoundrel Nabal. For as his name is, so is he: Nabal is his name, and folly is with him! But I, your servant, ask you to hold back from coming in bloodshed and from avenging Yourself with Your own hand. Now then, let your enemies and those who seek harm for my Lord be as Nabal, but as for me and my house, please forgive the sins of your servant and let our lives be bound in the bundle of the living, the living people, who follow You with all their hearts. Amen and let it be so.

Night-Whisper | **DANGER**

The dire desire of a deadly divinity

Somewhere in New York, an old Italian guy secretly watched his son, day after day, leave the apartment block and walk down the road towards his stop to catch the bus for school. Day after day, the old, Italian father saw his son bullied by the members of a local neighborhood gang. Day after day, his son would go hungry at school because the older boys would steal his lunch money and day after day, his son would return from school, stiff with the beatings he had taken on his body. The son never said a word to his father and the father never told the son that he secretly observed and knew everything that was happening to him.

The old father couldn't tell you when he made the decision but in his heart the sails were set, the rudder was pressed away from him and he had now come about to a very different course. One day soon, unexpectedly, he would kill those gang members who had robbed and abused his son for now so very, very long. Not yet, but soon, he would punish those perpetrators of such violent abuse and miscreant injustice carried out daily against his very own beloved son.

The top two levels of fear I have experienced in my life, and yes there have been many levels, has been first of all, the outburst of violent emotional anger. Yes. passionate crime, like a summer storm, can be devastating, but nevertheless, it is

1 Samuel 2:22-25

"Now Eli was very old; and he heard everything his sons did to all Israel, and how they lay with the women who assembled at the door of the tabernacle of meeting. So he said to them, "Why do you do such things? For I hear of your evil dealings from all the people. No, my sons! For it is not a good report that I hear. You make the Lord's people transgress. If one man sins against another, God will judge him. But if a man sins against the Lord, who will intercede for him?" Nevertheless they did not heed the voice of their father, because the Lord desired to kill them."
NKJV

often over very quickly and frankly its violence is usually so widely spread, that in its effect, most of the time anyway, those valuables of ours, those vital interests we cosset, are often spared its angry and unexpected onslaught. When this quick anger erupted from me, it was scary, it was tempestuous, but the violence it generated was in the end, its own means of dissipation.

The second most fearful thing I have experienced has been that more terrifying settling of anger, which I have observed first to begin first in the eyes of a man, only to flow slowly, like thick molasses down the side of an open jar, and fix itself like motorway bridge concrete in the deep foundational depths of his soul. When this firm, fixed and set decision of destructive and planned devastation, slots quietly like a key into the lock of the door of death, the icy countenance it produces, chills the very spirit of those who see and know that in a certain and terrifying expectancy, that now full formed and deep rooted hatred has finally come to visit them.

There is no escape from this kind of anger, for there is no dissipation of the same.

There is no escape from this kind of anger, for there is no dissipation of the same. Once hardened anger is released, it buys a big bad boat and sets its course for death filling its own black and bellowed sails with undeterred desire. Surely, there is no greater terror, than when a decision of death is turned into an active and unstoppable purpose to fulfil it?

The sooner we tremble at the quietness of God's capital decisions the sooner we will seek to both calm and expiate, His so great, His so fixed and His so focused and purposed anger. This calm and confident, fixed and icy stare of the Most High God, is one our world needs to be made much more familiar with and that right quickly, for I hear the deep long intake of angry, angelic breaths and the soft sound of golden trumpets, being pressed to pursed lips.

The gracious Son of God has been daily abused. The Father's judgment is coming. Be ready.

Listen: *"Then the sixth angel sounded: And I heard a voice from the four horns of the golden altar which is before God, saying to the sixth angel who had the trumpet, "Release the four angels who are bound at the great river Euphrates." So the four angels, who had been prepared for the hour and day and month and year, were released to kill a third of mankind. Now the number of the army of the horsemen was two hundred* *million; I heard the number of them. And thus I saw the horses in the vision: those who sat on them had breastplates of fiery red, hyacinth blue, and sulfur yellow; and the heads of the horses were like the heads of lions; and out of their mouths came fire, smoke, and brimstone. By these three plagues a third of mankind was killed - by the fire and the smoke and the brimstone which came out of their mouths. For their power is in their mouth and in their tails; for their tails are like serpents, having heads; and with them they do harm. But the rest of mankind, who were not killed by these plagues, did not repent of the works of their hands, that they should not worship demons, and idols of gold, silver, brass, stone, and wood, which can neither see nor hear nor walk. And they did not repent of their murders or their sorceries or their sexual immorality or their thefts." (Revelation 9:13-21 NKJV)*

Pray: Amen. Even so, come, Lord Jesus! Revelation 22:20 NKJV

| Vol 01 | Q1 | NW00085 | March 25th |

Night-Whisper | **WORK**

The 7 marks of a dream maker & 3 scales to measure them by

Having just flown back from America to my home in the United Kingdom, I found myself taking a vow. You see, from leaving my pleasant lodgings in Fort Lauderdale, I drove to Miami, flying from there to Boston and then on to Heathrow, where I was picked up at the airport by my son who drove me home, then carried my luggage up the stairs to our apartment as I limped behind him, dazed and thoroughly exhausted.

Proverbs 18:9

"He who is slothful in his work is a brother to him who is a great destroyer." NKJV

The whole journey had taken me twenty six hours from door to door, the real frustrations being a delay in Miami, the need to change two deflated aircraft tires in Boston and an extra hour of frustrated waiting, on the tired tarmac in London. Despite hot food, copious amounts of coffee, blankets, pillows, a fine selection of entertainment and polite, sweet smelling cabin crews, I classed it as my worst journeys yet and vowed never to make it again, that is, not unless I crossed the pond in the style that only a first class cabin can offer!

In the 17th century, the sea crossing to Boston could take anything from six to 28 weeks depending on the wind and the weather. With no bathrooms, no running water, save that beneath the keel, sour beer, moldy cheese, overcrowding, danger and sickness, George Whitfield that greatest of Christian orators, made that particular crossing, there and back mind you, some thirteen different times! If that wasn't enough to make this present poor preacher feel any more of a whining wimp, Whitfield went on to preach over 10 sermons per week, some 160,000 in his lifetime. On top of this, he corresponded widely, headed up major theological and charitable causes and raised money for them both! In Georgia in particular, just outside of Savannah on the Moon River, Whitfield, today in 1847, aged then just 25 years, began construction on the buildings of the 'House of Mercy,' Bethesda, a new orphanage for the provinces, that exists even today, as 'Bethesda Boys Home.'

Whitfield was burdened with the debt of this and therefore was burdened with the fundraising for this orphanage for the rest of his life. Indeed, after his death, that burden was even passed along to his Champion and sister in the Faith, Selina, Countess of Huntingdon. Mismanagement, revolution, fire, storm and hurricane, all raised themselves up against the continuance of Whitfield's long established dream of an orphanage for the provinces, yet despite it all, his dream, though in more modern form, it still continues today and has done great good for now over two centuries.

> *Great dreams require great endeavors. Great dreams require great dreamers with dirt underneath their fingernails.*

Great dreams require great endeavors. Great dreams require great dreamers with dirt underneath their fingernails. I have found that there is a great difference between the day dreamer and the dream maker and it is a difference of seven degrees, each one marked by prayers, blood, sweat, tears, tiredness, worry and vomit. What are you tonight? A day dreamer or a dream maker? If you would like to know which you are, sniff your armpits, then check your sick bag and your bank account, for those are the three best scales that you shall ever use, to truly discern yourself.

Listen: *"He who tills his land will be satisfied with bread, but he who follows frivolity is devoid of understanding." (Proverbs 12:11 NKJV)*

Pray: Lord, in all my dreaming, in all my visualization of goals and in all my applications of 'laws of attraction,' HA! Help me to get off my backside, to stop whining and to get on with what you have told me to do! In Jesus name I pray, amen, and let it be so.

When you bust a gut

1 Kings 19:3,4

"And when he saw that, he arose and ran for his life, and went to Beersheba, which belongs to Judah, and left his servant there. But he himself went a day's journey into the wilderness, and came and sat down under a broom tree. And he prayed that he might die, and said, 'It is enough! Now, Lord, take my life, for I am no better than my fathers!'" NKJV

Like I said, I had just arrived back from a visit to the USA. Since 9/11, travel is no longer any fun and pulling 4 bags with a total weight of around 150lbs from the circulator of a baggage claim and then carting it to your next destination can be harmful to a man in his late 40's, especially after 8 hours on a plane bent double and eating bad, very bad, beef lasagna. So anyway, that accounts for my pain of today. I won't tell you where, but only a man gets pain there. Ouch! As far as I can tell, rest and maybe antibiotics are the only remedy for this kind of over exertion.

Now, believe me when I tell you there is a spiritual parallel here, for I know that spiritual over exertion can lead to the same bow legged walking pain, can lead to reproductive incapacity, can lead to embarrassment and if left untreated, it can also lead to painful depression, even a depression that tends to thoughts of checking out without even exchanging your chips. This was Elijah's problem. You see, despite a couple of thousand unbent knees to Baal, he was nevertheless, the only one to be bending his knees in lifting the heavy and dead weight of a backsliding Israel.

It is amazing just how many ailments, physical, emotional, mental and even spiritual, that can be cleared up with rest, relaxation, good food and medication, provided nothing's busted of course! If that happens you need surgery, and then rest, relaxation, good food and medication.

Be careful what you are lifting out there fella. If you can get help, for apparently there's always a thousand strong backs somewhere, then get it!

If, however, these one thousand who have not yet bent the knee to Baal are well hidden, them make sure, you pace yourself, train yourself, and if necessary get yourself a truss!

My jocularity belays some very serious stuff here though. Spiritual over exertion can so drain you, so empty you, so exhaust you, that the consequence of ills it can bring upon you, can fill that tired painful and aching emptiness with such a death, that it can destroy your ministry, destroy your testimony, and even kill you dead. Believe me, I have seen it happen and here tonight, it was happening to Elijah and frankly, he didn't give two hoots.

If your spiritual exertion has led to pain, then you had better rest up. I tell you, it's a sin to let the lack of a few days regular rest to rob you of further weeks, months and even years in the ministrations of your God.

Spiritual over exertion can so drain you, so empty you, so exhaust you, that the consequence of ills it can bring upon you, can fill that tired painful and aching emptiness with such a death, that it can destroy your ministry, destroy your testimony, and even kill you dead.

Listen: *"So Elisha turned back from him, and took a yoke of oxen and slaughtered them and boiled their flesh, using the oxen's equipment, and gave it to the people, and they ate. Then he arose and followed Elijah, and became his servant." (1 Kings 19:21 NKJV)*

Pray: Lord, strengthen my back, give me the humility to ask for help and then Father, when I bust a gut, help me rest, even renew my youth like the eagles and then give me also, this same raptor's keener sense of sight, to view the coming prosperous years that will spring from this my rest. In Jesus name I pray, amen and let it be so.

Night-Whisper | **RESCUE**

Cow zombies

So God desired to kill the sons of Eli. Thus Hophni and Phineas were killed when the Ark of God, that box of the presence of the Lord amongst the His people was also lost to the Philistines in battle.

1 Samuel 6:3-9

> *"So they said, 'If you send away the ark of the God of Israel, do not send it empty; but by all means return it to Him with a trespass offering. Then you will be healed, and it will be known to you why His hand is not removed from you.' Then they said, 'What is the trespass offering which we shall return to Him?' They answered, 'Five golden tumours and five golden rats, according to the number of the lords of the Philistines. For the same plague was on all of you and on your lords. Therefore you shall make images of your tumours and images of your rats that ravage the land, and you shall give glory to the God of Israel; perhaps He will lighten His hand from you, from your gods, and from your land. Why then do you harden your hearts as the Egyptians and Pharaoh hardened their hearts? When He did mighty things among them, did they not let the people go, that they might depart? Now therefore, make a new cart, take two milk cows, which have never been yoked, and hitch the cows to the cart; and take their calves home, away from them. Then take the ark of the Lord and set it on the cart; and put the articles of gold, which you are returning to Him as a trespass offering in a chest by its side. Then send it away, and let it go. And watch: if it goes up the road to its own territory, to Beth Shemesh, then He has done us this great evil. But if not, then we shall know that it is not His hand that struck us — it happened to us by chance.'" NKJV.*

Like just another trophy of just another locally conquered God, the Ark, was then placed by the Philistines in the presence of their own god, Dagon. After all, surely two gods = double the power. What follows however, is nothing short of disastrous for the Philistines in that they were plagued with testicular tumors and overrun with rats and all their associated infestations and infections. To top it all, their idol of Dagon was found on several occasions to be laid prostrate and broken before the Ark of the Lord. This didn't do too much for the reputation of their own local god in that:

"neither the priests of Dagon nor any who come into Dagon's house tread on the threshold of Dagon in Ashdod to this day." 1 Samuel 5:5.

Yes, the Dagon shrine at Ashdod was forever rubbished by the presence of the real and only God.

The five Lords of the Philistines seemed to be passing the problems associated with the presence of the Ark of God, from one of their ruling provinces to the next. That is, until a vocal group of NIMBY's (Not in My Back Yarders) kicked up such a fuss, that the problem needed to be properly addressed at last. It's always the way, thus through divination, the priests of the Philistines came up with the solution laid out in our text for tonight and so, they loaded up the cart and watched the outcome from afar.

It would appear then that these cows knew their true Master, knew their great Owner, and were following His commands, even to their death, above and despite their own natural cow like inclinations.

God now did what Dagon could never do: He guided the cows, who unaccustomed to the yoke newly placed upon them, nevertheless, drew the load equally and securely, kept their attention on the right road, overcame their strong and natural desire to go to their calves, and brought the cart and the Ark in a straight line, without missing one turn in the road, straight away to the priestly city of Beth Shemesh. Let me emphasize that these cows went contrary to their own inclinations in that they had not forgotten their offspring and were not therefore moved ahead in some disassociated Zombie Cow like state, no, they were still lowing for their young ones, calling them, even pining for them. It would appear then that these cows knew their true Master, knew their great Owner, and were following His commands, even to their death, above and despite their own natural cow like inclinations. The following and watching Philistines, in observing these continually lowing kine, saw the majesty and the power of God over nature. It was enough to cause them to acknowledge that the judgment of God, had indeed been upon them.

We all, in our home nations of this day, seem to neither know nor even consider that the judgment of God may be upon us. Unlike the pining cattle of our text, we are in fact worse than any zombie-like cows all trotting not so merrily down the road, but are rather, like a drug and voodoo'd zombie, lumbering in Frankenstein like steadiness, in stupor to the slaughterhouse, being covered in tumors of STD's (did you know that even in 2003, a federal study revealed that 25% of American teenage girls carry a sexually transmitted disease!) and piling up our young men like so much dead meat on various battlefields around the watching world. I cannot help but believe that this is but the beginning of our sorrows, for zombie like cows, lost in a self-indulgent, cud chewing, mindless mooing stupor, rarely listen to the Gospel of Jesus Christ presented to them, for God has hardened their heart and settled them in their Christ rejecting state.

> *I cannot help but believe that this is but the beginning of our sorrows, for zombie like cows, lost in a self-indulgent, cud chewing, mindless mooing stupor, rarely listen to the Gospel of Jesus Christ presented to them*

The whole truth of the Bible, presents a disturbing picture of a Holy and a good God, coming into contact with a dirty and a bad mankind. Our only hope is to pray God's mercy over our zombie-cattled nations, which are moving headlong to the slaughterhouse. You see, truly the answer to our problems is not better programs to pander to the masses, not hipper presentations to hype them into the Kingdom, not the coolest of music to con them into more consumerist tendencies, but rather, it is to pray to God that He would unharden their hearts and unblock their ears before they are slaughtered before His presence.

It's not a merry message, but it is one that needs proclaiming.

Listen: *"The ox knows its owner and the donkey its master's crib." (Isaiah 1:3 NKJV)*

Pray: What passing-bells are there for these who die as cattle? Lift O Lord, the zombie like stupor that has fallen like death cauls around all the newborn of these wayward generations. Lord, grant to your church the right kind of cattle prod to issue a most timely wake up call to one and all, in Jesus name we pray, amen, and let it be so.

Night-Whisper | **PERSEVERE**

Catch the wind

This weekend and next, my present ministerial activities take me to the Kent countryside and Royal Tunbridge Wells in particular. Which is of course, also the birth-place of the great, Rev. Frank William Boreham, who lived from 1871-1959. As an ordained Baptist preacher ministering in England, New Zealand and Australia, he was probably the last student to be interviewed by CH Spurgeon, for entry into his Pastor's college!

Exodus 2:11-15

"Now it came to pass in those days, when Moses was grown, that he went out to his brethren and looked at their burdens. And he saw an Egyptian beating a Hebrew, one of his brethren. So he looked this way and that way, and when he saw no one, he killed the Egyptian and hid him in the sand. And when he went out the second day, behold, two Hebrew men were fighting, and he said to the one who did the wrong, 'Why are you striking your companion?' Then he said, 'Who made you a prince and a judge over us? Do you intend to kill me as you killed the Egyptian?' So Moses feared and said, 'Surely this thing is known!' When Pharaoh heard of this matter, he sought to kill Moses. But Moses fled from the face of Pharaoh and dwelt in the land of Midian; and he sat down by a well." NKJV

Boreham's prolific writings in the form of essays in particular, number in their thousands and he has and continues to influence many great speakers and theologians which came after him.

Boreham's tantalizing titles, descriptive and poetic prose and stories rooted in the common pictures of his day, all go to make his writings attractive, instructive and memorable. For example, in describing an old lady of a village who was both of strong and courageous character, a Godly woman and deeply respected and especially visited by many for her personal counsel, he writes that: "Like the sturdier of the poplars by my gate, she had gathered into herself the force of all the cruel winds that had beaten so savagely upon her." I like that.

Hardships and failures are often, in worked out practicality, fled from, rather than fed upon! We mostly turn our back upon our failures and maybe, even flee to greener pastures new, where no bitter remembrance of them can ever flower from our better plantings in the now new, fresh and fertile ground. I have often observed that these two courses of action, forgetting and fleeing that is, though frowned upon by folk not overly familiar with good intentions gone terribly bad, are often and nevertheless, absolutely necessary practices for both the safety and for sometimes the sanity of the individual. I believe that this was the case in our text for tonight regarding Moses and his current enrolment into the true college of faith and worship, situated in the mountainous halls and barren sandy plains of the backside of the dead and disappointing desert.

> *on the wings of angelic beings, who inhabit and play, and war and pray among these same stormy winds of protection and provision, even God Himself, was seen to ride!*

In this same desolate desert, Moses, that great past leader of Egyptian men and monarchy and future desert Pastor to former slaves who would become the servants of the Most High God, over the next 40 years would gather into himself all the force of the cruel winds that had beaten so savagely against him. So much so, that when actually commissioned by God to fulfil his destiny, his prayers would call forth these very same stormy winds, which would then be employed to blow away the eating locust into the seas and to bring from those same seas: mountains of Quail for complaining men, and then even pour these same gathered and destructive winds over the pursuing and angry army of Pharaoh's men, all still intent on further slaughter and bent on future enslavement. Brethren, I tell you tonight that on the wings of angelic beings, who inhabit and play, and war and pray among these same stormy winds of protection and provision, even God Himself, was seen to ride! Let me ask you: "Have you seen Him there?"

For some of you tonight, it is time to stop fleeing those stormy winds and time to turn and feed upon them, for surely, God shall be found in them, surely, provision shall be gotten out of them, and surely, protection shall be rolled along by them.

By the armfuls then, gather into yourself the force of all the cruel winds that have beaten so savagely upon you and feed on them, even making them your friends, for they shall in the end, both prosper your deliverance and power your destiny.

Listen: *"He rode upon a cherub, and flew; and He was seen upon the wings of the wind." (2 Samuel 22:11 NKJV0*

Pray: Now then O my Father, arms open wide, I call to my mouth, and command to my lungs, from the North, and the from the South, from the East and from the West, all the stormy winds of bitter disappointment and cruel adversity. Teach me to eat them and to digest them for my benefit and for my future deliverance, that they may indeed, become the power of my destiny in You, for Your eternal glory I ask this, in Jesus name, amen and let it be so!

Night-Whisper | **WISDOM**

Messing with the Marabouts

One of the dominant characteristics of Islam in Medieval North Africa and Algeria in particular, was the cult of holy men, or Maraboutism.

Exodus 7:11-13

"But Pharaoh also called the wise men and the sorcerers; so the magicians of Egypt, they also did in like manner with their enchantments. For every man threw down his rod, and they became serpents. But Aaron's rod swallowed up their rods. And Pharaoh's heart grew hard, and he did not heed them, as the Lord had said." NKJV

The Marabouts were believed to possess 'baraka,' that is, divine grace, (sounds like a president) and this was reflected in their amazing ability to perform miracles! Recognized as being both just and spiritual men, these Marabouts often had extensive followings both locally and regionally and therefore great influence along with it! To that end, when Algeria was under the domination of French colonialism, it was these same Marabouts, who, using their great influence and backing up their spiritual rhetoric and liberation theology with 'signs and wonders,' almost stirred the whole region up into a bloody uprising. I say almost, because France averted the uprising with some other 'signs and wonders.'

Yes, in 1856, the French response to such 'revolution' was not in terms of military might but in the sending in of a simple person called Jean-Eugène Robert-Houdin, a well-known magician from the city of Blois.

When Robert-Houdin met the Marabouts, his magical ability was simply that much more better than the 'signs and wonders' of the Algerian 'holy men,' and with their magical might now put to open shame and in subjection to the more powerful French Magician and Magic, the Marabouts lost their influence and thus the bubbling Algerian uprising was quelled without a single shot. (Well actually it was quelled with one shot and with Robert-Houdin catching it in his teeth, but that's another story for another night!)

The kingdoms of this world can be that much more easily overcome if the conquerors of those lands possess simply a better box of tricks. You might carry that box of tricks in a the back of a wagon, or carry them hid up your sleeve or even buried in the bowels of a Tomahawk missile but they are still a box of tricks! Yes, nice or incredibly nasty, they remain still nothing but tricks to mock and to subjugate inferior and frightened folk.

We can be so impressed by the power that these boxes of tricks seem to offer us that we might even want to get some ourselves! Maybe even change our name in honor of the great French trickster, say from Erik Weisz to Harry Houdini and then set up our own impressive travelling show and put the wind up a few other feeble and frightened folk impressed by tricksters.

When the real and God appointed leaders turn up, all they have is a shepherds staff and that alone will swallow up all the snakes of the enemy and part all rivers, to make a way into the promised land.

Ungodly rulers always have counterfeit power and always have a better box of tricks to dupe the people into following their will. However, when the real and God appointed leaders turn up, all they have is a shepherds staff and that alone will swallow up all the snakes of the enemy and part all rivers, to make a way into the promised land. Don't be impressed by boxes of tricks, or the many forms of fake signs and wonders we have seen far too much of recently.

Listen: *"'Return, O backsliding children,' says the Lord, 'for I am married to you. I will take you, one from a city and two from a family, and I will bring you to Zion. And I will give you shepherds according to My heart, who will feed you with knowledge and understanding.'" (Jeremiah 3:14-15 NKJV)*

Pray: Lord, though they be so very impressive, help us discern the charlatan. Then Lord, send us leaders, gifts from on high, endued with power from high, to lead us into Beulah land. In Jesus name I pray, amen, and let it be so.

Night-Whisper | **CHANGE**

Crushing the cockroaches of crowd pleasing

Did you know that our sinful appetites get worried when the source of their sustenance becomes lessened in some way, become if you will, even somewhat inaccessible compared to how previously open the source once was? This wobbling worry then manifest in our sinful appetites, if not averted by full and renewed access to the original source of their sustenance, can quickly turn such sinful appetites not only from worry into quivering fear, but then to bitterness, anger, hate and eventually murdering madness, for sinful appetites, must at all costs, get back to the source of their sustenance. At all costs I say, else they shall threaten to destroy you.

1 Samuel 18:7-9

"So the women sang as they danced, and said: 'Saul has slain his thousands, and David his ten thousands.' Then Saul was very angry, and the saying displeased him; and he said, 'They have ascribed to David ten thousands, and to me they have ascribed only thousands. Now what more can he have but the kingdom?' So Saul eyed David from that day forward." NKJV

King Saul was a crowd watcher, nay, more than that, King Saul was a crowd pleaser, even a crowd sucker if you will, his most sinful appetites, gaining strength and sustenance from the fickle crowd's vocal approbation of him, and so, when this same large teeted, local crowing, mass of humanity, the source of his sinful appetite, poured their milk of praise more over David than they did over the bad and sad King Saul, mad trouble was a brewing! Yes siree, raving, insane, open to the demonic lunacy was a crackling away under the hot coals of Saul's terrified and perpetually hungry sinful little heart.

I thoroughly dislike reading about the life of King Saul, for when I do so, I hear and feel the cockroach like scurrying of that same darkness which resides too much still within me, as it flees to hide under the rocks of my own dark heart, from the light of the terrible texts which shines so clearly upon them, revealing them for the black dung beetles which they truly are. Nevertheless, this exposure to the light is a good exercise and providing the source of the sustenance of my own sinful appetites are removed, even if they are but crumbs, this good exercise can become a profitable exercise, as my sinful appetites will then begin to die in this so great textual lighting.

Far better though, that despite their threats of our destruction should they not be fed, once they are recognized, that these same sinful appetites are then immediately crushed underneath our well-booted and stamping feet. Far better we kill them quick by so thoroughly stamping them out! Acknowledgement with confession and repentance followed by stamping substance, have always been the best cocktails of extermination for such sinful infestations. Try it.

Acknowledgement with confession and repentance followed by stamping substance, have always been the best cocktails of extermination for such sinful infestations.

Before you get to stamping though, I wonder if you first need to see the infestation. So, let me ask you tonight, what darkness rises in you when you are, like Saul, publicly lowered and somewhat lightly esteemed, even overlooked? Yes, when the wind of fickle change, bows the wheat like heads of the milling masses which once sang your praises, all at once to now lay their heads in the opposite direction to you, what darkness rises in you, in response to this? Preacher, Pastor, leader, oh woman of renown, what darkness rises in you, when the crowd stops feeding you the bread you think you so richly deserve and always believe you so rightly crave?

Maybe it's time to start killing some cockroaches. Before they kill you.

Listen: *"Then Saul sought to pin David to the wall with the spear, but he slipped away from Saul's presence; and he drove the spear into the wall. So David fled and escaped that night. Saul also sent messengers to David's house to watch him and to kill him in the morning." (1 Samuel 19:10-11 NKJV)*

Pray: So my Lord, my sinful appetites will always try to kill the King of selfless love, residing in my heart. Despite my revulsion to the sound of the scurrying within my soul, Lord, send the light! And with it, send a big pair of size nine boots. Then my Lord, send the power and resolve to set my feet to stomping, in Your great name I ask it, amen and let it be so.

Night-Whisper | **PREPARE**

Stones of fire on the mount of angels

The old Celtic legend says that this particular saint had power over wild beasts, and in particular, had power over a 'chrysalides' type of gigantic cow, which was of use to him as a kind of ancient, all in one, U-Haul and milk truck!

Ezekiel 28:14c

"You walked back and forth in the midst of fiery stones." NKJV.

Now, this particularly large cow had the care and oversight of a wild wolf, who one day came and prostrated himself before the saint, repentant and forlorn, as he had failed in his protective commission over the cow, when a passing King had killed his charge for food. The cow-killing King, however, having placed pieces of the now dead behemoth of a bovine in a cooking pot, despite the fierceness of the fires set under it could not get the water to boil! Thus the king, discerning both the power of God and their culpability in killing the saint's large cow, eventually also came, and like the wolf, prostrated himself before the saint, as he and his entourage sought both his forgiveness and his protection from God's wrath. These two things, St Brynach provided, and to prove the efficacy of his word, Brynach then raised the giant cow from the dead, restoring him to the care of the wild wolf. For such devoutness, magnanimity and power, the king gave St Brynach land for a monastery and a church and also freedom from taxation to boot, and frankly, who wouldn't have!

Interestingly, it was this same given land, to which an angel of the Lord had previously directed Brynach to proceed to as he was praying on the mount of his visitation. This mount is now named, Carn Ingli, or the Mount of Angels. Yes, this marvelous and still mystical region in the West of Wales, from which the magical and healing blue rocks of the Neolithic masterpiece we have come to know as Stonehenge were once hewn and quarried, was apparently first footed and owned by the angels, and became to all spiritual peoples, a listening post, a meeting place, indeed, a sacred place of practical business between the material and spiritual realms. Wales is, and always has been, a very strange place!

In noting God's delight in all things material, I have observed from the Scripture, God's particular fascination and delight with untouched stone, stone shaped only by those four distinct tools at His command and in His hand. That is: time and water, wind and weather. The Celts might have said that "These four Divine tools, make shapes among the rocks and amidst the standing stones, and in forming an interface between the spiritual and material realms, they scoop out conduits of power, make places of interaction and interface, and allow heaven to touch the earth!"

In the same way dear friends, God takes the passing of time, the wind of adversity, the water of His sanctification and the weather of our journey, to rightly shape His living stones of healing, His present saints, the church of His own dear Son, to change them into a listening post, even a proclaiming place of power, where heaven can touch the earth once more. Surely, when the living healing stones of Christ and the Holy priests of the Most High God, gather in the standing circle of His love, surely then, from within that sacred place and out of that true and magical Royal Blue Kingdom of the Son, anything is possible and anything can happen? From there, maybe even wolves could begin to care for giant cows once more and the Kings of the earth might come to us again, for healing, for protection, for power and for provision.

> *It is time that the spiritual and the material once again meet together in the church of the living God.*

Stonehenge is being excavated once more, so that it's secrets may be found, whilst the church in these ancient lands and of these ancient lands, continues in its horrific decline into uncared for and unheeded 'laughability.'

It is time that the spiritual and the material once again meet together in the church of the living God.

Listen: *"But He answered and said to them, 'I tell you that if these should keep silent, the stones would immediately cry out.'" (Luke 19:40 NKJV)*

Pray: So set a fire underneath Your standing stones O God, the heat of which would crack open our clam like mouths to speak forth the sweetest of praise to the greatest of names on the earth, under the earth and in the earth and in that great name of heaven we so confidently and rightly pray to you and shout out tonight. Jesus hear us! Amen, and let it be so.

THE MISSION STATEMENT OF THE 66 BOOKS MINISTRY

WWW.66Books.tv | Our Mission is:

1. "To proclaim Jesus, the Savior of the whole world, from the whole Bible, because He is wonderful!"

2. Indeed, we are constrained by the love of God, to communicate the rawness of the Bible to real people, in real ways, and our driving and major project of '66Cities' shall take us to the 66 most influential cities of the 250 nations of the world in the next 25 years. That's 16,500 cities!

3. We are aiming to build relationships with grass roots, real people, that is, ordinary people, who, in their own countries and cities, want to do extraordinary things for Jesus and the Kingdom of God, to bring a Biblical Gospel message that is relevant to now, in a world that has come to believe that Jesus is irrelevant to their lives.

If you would like to partner with us in this great task. Then we want to hear from you! Contact me today on vr@66books.tv

MORE ABOUT 'THE 66 BOOKS MINISTRY'

<u>WWW.66Cities.com</u> | By the year 2047, by the grace of God and according to His will and favor, The 66 Books Ministry shall be preaching consecutively from each of the 66 Books of the Holy Bible, the Gospel of the Lord Jesus Christ in 16,500 of the most influential cities of the world on an annual and ongoing basis!

We do not underestimate the quality teams of trained people that this will take, together with the need for vast amount of materials and finances which will also have to be raised. However, as most futurists indicate that the growing global population will be gathered mostly in major world cities in the coming years, there is a necessity laid upon the church to present and proclaim the God of the whole Bible, through the primacy of preaching in these cities. We are convinced that this is a paramount and pressing concern.

"For since, in the wisdom of God, the world through wisdom did not know God, it pleased God through the foolishness of the message preached to save those who believe" 1 Corinthians 1:21NKJV

"Preach the Word! Be ready in season and out of season. Convince, rebuke, exhort, with all longsuffering and teaching." 2 Timothy 4:2NKJV

The church is looking for a revival. The 66 Books Ministry, however, is trying to start a revolution of a return to the preached Word, from the whole of the Bible as a precursor to any and all coming revival.

For "whoever calls on the name of the Lord shall be saved." How then shall they call on Him in whom they have not believed? And how shall they believe in Him of whom they have not heard? And how shall they hear without a preacher? And how shall they preach unless they are sent? As it is written: "How beautiful are the feet of those who preach the gospel of peace, Who bring glad tidings of good things!" Romans 10:13-15 NKJV

We are unashamedly looking for and seeking to foster a massive, huge, releasing, transformative, and exceptionally disruptive reversal and revolutionary change, both within the church and then in the world. We are not just another mission trying to do the same as every other mission. We are intent on revolution!

To this revolutionary end, we have no fear of seeming failure and will cultivate that audacious atmosphere within our ministry. We want to attract grass roots people who are people of faith risk takers, for we believe it is people of such life hazarding attitudes that are used by God to make breakthroughs in the world for the Kingdom of God. Hanging back for fear of seeming failure, hanging back and waiting for the trained professionals, both wastes the time of the church time and kills the spirit of victory.

In that spirit then, we therefore are believing that this task can be accomplished by such people within the time frame we have given ourselves.

Fully assured then, that we are in full obedience with the great commission of our great God and Savior Jesus Christ, we do, with great confidence in Him, turn ourselves happily to this so great a task in the hope that, like a happy hound straining at the leash to be let loose, we believe that many other people will smile along with us and be part of this brand new grass roots 21st Century Global City Mission.

If you want to know more and want to be part of what we are doing then go to www.The66BooksMinistry.com or call us in the USA on **855 662 6657**, or email V.R. directly on vr@66Books.TV

AUTHOR BIO | PURPLE ROBERT

It won't take too much investigation for you to find out that Purple Robert is in fact, Victor Robert Farrell (Born 1960 and alive until now and still kicking) was born in Chesterfield England to Scottish parents with Irish grandparents, which is an obvious recipe both for writing and emotional disaster if ever there was one!

He grew up a culturally excluded Roman Catholic (his parents were divorced,) which is one of the reasons why he hates religion with a passion, and that's an interesting enough fact by itself, because he is also an ordained protestant minister to boot.

Purple Robert. became a Christian whilst serving on board a Polaris Submarine at the end of the cold war. He has gone on to do many things, including being a broadcaster, App developer, performance poet, and the long-time author of 'Night Whispers,' which is read in over 100 counties and is also translated into Spanish (see www.Night Whispers.com)

Currently, Purple Robert is also President of The 66 Books Ministry: a grass roots global city mission endeavor. I suppose it is this concoction of background and experience which means Purple Robert's communication is always raw and emotive. After all, and as he says, *"If Christianity can be relevant on a Monday morning, several hundred feet underneath an unknown ocean, in a pornographic sewer pipe carrying enough nuclear weapons to destroy a continent whilst hiding from the Russians, then it can be relevant anywhere and everywhere!"*

Purple Robert sees himself as a servant of the 'Word of the Lord' to tasked communicate the God of the whole Bible. His proclamation of the same is done in very raw terms to very real people, is both his burden and his passion.